OECD ECONOMIC SURVEYS

1992-1993

UNITED STATES

ORGANISATION FOR ECONOMIC CO-OPERATION AND DEVELOPMENT

ORGANISATION FOR ECONOMIC CO-OPERATION AND DEVELOPMENT

Pursuant to Article 1 of the Convention signed in Paris on 14th December 1960, and which came into force on 30th September 1961, the Organisation for Economic Co-operation and Development (OECD) shall promote policies designed:

— to achieve the highest sustainable economic growth and employment and a rising standard of living in Member countries, while maintaining financial stability, and thus to contribute to the development of the world economy;
— to contribute to sound economic expansion in Member as well as non-member countries in the process of economic development; and
— to contribute to the expansion of world trade on a multilateral, non-discriminatory basis in accordance with international obligations.

The original Member countries of the OECD are Austria, Belgium, Canada, Denmark, France, Germany, Greece, Iceland, Ireland, Italy, Luxembourg, the Netherlands, Norway, Portugal, Spain, Sweden, Switzerland, Turkey, the United Kingdom and the United States. The following countries became Members subsequently through accession at the dates indicated hereafter: Japan (28th April 1964), Finland (28th January 1969), Australia (7th June 1971) and New Zealand (29th May 1973). The Commission of the European Communities takes part in the work of the OECD (Article 13 of the OECD Convention).

Publié également en français.

Table of contents

Box

Tables

Text

Diagrams

Text

BASIC STATISTICS OF THE UNITED STATES

THE LAND

Area (1 000 sq. km)	9 373	Population of major cities, including their metropolitan areas (1.4.1990 estimates):	
		New York	18 087 000
		Los Angeles-Anaheim-Riverside	14 532 000
		Chicago-Gary-Lake Country	8 066 000

THE PEOPLE

Population, 1992	255 414 000	Civilian labour force, 1992	126 982 000
Number of inhabitants per sq. km	27.3	*of which:*	
Population, annual net natural increase (average 1978-89)	2 619 200	Employed in agriculture	3 207 000
		Unemployed	9 394 417
Annual net natural increase, per cent (1978-89)	1.02	Net civilian immigration (annual average 1985-88)	666 000

PRODUCTION

Gross domestic product in 1992 (billions of US$)	6 038.5	Origin of national income in 1992 (per cent of national income[1]):	
GDP per head in 1992 (US$)	23 642	Agriculture, forestry and fishing	2.1
Gross fixed capital formation:		Manufacturing	18.4
Per cent of GDP in 1992	13.1	Construction and mining	4.4
Per head in 1992 (US$)	3 090.0	Government and government enterprises	15.1
		Other	60.0

THE GOVERNMENT

Government purchases of goods and services, 1992 (per cent of GDP)	18.7
Revenue of federal, state and local governments, 1992 (per cent of GDP)	30.6
Federal government debt as per cent of receipts from the public, 1992	109.9

Composition of the 103rd Congress 1993:

	House of Representatives[2]	Senate
Democrats	258	56
Republicans	175	44
Independents	–	–
Vacancies	1	–
Total	435	100

FOREIGN TRADE

Exports:		Imports:	
Exports of goods and services as per cent of GDP in 1992	10.6	Imports of goods and services as per cent of GDP in 1992	11.1
Main exports, 1992 (per cent of merchandise exports):		Main imports, 1992 (per cent of merchandise imports):	
Machinery and transport equipment	47.7	Machinery and transport equipment	43.0
Food and live animals	7.8	Food and live animals	4.5
Crude materials (inedible)	6.0	Crude materials (inedible)	2.8
Chemicals	10.4	Chemicals	5.2
Manufactured goods	8.6	Manufactured goods	11.5
All other	19.5	All other	33.0

1. Without capital consumption adjustment.
2. As of July 31, 1993, Michigan had one vacancy.

Note: An international comparison of certain basic statistics is given in an annex table.

This Survey is based on the Secretariat's study prepared for the annual review of the United States by the Economic and Development Review Committee on 9th September 1993.

•

After revisions in the light of discussions during the review, final approval of the Survey for publication was given by the Committee on 30th September 1993.

•

The previous Survey of the United States was issued in November 1992.

Introduction

The United States has enjoyed the fruits of a moderate economic expansion over the past year. The pace of output growth has picked up somewhat, as has that of job creation, and unemployment has begun to fall. Inflation has remained subdued, but there are signs that further declines may be difficult to achieve, despite the excess capacity that still seems to exist in both product and especially labour markets. While the external accounts have deteriorated, the bulk of the widening in the current-account deficit is attributable to higher domestic demand growth in the United States than in the rest of the OECD area. The outlook for the next 18 months is for a continuation of these trends: a further slight pick-up in the rate of output growth to around 3 per cent, another moderate drop in the unemployment rate, slightly declining inflation in the 3 per cent range and a continued modest enlargement of the current external deficit. While this may appear to some as a disappointing picture, it is actually rather satisfactory, given the weakness of export markets and the ongoing structural adjustments that must be faced: the defence downsizing, the budget deficit reduction, the restructuring of many of the nation's largest corporations and the overhang of commercial office space.

International observers including the OECD have for a long time urged the United States to deal with its huge federal budget deficit, not only because it is unsustainable, but also because it is a major drag on U.S. and global savings and a contributor to high interest rates world-wide. The recent passage of the legislation to cut the deficit substantially over the next few years, both by increasing taxation and by paring expenditure, has therefore been widely welcomed. Chapter II discusses the details of the package, as well as its main medium-term effects. It also reviews the dilemma facing monetary policy makers who must decide when to rein in the stimulus that has been provided over the past few years.

The new Administration has been active not only on the deficit-reduction front. It has brought with it a new approach to the longer-term problems of productivity and competitiveness confronting the nation. The third Chapter is devoted to an analysis of these problems. After an examination of the historical record, the chapter moves on to explore the role of inadequate saving and investment before scrutinising the effect of structural change and the downsizing of the military. It then surveys the Administration's proposals on a number of other matters that are likely to influence productivity outcomes to an important degree: investment in public infrastructure, education and human capital, research and development and social and economic regulation. The chapter ends with an investigation of several other possible problem areas which have as yet drawn little Administration attention: corporate governance, workplace issues, and tort and bankruptcy reform. Chapter IV then describes the trade policy positions of the new Administration and points out some of the risks involved. Finally, it briefly summarises some of the main structural reforms in areas not covered elsewhere. Overall conclusions are presented in a final chapter.

I. Recent trends and prospects

A moderate expansion in output and expenditure

The economic recovery since the business cycle trough in early 1991 has remained relatively sluggish, notwithstanding the likely rebound in GDP growth in the second half of 1993. Activity has responded noticeably to lower interest rates; however, fiscal changes and structural imbalances held down average real GDP growth to 1.7 per cent during the year after the trough and 2.9 per cent in the most recent four quarters ending mid-1993. Over the previous five business cycles dating back to 1959 (omitting the four-quarter recovery of 1980-81), GDP growth in the eight quarters following the trough averaged 5 per cent at an annual rate, compared with only 2.5 per cent in the present upswing. The erratic timing of defence procurements, recurring swings in consumer sentiment, along with hurricanes, flooding and winter storms, have made the recovery seem relatively choppy, causing sharp quarter-to-quarter volatility in income, consumption and inventory accumulation. In the weaker quarters of the recovery, output growth has fallen well below long-run trend rates. However, the size of such fluctuations in growth is perfectly normal for a recovery period (Table 1): what is unusual is the modest average rate of growth since the trough (Diagram 1).

For a while, it was plausible to cite "the jobless recovery" as one explanation (along with fiscal adjustments) for why GDP growth has been so disappointing since the trough. Until the end of 1992, productivity had increased as hiring lagged the pick-up in output growth – delaying the sustained recovery in employee compensation growth needed to drive an acceleration in consumption spending. Such an acceleration in productivity growth has been a feature of all past recoveries, too, but the wide publicity given to large-scale manufacturing layoffs and "restructuring" suggested overall productivity growth might have been unusually strong in the current recovery. However, services employment

Table 1. **Growth and variability of GDP during recovery periods**

Annualised growth at constant 1987 prices

Recoveries	GDP			Private consumption			Government consumption		
	STD	Mean	CV	STD	Mean	CV	STD	Mean	CV
Q2 1958-Q1 1960	3.31	5.14	0.64	1.50	4.43	0.34	5.08	0.16	31.97
Q1 1961-Q4 1962	2.41	4.44	0.54	2.00	4.06	0.49	3.46	3.65	0.95
Q1 1971-Q4 1972	3.00	5.10	0.59	1.91	5.65	0.34	2.13	–1.14	–1.87
Q2 1975-Q1 1977	2.32	4.86	0.48	1.65	5.23	0.32	2.42	0.03	82.68
Q4 1982-Q3 1984	3.29	5.40	0.61	1.77	4.93	0.36	2.78	2.86	0.97
Q2 1991-Q1 1993	1.63	2.47	0.66	1.86	2.47	0.75	3.39	–0.87	–3.90
Average of 5 recoveries	2.87	4.99	0.57	1.76	4.86	0.37	3.17	1.11	22.94
	Change in stocks			Private non-residential investment			Residential investment		
	STD	Mean	CV	STD	Mean	CV	STD	Mean	CV
Q2 1958-Q1 1960	2.67	2.34	1.14	10.61	4.96	2.14	23.51	18.15	1.30
Q1 1961-Q4 1962	1.91	2.23	0.86	6.89	4.23	1.63	8.17	7.58	1.08
Q1 1971-Q4 1972	1.16	2.94	0.40	6.74	7.08	0.95	12.86	20.08	0.64
Q2 1975-Q1 1977	2.42	1.48	1.64	7.76	5.00	1.55	20.80	23.06	0.90
Q4 1982-Q3 1984	4.59	2.45	1.87	12.92	9.33	1.38	26.35	31.89	0.83
Q2 1991-Q1 1993	1.13	0.39	2.90	7.37	4.11	1.79	10.91	14.13	0.77
Average of 5 recoveries	2.55	2.29	1.18	8.98	6.12	1.53	18.34	20.15	0.95
	Total domestic demand			Exports of goods and services			Imports of goods and services		
	STD	Mean	CV	STD	Mean	CV	STD	Mean	CV
Q2 1958-Q1 1960	3.53	5.12	0.69	25.80	10.73	2.40	11.79	7.70	1.53
Q1 1961-Q4 1962	2.47	4.73	0.52	14.76	3.22	4.49	6.37	8.68	0.73
Q1 1971-Q4 1972	2.60	5.32	0.49	26.55	9.94	2.67	24.74	12.06	2.05
Q2 1975-Q1 1977	2.97	5.69	0.52	8.96	2.52	3.56	17.65	15.20	1.16
Q4 1982-Q3 1984	3.96	6.76	0.58	7.93	2.74	2.89	15.27	19.32	0.79
Q2 1991-Q1 1993	1.75	2.84	0.62	6.71	6.61	1.02	3.76	9.50	0.40
Average of 5 recoveries	3.10	5.52	0.56	16.80	5.83	3.22	15.16	12.59	1.25

STD = the standard deviation.
CV = the coefficient of variation, *i.e.* the standard deviation divided by the mean.
Source: U.S. Department of Commerce.

Diagram 1. **REAL GDP IN THE "PROTOTYPE RECOVERY" AND IN THE CURRENT RECOVERY**

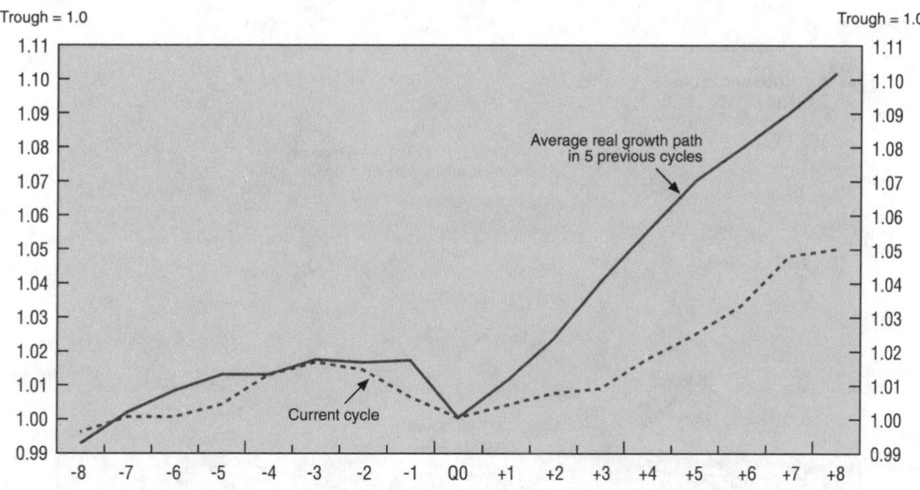

Source: Department of Commerce and OECD.

growth has been quite strong in 1993, given weak growth of output. In light of the relatively mild recovery, cumulative employment growth is by now similar to what past experience would have suggested[1] (Diagram 2). Thus, cyclical productivity increases may explain the slow growth of labour incomes and consumer spending in the initial stages of the current and past recoveries, but not the overall weakness of recent GDP growth relative to past recoveries.

In fact, productivity changes have a positive effect during recoveries. Cyclical productivity increases tend to boost the returns to capital and the funds available for new investment. Furthermore, together with vigorous competition, the recent extraordinary growth of productivity in the computer industry has led to very sharp computer price declines in the last year or two, allowing firms' investment dollars to stretch much further (Diagram 3). Thus, while the volume of non-computer equipment investment increased a healthy 10 per cent over the past year, computer investment has surged a spectacular 36 per cent. Of course, another reason for the boom in equipment investment over the last year or so is the fall in interest rates on corporate bonds, which has reduced the cost of new borrowing and freed up internal funds for investment by reducing the business

Diagram 2. **HAS THIS BEEN A JOBLESS RECOVERY?**

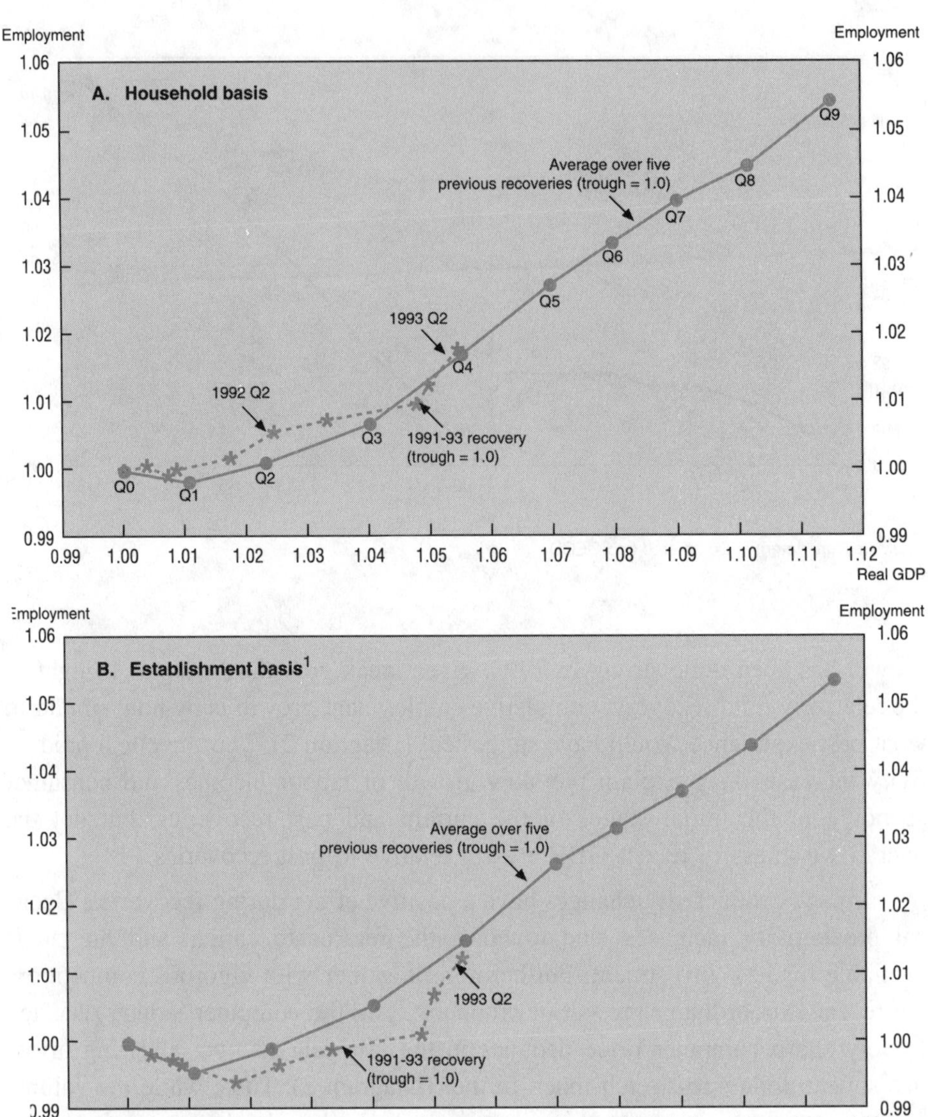

Establishment-survey-based non-farm business employment plus household-survey-based employment in iculture and government, and the self-employed.

ırce: Department of Commerce and OECD.

Diagram 3. **EQUIPMENT INVESTMENT**

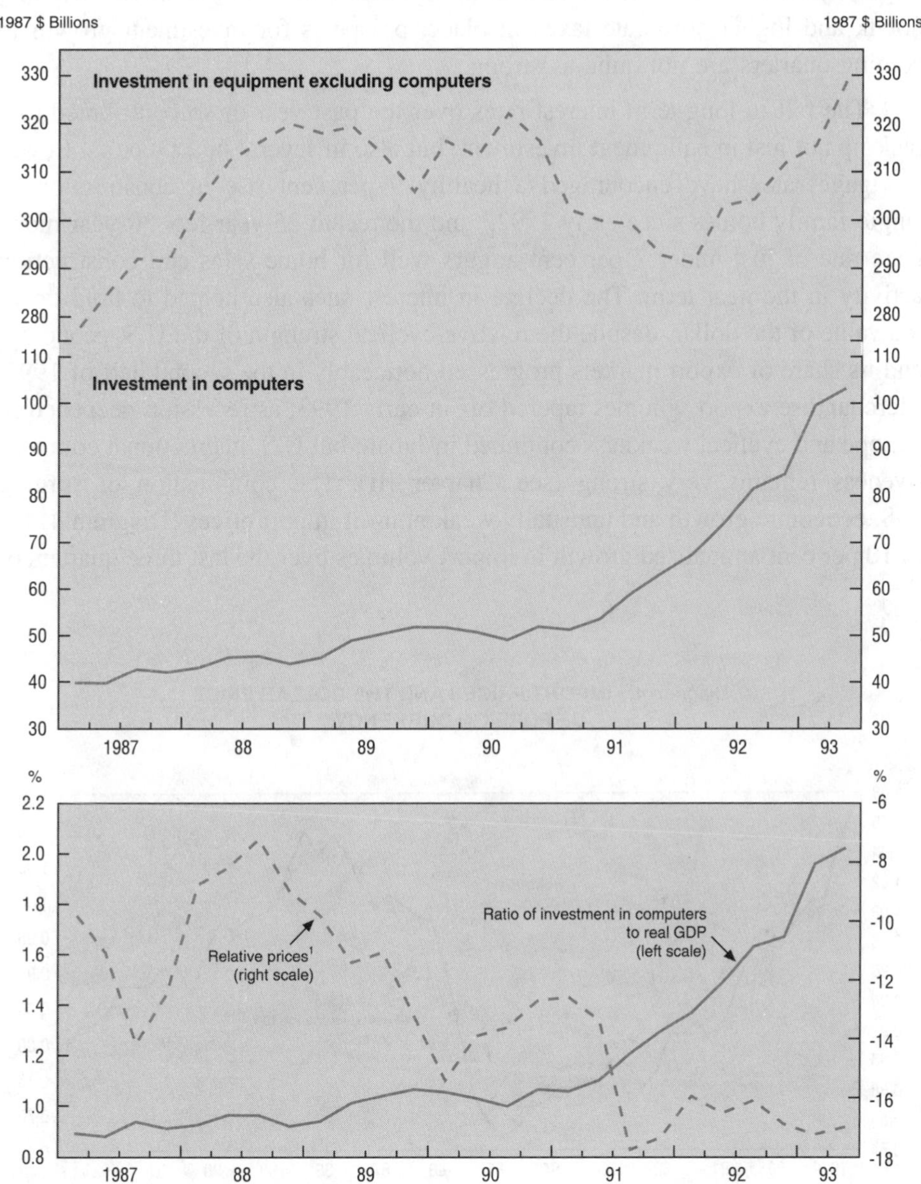

1. Percentage change over four quarters in the ratio of the deflator for computers to the GDP deflator.
Source: Department of Commerce.

sector's debt-service burden. But with the cyclical boom in productivity winding down, and higher corporate taxes in place, prospects for investment growth in coming quarters are not quite as strong.

The fall in long-term interest rates over the past year or so contributed to a pick-up not just in equipment investment, but also in several other sectors. Lower mortgage rates have encouraged a healthy 9 per cent rise in construction of single-family homes since early 1992,[2] and the recent 25-year-low 30-year mortgage rate of just under 7 per cent augurs well for home sales and construction activity in the near term. The decline in interest rates also helped to hold down the value of the dollar, despite the relative cyclical strength of the U.S. economy, and its share of export markets progressed noticeably in the second half of 1992. Merchandise export volumes tapered off in early 1993, as recession deepened in Europe and cyclical weakness continued in Japan, but U.S. international competitiveness remains very strong (see Chapter III). The combination of surging U.S. economic growth and unusually weak non-oil import prices (Diagram 4) led to 10 per cent annualised growth in import volumes over the last three quarters of

Diagram 4. **IMPORT PRICES AND THE DOLLAR PRICE OF FOREIGN CURRENCY**

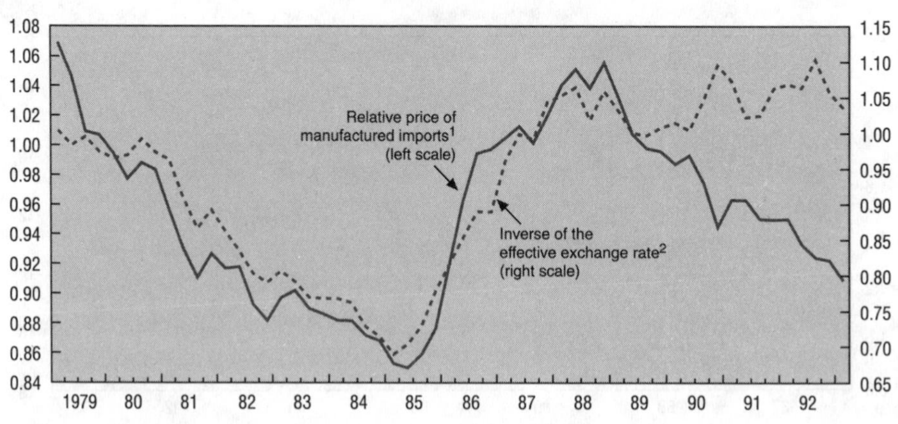

1. Ratio of manufactured import prices to producer prices of industrial goods.
2. The average dollar value of trading-partners' currencies.

Source: OECD.

1992, and import growth was even a bit faster in the first half of 1993, despite the slowdown in domestic demand. Thus, net exports have contributed negatively to output growth since early 1992, the first such sustained reduction since 1986.

Consumption growth has been erratic over the last year or so (Table 1). Post-election optimism may have contributed to an upswing in spending late in 1992, while unpleasant surprises on federal tax bills and a huge winter storm in March held down consumption in early 1993. Looking through these fluctuations however, consumption growth has averaged about 3 per cent since early 1992 – similar to overall output growth. Nothing particularly surprising occurred to the determinants of consumption over the past year. The ratio of household net worth to disposable income has remained near its long-run average. The personal saving rate, at about 4½ per cent, remains rather low relative to the OECD average. Still, this second-quarter level is only slightly lower than the average for 1991 and 1992. In relation to the modest growth of GDP in recent quarters, private consumption demand appears to be neither a major driving force nor a constraint.

Inventories have served to damp the swings in GDP growth over the last four or five quarters. On balance, though, inventories have been a slight drag on the economy since early 1991, not quite keeping pace with real sales levels. There is little to suggest the existence of any inventory overhang which might pose a threat to growth in activity over the coming year.

The sectors holding down overall activity are those where structural adjustment continues: government and non-residential construction. Weakness in government spending has been the most severe drag on growth in aggregate demand. Defence downsizing has led to a 2½ per cent average annual rate of decline in real federal purchases in recent quarters, despite continued solid growth in non-defence purchases. The irregular timing of defence outlays contributed to the surge in GDP in the third quarter of 1992 and the downturn in GDP growth in early 1993. The pattern of outlays by state and local authorities has been less erratic, but, like the federal government, they have also had to pare spending. Their budget problems began well before the 1990-91 recession, and the spending correction continued through early 1993. Over the past year, real state and local purchases have stagnated, as governments have offset rising payrolls by cutting back on construction activity. Still, the states have a long way to go to correct fiscal imbalances. As of early 1993, overall state budgets excluding pension funds were, in aggregate, almost $60 billion in deficit: frequently, state governments have tapped their capital budgets to circumvent laws requiring that current operating budgets be in balance.

The weakness of investment in non-residential structures can be traced almost entirely to the commercial office building sector. The office construction boom of the 1980s left a legacy of excess office space, which caused a collapse in real construction activity from $45 billion (in constant prices of 1987) in the mid-1980s to $16 billion in early 1993. Even with little new office construction in recent quarters, the nation-wide average vacancy rate on office buildings remains about 18 per cent, compared with an early-1980s average of about 5 per cent. Thus, further declines in commercial construction are quite possible. However, the overall decline in non-residential construction appears to be slowing, as increases in construction of factories, utilities and other structures begin to outweigh the continuing decline in the dwindling office construction market. Indeed, a burst of natural gas drilling activity was enough to generate strong overall non-residential construction growth in the second quarter. However, the rebound is not likely to be carried through into the latter part of the year.

Slow labour-market improvement

Shifts in employment over the past year or two reflect the labour-market consequences of several structural trends. Defence downsizing certainly played an important part in restraining the pace of recovery in GDP, and the corresponding layoffs show up in the slow pace of overall employment growth since the trough: no growth at all in 1991 and only about 1 to 1½ per cent since early 1992. California, the biggest centre of defence production, has seen employment decline by almost 2 per cent over the past year, while most other states have had marked increases in employment since the trough. Employment has been held down not just by defence cut-backs, though, but also by widespread restructuring and productivity improvement in large manufacturing firms. Thus, manufacturing employment has declined since early 1989, while employment has expanded in the service sector – particularly in health services, restaurants and business services. The strength of employment growth in health services reflects the rising demand for health care, while the rise in demand for workers in business services reflects increased use of temporary hiring agencies[3] – not particularly encouraging, if one is looking for signs of solid long-term gains in labour demand.

Increases in the cost of doing business have had a major effect on employment in recent quarters.[4] The continued rapid growth in benefit costs relative to wages has encouraged many employers to make greater use of part-time, rather than full-time workers. Thus, the number of those working part-time because they could find only part-time work rose 4.2 per cent over the past year – much faster than overall employment growth. Increased costs of employing additional workers have also encouraged firms to rely on overtime to a greater extent than in the past: since its 1991 trough the average workweek for all non-supervisory workers has risen by 0.7 hours to 34.7 hours in August.

The U.S. labour market continues to demonstrate a fair degree of flexibility. Even though manufacturing employment has fallen about 4 per cent over the past two years, the number of unemployed manufacturing workers has declined. Furthermore, the decline in manufacturing unemployment has been faster than the decline in overall unemployment, suggesting that many workers formerly employed in manufacturing may have found jobs in other sectors.[5] Many of the new jobs may not be as rewarding for the relocating workers (financially or otherwise), but this does suggest that defence downsizing and manufacturing-sector restructuring may not lead to severe long-term structural unemployment. Another positive indicator for the long term is the decline in median length of unemployment in recent months: from a peak of 9.4 weeks in December 1992 to 8.4 weeks in August 1993.[6] However, the median length of unemployment has not declined quite as much as would normally be the case, given the drop in the overall unemployment rate since mid-1992. Greater reduction in long-term unemployment may have been hampered by the unusually large fraction of permanent versus temporary job losses in the 1990-91 recession. Two other contributing factors may be the successive extensions of unemployment insurance benefits, and some permanent shifts in the sectoral and skill mix of labour demand in recent years.

With the overall unemployment rate at 6.7 per cent in August, the decline in joblessness has been small relative to the corresponding stage of past recoveries – due to the weaker expansion, the disincentives to job search from extended unemployment insurance (see Chapter II), and the difficulties and delays involved in relocating laid-off defence workers in new sectors. Estimates in

Chapter III suggest that in mid-1993 productivity is near trend levels. Thus, a further decline in the unemployment rate over the next few quarters may come about even if the recovery continues to be relatively subdued.

No clear downturn of inflation

The continuing excess of unemployment over most estimates of the NAIRU suggests that downward pressure on wage growth might still be expected, even this far into the recovery. However, growth of hourly compensation rates (as measured by the employment cost index) has flattened out over the past year or so: the 3½ per cent growth over the past four quarters is no lower than in the previous year. If anything, there has been a slight increase. While a little surprising, this is not yet cause for alarm. Given strong productivity growth up to the end of 1992, unit labour costs increased very little until early 1993. Nonetheless, underlying consumer price inflation through August has not yet shown a clear downturn from the 3 per cent range. In part this may reflect a cyclical increase in the mark-up over unit labour costs, back closer to historical norms (Diagram 5). The increase in mark-up is probably related to the pick-up in capacity utilisation, which has retraced more than half the decline which occurred from the January 1989 peak to the March 1991 trough. By this measure, the remaining economic slack is similar to that in labour markets: since the June 1992 peak, the unemployment rate has made up a little over half of its excess over the Secretariat's estimate of the end-1993 NAIRU (roughly 6 per cent of the labour force).

Consumer prices of food and energy increased relatively slowly over the course of 1992,[7] although they contributed noticeably to swings in aggregate inflation. The "core" CPI excluding food and energy, often a better indicator of underlying price trends, increased at roughly a 3½ per cent rate in 1992 (Diagram 6). In the first quarter of 1993, core CPI growth moved up to a 4.3 per cent annual rate, leading to concern that inflation might be picking up again, despite slack in labour and product markets and slow growth in import prices. However, there was no acceleration in the corresponding personal consumption deflator,[8] and many analysts blamed the acceleration on seasonal-adjustment difficulties and other measurement problems, rather than any underlying price pressure. Indeed, CPI growth from May through July was minimal:[9] reading through the

Diagram 5. **COSTS OF PRODUCTION AND UNIT PROFITS**
Non-financial corporate sector

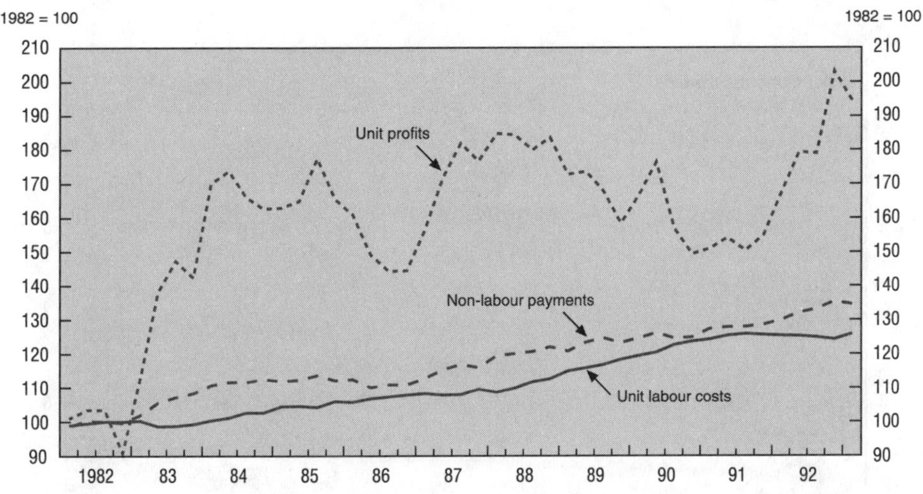

Source: Bureau of Labor Statistics.

quarterly swings, underlying consumer price inflation appears to have remained in the 3 per cent range.

Since productivity growth in recent years has been more rapid in computers and other investment goods than in most household goods and services, rates of inflation for producer durable equipment have been correspondingly slower. In particular, the price deflator for computing equipment has fallen 15 per cent in the past four quarters. Price growth for other producer durables has also been weak, though not quite as dramatically so – their deflator rose 1.6 per cent. Overall, prices for total equipment investment showed little change in 1992.[10] Prices of new structures, however, began to increase more rapidly in the second half of 1992, after a pick-up in construction activity had pushed up costs of lumber and other raw materials. Over the past four quarters, the residential investment deflator has increased at a 4 per cent annualised rate, after stagnating in 1991 and early 1992.

The federal purchases deflator increased almost one per cent faster than consumer prices in 1992 and at about a 9 per cent annual rate in the first quarter

Diagram 6. **AN END TO WAGE/PRICE DECELERATION?**
Year over year percentage change

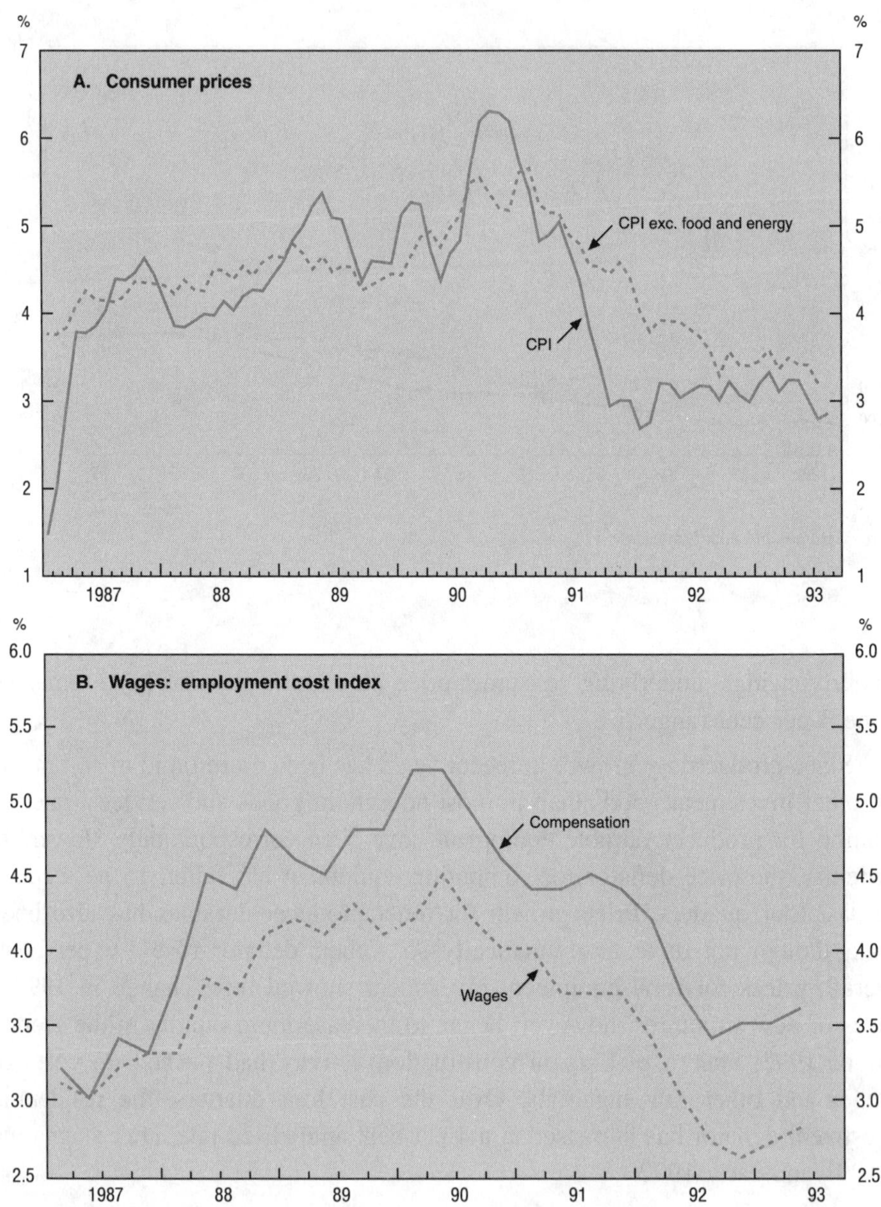

Source: Bureau of Labor Statistics.

of 1993. This inflationary surge was not caused by a rise in prices of goods purchased by the government, but rather by the relatively strong growth of federal employee compensation. From the first quarter of 1992 to the first quarter of 1993, the deflator for employee compensation increased 5.3 per cent. This figure is probably overstated by about a percentage point, due to conceptual problems in measuring the government deflator.[11] Nonetheless, the federal compensation deflator increased far more rapidly than inflation economy-wide – or even compensation in the rest of the economy. However, second-quarter growth in the federal compensation deflator was in line with overall inflation rates economywide, and the 1994 Budget incorporates a temporary pay freeze for civilian employees, which will hold down measured inflation next year.

Overall, the GDP deflator increased at a 3 per cent annual rate in the first half of 1993. This increase, similar to the 1992 average rate of 2.9 per cent, may overstate actual inflationary pressures, for reasons discussed above. However, the Blue Chip survey of business economists indicates that many expect consumer price inflation to continue to edge upward in 1994, despite the modest pace of economic recovery. They may well turn out to be wrong, but such pessimistic inflation expectations may be affecting current wage- and price-setting decisions – another reason why inflation has not declined further in the past year or so, despite the slack in the economy.

Cyclical deterioration in the external balance

The current-account deficit has widened in the past year or so, from a Gulf War-adjusted level of $51 billion[12] in 1991 to $66 billion in 1992. However, export volumes in 1992 were actually quite strong. The U.S. share of foreign markets continued to increase (though at a slowing pace), and thus real merchandise exports increased more than 6 per cent, despite deceleration in foreign activity. Real service exports increased similarly, and the surplus on services rose by about $8 billion. The deterioration in the external balance came in two other items, receipts of factor income and merchandise imports. The first of these reflects in part a cyclical deterioration in earnings on direct investment abroad (though these receipts of factor income did rebound in the first half of 1993). More fundamentally, the weakening of net factor income results from the long-run deterioration in the U.S. net asset position internationally. Years of large

Table 2. **Current account**

$ billion, seasonally adjusted annual rates

	1990	1991	1992	1992				1993	
				Q1	Q2	Q3	Q4	Q1	Q2
Current account balance	–92	–8	–66	–27	–73	–71	–95	–89	–108
Exports of goods, services and income	689	708	730	729	726	728	739	736	751
Imports of goods, services and income	747	724	764	726	767	771	792	795	831
Balances									
Goods	–109	–74	–96	–71	–99	–110	–104	–117	–138
Non-factor services	31	46	56	56	55	61	54	58	59
Investment income	20	13	6	18	4	7	–3	0	–1
Private transfers	–13	–14	–14	–15	–15	–14	–14	–13	–14
Official transfers	–20	20	–18	–14	–17	–15	–27	–17	–14

Source: U.S. Department of Commerce, *Survey of Current Business.*

federal deficits, combined with falling private saving, have boosted capital inflows in the form of foreign direct investment[13] and foreign borrowing – and this has taken its toll on the nation's income. For the first time ever, the investment income balance was negative in the fourth quarter of 1992, and the balance remained in deficit in the first half of 1993.

Merchandise import volumes rose 10 per cent in 1992. In part, this reflected an increase in demand for consumer goods from China and Latin America, as the relative prices of these consumer-good imports have fallen noticeably since 1990. However, the main factor behind the import surge was a 43 per cent increase in the volume of computer imports, paralleling the boom in domestic computer demand. Falling computer prices held down overall growth of merchandise import prices to 1.4 per cent; nonetheless, the overall increase in nominal spending on merchandise imports brought to an end a four-year period of steady shrinkage in the foreign trade deficit. This increase is not necessarily a cause for concern: importing computers to boost domestic investment seems a much sounder reason for increased foreign borrowing than in the mid- to late-1980s, when the widening deficit reflected instead a sharp decline in personal and government saving rates and an increased focus on government consumption.

The merchandise trade balance deteriorated sharply in the first half of 1993, reflecting both a deceleration in exports (with recession in Europe and Japan), and continued rapid growth of imports, notably imports of computers and automobiles. However, international cost competitiveness remains very strong: growth in unit labour costs was very low through 1992, though accelerating in early 1993. With very favourable relative costs and prices, the United States is well-positioned to expand export volumes once the cyclical downturn in Europe and Japan is over.

Short-term prospects

In coming quarters, a combination of defence cut-backs, federal tax increases, state and local budget problems, persistent weakness in export markets and the continuing glut of commercial office space will serve to hold growth of aggregate demand below the pace of past recoveries. However, the profits and overall balance-sheet positions of firms have improved substantially over the past year or so. As firms begin to spend more of their increased cash-flow to hire workers and expand the scope of their operations, real output growth is expected to pick up again in the second half of the year. Output growth in the 3 per cent range is expected through the end of 1993, with similar growth in 1994. This cyclical rebound, combined with the higher corporate, personal and indirect taxes contained in the budget reconciliation bill passed this summer, is projected to reduce the federal deficit on a national accounts basis to 3.9 per cent of GDP in 1994.[14] Of course, the prospect of higher taxation and uncertainty about health-care reform could lead firms to slow the pace of expansion and households to boost saving over the next quarter or two. However, if Congress settles on a national health-care package that is not too expensive, business cost increases will probably not fully offset the stimulative effects of low corporate bond rates and much-improved profit margins. Thus, while equipment investment is expected to slow in mid-1993 from the rapid rates of the past four quarters, the fundamentals suggest further medium-term stimulus to activity from investment growth.

Even a modest recovery like the one projected would typically generate at least 1 per cent annual growth of employment. However, an unusually long average workweek as of mid-1993 could affect the normal relationship between

Table 3. **Near-term outlook**

Percentage change from previous period, seasonally adjusted at annual rates, volume (1987 prices)

	1987 current prices $ billion	% of GDP	1992	1993	1994	1992		1993		1994	
						I	II	I	II	I	II
Private consumption	3 052.2	67.2	2.6	3.2	2.8	2.6	3.9	2.6	3.5	2.6	2.6
Government consumption	881.5	19.4	–0.1	–0.6	–0.3	0	1.4	–2.6	1.4	–0.9	–0.7
Gross fixed investment	723.0	15.9	6.2	9.5	9.2	7.8	9.1	11.0	7.1	10.0	9.7
of which:											
Residential	225.2	5.0	16.3	7.4	8.6	18.9	13.5	5.4	5.5	10.0	8.8
Non-residential	497.7	11.0	2.9	10.4	9.4	4.0	7.5	13.2	7.7	10.0	10.0
Final domestic demand	4 656.5	102.6	2.5	3.4	3.2	2.8	4.2	2.9	3.7	3.1	3.1
Stockbuilding [1]	26.1	0.6	0.3	0.2	0.1	0	0.2	0.5	–0.3	0.3	0
Total domestic demand	4 682.6	103.2	2.9	3.6	3.3	2.8	4.4	3.3	3.4	3.4	3.1
Exports of goods and services	363.8	8.0	6.4	3.1	4.9	5.5	5.3	1.8	3.4	5.1	5.9
Imports of goods and services	506.9	11.2	8.7	9.3	7.3	7.4	9.9	10.5	6.3	7.7	7.5
Foreign balance [1]	–143.1	–3.2	–0.3	–0.8	–0.4	–0.2	–0.6	–1.1	–0.4	–0.4	–0.3
GDP at constant prices			2.6	2.8	3.0	2.6	3.8	2.3	3.0	3.0	2.9
GDP price deflator			2.9	2.6	2.3	3.2	2.1	3.2	2.1	2.4	2.4
GDP at current prices	4 539.6	100.0	5.5	5.6	5.4	5.9	6.0	5.5	5.1	5.5	5.3
Memorandum items											
Private consumption deflator			3.3	2.8	2.7	3.8	2.6	3.1	2.2	2.9	2.8
Unemployment rate			7.4	6.8	6.5	7.4	7.4	7.0	6.7	6.6	6.4
Household saving rate			5.0	4.6	4.2	5.3	4.8	5.2	4.1	4.2	4.2
Three-month Treasury bill rate			3.4	3.0	4.1	3.8	3.1	3.0	3.0	3.7	4.5
Ten-year Treasury note rate			7.0	5.9	5.5	7.3	6.7	6.1	5.6	5.5	5.6
Net lending of general government											
$ billion			–269	–244	–195	–	–	–	–	–	–
Per cent of GDP			–4.5	–3.8	–2.9	–	–	–	–	–	–
Current account balance											
$ billion			–66	–107	–135	–	–	–	–	–	–
Per cent of GDP			–1.1	–1.7	–2.0	–	–	–	–	–	–

1. The yearly and half-yearly rates of change refer to changes expressed as a percentage of GDP in the previous period.
Source: OECD estimates.

output and employment growth in the very near term. The average workweek is likely to ease, with rising output in the next few quarters yielding a 1½ to 2 per cent annualised growth of employment and a slow decline in the unemployment rate to below 6½ per cent in late 1994. This rise in employment and a slight increase in real compensation rates will tend to boost personal income next year; on the other hand, higher taxes will reduce growth in disposable income and the saving rate is expected to rise moderately from the flood-distorted lows of mid-summer. Thus, growth of real private consumption is expected to ease back to the 2½ per cent range. Combined with healthy investment growth, that should be sufficient to sustain the pace of expansion, despite the structural weaknesses mentioned above. U.S. growth is likely to exceed the pace in Europe, leading to a cyclical widening in the current-account balance, from 1.1 per cent of GDP in 1992 to 2 per cent in 1994. Nonetheless, the very favourable cost position of U.S. manufacturers ought to boost the U.S. share of export markets, unless more serious trade disputes arise: for example, if the Uruguay Round negotiations end in failure.

Rising mark-ups over unit labour cost have sustained consumer price inflation in the 3 per cent range in past quarters, despite slow growth of labour costs. For several reasons, these mark-ups are likely to stabilise in coming quarters. First, investment has been strong enough and output growth mild enough to avoid substantial pressure of output on capacity. Second, slow activity growth internationally should hold down price growth for industrial raw materials such as oil, lumber, copper and scrap metals. Prices for agricultural commodities may be higher in 1993-94, due to weather-inflicted crop damage, but this should affect primarily food prices, with little implication for economy-wide core inflation. Instead, the slow growth of labour costs should cause underlying consumer price growth to ease slightly, to just below 3 per cent.

Even with inflation under control as projected, near-zero real short-term interest rates will no longer be appropriate when the unemployment rate edges downward toward its full-employment level and excess capacity dwindles: accordingly, a process of monetary tightening is likely to get underway. An initial minimal increase in the Federal Funds rate is expected in late 1993, serving mainly as a signal to calm inflation worries in bond markets. By late 1994, the Funds rate is expected to rise by some 150 basis points – though economic activity is more sensitive to changes in long-term rates, which are projected to remain fairly stable.

Risks to the projections

Economic growth could be substantially more favourable than projected here – more in line with a normal recovery – if several favourable events occurred. First of all, the cost savings from corporate restructurings implemented over the past few years could slow the rate of price inflation more than projected, and thereby boost growth of aggregate demand and output. Also, prompt introduction and passage of a relatively low-cost health care reform bill would markedly improve business confidence, boosting investment and hiring. Finally, export markets could expand more than assumed here, if recovery in Europe and Japan gets underway already later this year.

On the downside, the health-care debate could drag on into mid-1994, with a relatively high-cost option finally chosen. Firms and households might then attempt to increase savings in order to consolidate their financial positions further as a precaution against a possible economic slowdown in 1994-95. Higher private saving rates would most likely be a plus for the long term, but in the coming few quarters the effect could be a slowdown in spending on consumption and investment goods, as well as weak hiring. Lastly, widening trade disputes could lead to a sequence of protectionist measures, reducing income and activity at home and abroad.

II. Macroeconomic policies

Progress in deficit reduction

Recent outcomes

In 1990, after great efforts, the U.S. authorities managed to pass the Omnibus Budget Reconciliation Act (OBRA90), which was intended to generate the largest deficit reduction in the nation's history (some $485 billion) during the first half of this decade. Within short order it became clear that deficit reduction was not being achieved: the actual federal deficit rose from $221 billion (4.0 per cent of GDP) in fiscal 1990 to $290 billion (4.9 per cent of GDP) in 1992 (Diagram 7). Deficit projections made by the Congressional Budget Office (1993*c*) (CBO) in March 1993 showed a cumulative 1991-95 baseline deficit of $1 433 billion, nearly twice that projected at the time of OBRA90 (Table 4). It is widely understood that a major reason for the overrun is the poor economic growth performance that has been recorded in recent years: the CBO attributed nearly 40 per cent of the deterioration to this factor. Otherwise, the control mechanisms have worked well, as policy changes in the interim have had virtually no impact on the cumulative deficit. It is the so-called ''technical changes'' (all other residual sources of discrepancies) which have been responsible for over 60 per cent of the $663 billion cumulative worsening of the baseline deficit through fiscal 1995. Most of this has occurred on the spending side, especially on the two public health-care programmes. Other major benefit programmes have also turned out to be unexpectedly costly, and debt service estimates have been raised because of higher deficits than had been projected. Covering the losses of depositors in failed financial institutions, on the other hand, appears likely to cost substantially less than expected in 1990. Finally, elasticities of tax revenues with respect to their respective bases were systematically overestimated, and revenue shortfalls independent of economic conditions amount to $178 billion over the five-year period.

Diagram 7. **FEDERAL RECEIPTS, EXPENDITURES AND DEFICIT**[1]

Per cent of GDP, fiscal-year basis

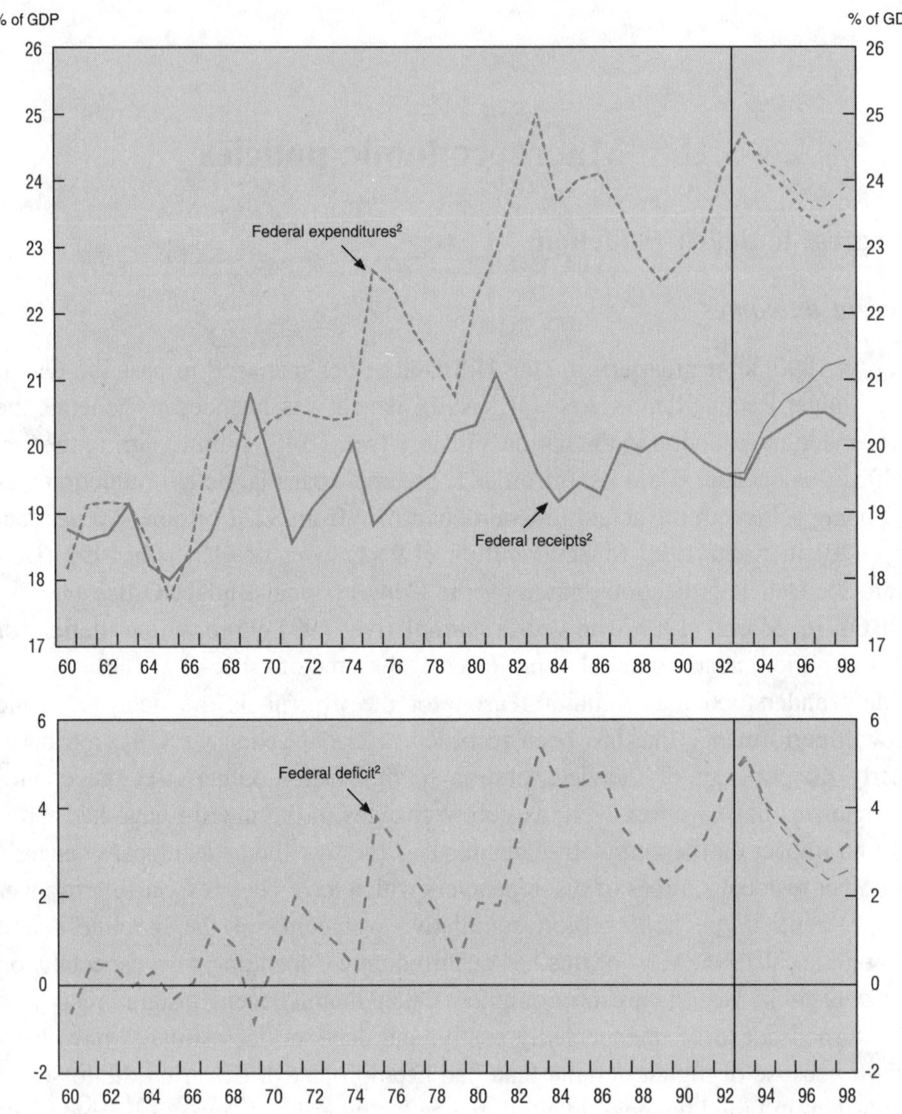

1. OECD definitions for receipts and expenditures. Forecast data based on Office of Management and Budget (1993*b*).
2. Darker lines refer to forecast assuming "baseline economics"; lighter lines refer to forecasts assuming "Administration economics".

Source: OECD.

Table 4. **Changes in CBO deficit projections since OBRA90**

By fiscal year, in $ billion

	1991	1992	1993	1994	1995	Cumulative total
December 1990 projection	253	262	170	56	29	770
Policy changes						
Revenues	–1	3	5	0	0	7
Outlays	–19	15	14	4	2	16
of which:						
Net outlays on Desert Storm	–20	8	10	2	1	1
Deficit	–19	13	9	4	2	9
Economic changes						
Revenues	–31	–58	–78	–90	–102	–359
Outlays	1	–9	–31	–38	–34	–111
Deficit	32	49	47	52	68	248
Technical changes						
Revenues	–24	–38	–42	–38	–36	–178
Outlays	–21	–71	42	140	148	238
of which:						
Medicaid and Medicare	7	19	32	45	60	163
Deposit insurance	–28	–108	–38	46	37	-91
Deficit	3	-34	84	179	185	417
March 1993 baseline projection	270	290	302	287	284	1 433

Source: Congressional Budget Office (1993*a* and 1993*c*) and OECD.

On a national-accounts basis, the year 1992 saw a sharp widening of the federal deficit (including social security) from $203 billion to $276 billion, as well as a very slight narrowing of the state-and-local surplus (Table 5), the third straight annual decline. OECD figures suggest that the resulting degradation of some 1 percentage point of GDP in the general-government balance was largely due to cyclical factors, but that structural deterioration amounted to nearly ½ percentage point of GDP. A large part of the latter resulted from the previous Administration's decision in March 1992 to reduce the rate of federal withholding on personal income taxes, leaving the growth rate of federal personal tax receipts well below that of household income. The growth of outlays was also robust at both levels of government. While direct purchases were held down by defence cuts, and net interest paid eased marginally with further declines in market interest rates, non-defence purchases rose sharply at the federal level, and transfer payments once again recorded explosive growth.[15] They now represent some 43 per cent of total federal expenditures, compared with about 25 per cent

Table 5. **Government receipts and expenditures, 1992**

National accounts basis, $ billion

	Federal		State and local	
	Level	% change	Level	% change
Receipts	1 160.4	3.4	837.7	7.7
Personal taxes	474.1	0.1	153.2	5.4
Corporate taxes	115.0	12.2	25.2	17.1
Indirect business taxes	81.5	4.2	422.7	6.5
Social insurance contributions	489.7	4.6	63.7	5.1
Federal grants-in-aid			173.0	12.8
Expenditures	1 458.4	9.4	822.3	8.1
Purchases	449.1	0.4	665.8	3.5
of which:				
National defence	315.8	–2.5	0	–
of which:				
Compensation	135.4	2.1	0	–
Other	180.4	–5.6	0	–
Non-defence	133.4	7.9	665.8	3.5
of which:				
Compensation	63.7	7.2	454.9	4.4
Other	69.7	8.6	210.8	1.5
Transfer payments (net)	623.3	19.4	233.6	18.0
of which:				
To persons	608.0	10.5	233.6	18.0
To rest of the world (net)	15.3	n.m.[1]	0	–
Grants-in-aid to State and local governments	173.0	12.8		–
Net interest paid	186.7	–0.1	–43.8	–9.5
Gross subsidies	30.6	5.2	0.4	0
Current surplus of government enterprises	4.4	–26.7	23.7	3.0
Dividends received	0	–	10.0	5.2
Surplus/Deficit	–298.0	41.6	15.5	–9.4
of which:				
Social insurance funds	30.4	–39.3	57.5	–4.6
Other	–328.4	26.0	–42.1	–2.3

1. Not meaningful.
Sources: U.S. Department of Commerce, *Survey of Current Business* and OECD.

30 years ago (Diagram 8). Upward pressure on so-called "entitlement" (mandatory) spending continues unabated because federal transfers have a strong autonomous dynamic. This is attributable to factors specific to health care (discussed in detail in last year's *Survey*), Congressional concessions (for example, the expansion of the Earned Income Tax Credit (EITC) and the broadening of Medicaid in OBRA90), judicial decisions and the fading stigma of receiving public transfers.[16]

Diagram 8. **FEDERAL GOVERNMENT EXPENDITURES**

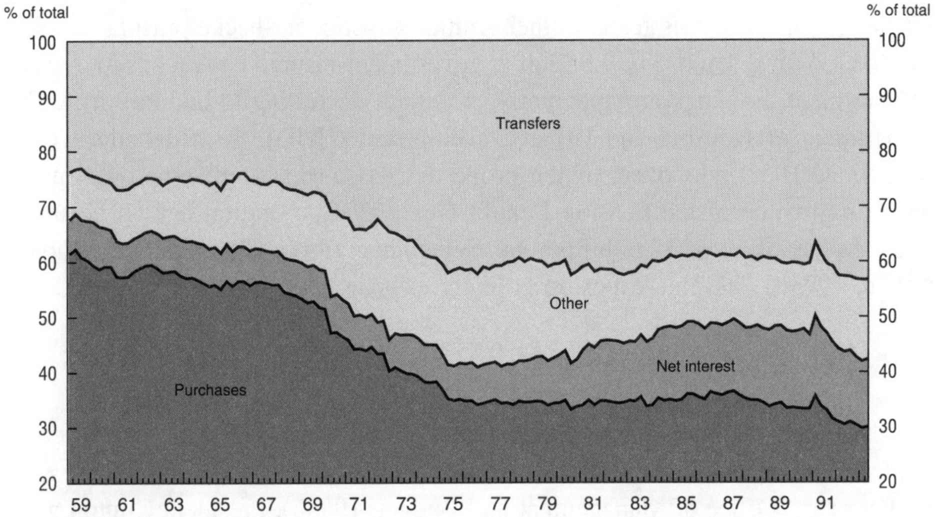

Source: Department of Commerce.

Indications are that the federal budget deficit for fiscal 1993 will be much lower than expected at the time of the 1993 budget ($352 billion) and could very well be much lower than 1992's $290 billion.[17] For the first eleven months of the fiscal year, the cumulated deficit was running about $30 billion below year-earlier levels. The main contributing factor is deposit insurance – excluding such outlays, the deficit is running slightly ahead of last year's pace. After the Resolution Trust Corporation Refinancing, Restructuring and Improvement Act of December 1991 appropriated only $25 billion for the resolution of insolvent thrifts in 1992, and then only provided that they occurred by end-March, the rate of resolutions fell off markedly. In 1993, the new Administration requested a further $45 billion in funding, but legislation moving through Congress at the time of writing is less generous, providing about $27 billion. Estimates differ as to how much is still needed to finish the job of thrift-institution resolution: the Administration believes $29 billion will suffice; the CBO pegs the need at $35 billion in present-value terms (Congressional Budget Office, 1993*d*).

While the deposit-insurance disaster looks likely to be less costly to the taxpayer than once was feared, other similar government-backed insurance bills may be looming. Up to $11.9 billion in government-insured bank loans to owners of apartment buildings are apparently in default according to auditors from the Department of Housing and Urban Development (HUD). Such defaults would necessitate HUD take-overs of the properties. Also, the single-employer insurance programme of the Pension Benefit Guaranty Corporation had an accumulated deficit of over $2½ billion by September 1991 (Congressional Budget Office, 1993*b*), and this exposure is likely to grow.

"A vision of change"

The new Administration quickly recognised the need to act in order to confront the problem of the deficit. Already in his State of the Union address of 17 February (Office of Management and Budget, 1993*b*), President Clinton gave the outlines of a package which would have cut the deficit substantially. In the Administration's view, the saving was to be a cumulative $460 billion to 1998 (a cut of nearly one-quarter), while the CBO evaluation of the impact of the plan was $355 billion (nearly one-fifth), comprising $652 in gross deficit reductions and $297 billion in gross deficit increases (Table 6).[18] Great political importance was attached to the relative weights given to tax increases and spending cuts. In the Administration's view, the latter comprised over 46 per cent of the total, but the CBO (1993*c*) credited changes on the spending side of the Administration proposals with only 25 per cent of the total. In any case, the package would have reversed the recent downward trend in the revenue share of GDP as well as the upward trend in the expenditure share (Diagram 7). One of the main components of the package was a so-called stimulus programme which comprised $16.3 billion (the amount by which 1993 appropriations were expected to fall short of the combined discretionary spending ceilings of OBRA90) of additional budgetary outlays in the short term, plus over $3 billion in extra trust-fund expenditures on transportation infrastructure. Although small in size and to some extent of an investment nature, the programme risked providing pro-cyclical stimulus to the economy. Faced with insurmountable opposition in the Senate, the majority of the programme was abandoned later in the spring.[19] Thereafter, the Congress began the process of designing the legislation to implement deficit reduction. The version passed by the House of Representatives was similar to the Administration

Table 6. **The evolution of federal deficit projections in 1993**

Fiscal years, except as noted

$ billion

	1993	1994	1995	1996	1997	1998	Cumulative total 1994-98
1. January (Bush) uncapped[1] deficit	327	309	307	324	384	426	1 750
With defence proposals	327	305	297	308	362	398	1 670
2. February (Clinton) uncapped[1] baseline (with defence proposals)	319	301	296	297	346	390	1 630
of which: Structural	246	242	264	286	341	381	1 514
Effects of February policy proposals	13	–39	–54	–92	–140	–148	–473
of which: Net spending changes	9	–5	–21	–40	–73	–83	–222
Net revenue changes	3	–33	–34	–51	–68	–65	–251
Resulting deficit	332	262	242	205	206	241	1 156
as a per cent of GDP	5.4	4.0	3.5	2.9	2.7	3.1	–
of which: Structural	258	203	209	194	201	233	1 040
as a per cent of GDP	4.2	3.1	3.0	2.7	2.6	3.0	–
3. April revised baseline	310	302	301	298	347	387	1 635
of which: Structural	240	243	266	287	341	379	1 516
Effects of policy proposals	12	–38	–54	–86	–133	–137	–448
Resulting deficit	322	264	247	212	214	250	1 187
4. September revised baseline	310	305	302	298	347	388	1 640
Effects of OBRA93[2]	6	–41	–82	–100	–128	–145	–495
Administration September deficit[3]	285	259	200	179	184	181	1 003
5. Congressional Budget Office view of uncapped[1] baseline deficit	302	296	302	301	327	361	1 587
CBO capped[1] baseline deficit	302	287	284	290	322	360	1 543
CBO evaluation of February policy proposals	7	–19	–27	–68	–117	–131	–362
of which: Net spending changes	7	9	12	–12	–45	–60	–96
Net revenue changes	0	–28	–39	–56	–72	–72	–267
CBO evaluation of OBRA93[2]	4	–26	–54	–82	–117	–143	–422
CBO September deficit[3]	266	253	196	190	198	200	1 037
On a national accounts basis	273	220	194	192	191	196	993
6. OECD projection, calendar year	247	207	n.a.	n.a.	n.a.	n.a.	n.a.

1. The terms "capped" and "uncapped" refer to the enforcement of the limits on discretionary spending through 1995 required to meet the terms of the Budget Enforcement Act of 1990. The Congressional Budget Office assumed that capped outlays are fixed in real terms thereafter.
2. The line also includes other legislative changes which raise the cumulative deficit by $10 billion (Administration) or $4 billion (CBO).
3. Including the effects of revised economic assumptions and technical re-estimates.

Sources: Office of Management and Budget (1993*b*, 1993*c* and 1993*d*) and Congressional Budget Office (1993*c* and 1993*f*).

proposals, but more important changes were wrought by the Senate. The final reconciliation bill (OBRA93) contained many of the major Administration proposals, with a Congressional claim of $496 billion in cumulative deficit reduction over the 1994-98 period (Table 7).[20]

Table 7. **Deficit reduction resulting from the Omnibus Budget Reconciliation Act of 1993**

Changes in $ billion

		1994	1995	1996	1997	1998	1994-98
Receipts		–27	–47	–54	–63	–59	–250
Outlays		–19	–36	–46	–66	–87	–255
of which:	Mandatory	–8	–14	–18	–22	–26	–87
	Discretionary	–10	–17	–18	–27	–36	–108
	Debt service	–1	–5	–10	–17	–26	–60
Total		–47	–83	–101	–129	–146	–505

Source: Office of Management and Budget (1993*d*).

Revenue-raising measures

OBRA93 contains a large number of proposed changes of varying importance. On the revenue side, the largest single change is a major increase in personal income taxes for high-income earners retroactive to 1 January 1993, yielding a projected $115 billion in extra revenues by 1998: raising the top marginal rate from 31 to 36 per cent, plus introducing a special surtax effectively raising it to 39.6 per cent for those with taxable incomes above $250 000. In addition, the ceiling on wages subject to the hospital insurance component of the social-security payroll tax (currently $135 000) has been repealed, generating $29 billion over the next five years. In effect, since this tax is widely believed to be paid ultimately by the employee, the effective top marginal rate on wage income has been raised to over 42 per cent.

While these changes were understandable on the basis of equity considerations,[21] given the major shifts in income distribution observed since 1980, the likely incentive effects and the resulting possibility of revenue over-estimation are a matter of concern.[22] First, with capital gains still taxed at a maximum rate of 28 per cent, there will be strong incentives to transform earned income into capital gains (assuming inflation rates stay low), to provide more executive compensation in tax-free or deferred form and to shift portfolios towards municipal bonds whose interest is untaxed.[23] Second, although the consensus view as to whether taxes influence real behaviour to any substantial degree has become more sceptical in the 1980s (Slemrod, 1992), the labour supply of those earning high enough incomes to face higher rates may be cut back by up to 2 per cent, based on available evidence of the relevant elasticities (MaCurdy, 1992). Spouses' labour-market participation decisions would also be affected: income effects would boost participation, but substitution effects would be negative and might well dominate in this income range. Third, the timing of transactions would shift: indeed, fearing just such a rise, the securities industry paid its employees early bonus payments of some $1.5 billion in December 1992. Official revenue estimators try to account only for the first effect (U.S. Congress, Joint Committee on Taxation, 1992).

Another personal tax change worthy of note raises the share of social-security (public pension) benefits subject to tax from 50 to 85 per cent (treatment similar to private-pension income) for couples with income over a ceiling of $44 000 ($34 000 for individuals) in order to generate $25 billion over the next five years. This is important because social security has long been regarded as sacrosanct in terms of deficit-reduction potential. It should be pointed out, however, that it provides another marriage tax penalty, and it would seem likely to generate a disincentive to save for those in or near retirement in the relevant income range.

Changes in business taxation are also significant.[24] The abandoned stimulus programme included a temporary marginal investment tax credit (ITC) for large firms and a permanent credit for small firms only (see Chapter III). With it, the Administration proposed to raise the corporate income tax rate from 34 to 36 per cent for the approximately 2 700 largest corporations with taxable income exceeding $10 million. The thrust of these changes would have run counter to the 1986 tax reform which was based on the belief that the tax base should be as broad as possible, allowing the lowest possible rates. With the abandonment of the ITC, the increase in the top corporate rate was eventually reduced to 1 percentage point, sufficient to raise about $15 billion in revenues over a five-year horizon.

Easily the most controversial move proposed by the Administration was to advocate an energy tax based in large part on the heat content of individual fuels (the so-called BTU tax). Phased in in three equal steps at mid-1994, mid-1995 and mid-1996, it would have generated $71 billion by 1998 in net terms ($110 billion in gross terms) and about $22 billion per year thereafter. Increased energy taxation is justified based on the inelasticity of its demand (from an optimal taxation point of view) and the negative externalities involved (from an environmental perspective). Rather than a pure carbon tax, which would have been more effective in reducing greenhouse gas emissions, the Administration decided to support this BTU-based approach which taxes coal less severely, primarily on the grounds of regional equity. However, for both environmental and national-security reasons, oil was to be subject to a surcharge. Recognising the regressive nature of the tax, the Administration suggested it be accompanied by a series of measures (expanded Food Stamps, EITC and energy assistance) worth about $22 billion over 1994-98 to low income earners. Nevertheless, in light of fears that it could easily be boosted once in place and that it might harm U.S. international competitiveness (despite the fact that U.S. energy taxation is amongst the lowest in the OECD), the tax quickly drew out armies of lobbyists seeking special exemptions and was eventually excluded from the final legislation. In its stead, the bill includes simply an increase of 4.3 cents per gallon on gasoline and other fuels effective 1 October 1993 (which will generate only $24 billion, one-third of the revenue expected from the BTU tax).

Finally, new revenues are being sought by boosting a wide variety of user fees and reducing related subsidies. Many of these changes are similar in nature to earmarked taxes. Changes in discretionary programmes would raise $7 billion in five years, and modifications of mandatory programmes would yield a further $20 billion. The single change generating the most extra revenue would be a move to auction the rights to that part of the electromagnetic spectrum under the control of the Federal Communications Commission. The Administration also proposed an innovative land-management programme involving, amongst other items, the phasing-out of below-cost timber sales, increases in public grazing fees (which tend to be less than half their fair market value), a permanent extension of the 1993 institution of annual hardrock mining claim holding fees and the imposition of a 12½ per cent royalty on the gross value of hardrock minerals extracted from public lands – altogether worth over $3 billion by 1998. But it withdrew proposals in this area early in the spring, at least temporarily, due to opposition from Congressional members in the western states.

Spending cuts

Besides the abandoned stimulus programme, there are also a wide variety of important changes on the spending side. Gross cuts over the five-year period amount to $329 billion. Quantitatively the most important are the further cuts imposed on defence outlays from the already substantially reduced adjusted baseline of the Bush Administration: about $112 billion (nearly 8 per cent) through 1998. No longer will such spending merely be frozen in nominal terms as in the Bush baseline, but by 1998 it will be cut by some 14 per cent from 1993 levels. Further details and analysis are given in Chapter III.

Spending will also be pared by eliminating 11 discretionary programmes outright, saving nearly $10 billion by 1998, and by various administrative efficiencies. Highlights of the latter are the elimination of 101 800 federal positions in the executive branch (mostly in the Department of Defense), nearly 5 per cent of the total (worth $10.5 billion through 1998); pay restraint involving the omission of a generalised increase in calendar-year 1994 and increases of 1 percentage point less than in the rest of the economy in calendar-years 1995 through 1997 (saving $11.3 billion over five years); taking over the student-loan programme currently handled by the commercial banks ($3.2 billion);[25] and an overarching (and unspecified) cut in administrative costs of 14 per cent by 1997 ($11.3 billion).

A significant number of adjustments to agricultural policies were made in the budget compromise. These include changes in the determination of the acreage reduction requirements for wheat, feedgrains, and cotton; and a cap on the purchase prices of certain dairy products and a reduction in the assessment for milk.[26] The Congressional Budget Office estimates that these policy changes will result in savings of $3 billion over fiscal years 1994-98. Fiscal year 1994 outlays for agricultural subsidies were earlier projected to fall to $12 billion from $17 billion in fiscal year 1993, but disaster assistance for flooding and drought is expected to alter spending estimates.

Another area where savings are being sought is debt management. In May 1993, the Administration announced the details of a major overhaul of its debt-issuance policy. Given that net interest payments represent some 3¼ per cent of GDP, this is a potentially crucial decision. The existing 7-year note will be discontinued ($41 billion were issued in 1992); the 30-year bond will henceforth be issued semiannually, rather than quarterly ($40 billion were issued in 1992, $28.5 billion will be issued this year and $22 billion in 1994); and the funding shortfall will be made up by greater reliance on 2- and 3-year notes and bills. The result is a projected shortening in the average maturity of privately-held federal debt from 5 years and 10 months at the end of 1992 to below 5 years (still well above the post-war trough of 2 years and 5 months recorded at the end of 1975) within a year. Together with the previously announced reduction in the minimum guaranteed rate on U.S. Savings Bonds from 6 to 4 per cent, the Administration expects to save $16.4 billion from the reform over the next five years (over 1 per cent of net interest outlays), although the CBO estimates the changes to be worth substantially less due to different baseline assumptions (Congressional Budget Office, 1993*e*).

Besides the near-certainty[27] of a reduction in interest costs on the public debt, the other possible advantage of a shift away from long-term debt is a reinforcement of lower interest-rate expectations and, therefore, reduced long-term rates. This has been the object of a great deal of academic research over the past decade, but with conflicting results. But there are, in fact, important risks to the move. Given that the Treasury already refinances some 37 per cent of total debt each year (down from 47 per cent in 1980), higher roll-over will make budgetary outlays and outcomes more sensitive to interest-rate fluctuations,[28] thereby possibly raising pressure on the Federal Reserve to keep monetary policy accommodative in order to avoid raising federal interest costs.

Medicare and Medicaid changes

Even before the Administration had finalised its proposals for comprehensive reform of the health-care system, it was forced, in order to meet its deficit-reduction targets, to seek savings in the two public health-care programmes, Medicare (for the elderly) and Medicaid (for some of the poor). The nation's health-care bill reached 14 per cent of GDP in 1992, led by Medicaid outlays which rose some 30 per cent.[29] Twenty-seven separate changes to Medicare are expected to generate $49 billion in cumulative expenditure reduction through 1998, and a number of changes to Medicaid are expected to shrink its cost by a further $7 billion over the same horizon. The highlights of these reforms are presented in Table 8.[30]

Independent of these cost-cutting proposals to modify Medicare and Medicaid, the Administration has been putting together a comprehensive overhaul of the health-care system. Its reform plan was originally scheduled to be released in the spring, but its announcement was delayed until September in order to let the deficit-reduction package clear the Congress first. The reform proposes a form of managed competition, rather than any kind of single-payer system. This implies

Table 8. **Major OBRA93 changes affecting health care**

	Savings through 1998 ($ billion)
1. Increased Medicare premiums beginning in 1996	11.6
2. Reduced supplementary payments to hospitals to cover indirect medical education	3.5
3. Move towards resource-based physician reimbursement system for practice expenses	3.0
4. Permanent extensions of reforms already implemented	7.6
5. Setting laboratory fee schedules for Medicare at market levels	4.5
6. Delaying update of Medicare hospital payments for in-patient services from 1 October to 1 January	6.0
7. Reduced increase in physician fee schedule for non-primary care by 2 percentage points in 1994	1.7
8. Reduced payments to hospitals by 1 percentage point in both 1994 and 1995	7.0
9. Maintaining optional nature of personal care under Medicaid, set to become mandatory in 1995 under OBRA90	5.8

Source: Office of Management and Budget (1993*b*).

that insurance will continue to be employer-provided but purchased through state-based cooperatives or alliances. The new system will aim to achieve near-universal coverage, thereby overcoming the problem of the 37 million Americans presently without medical coverage, as well as the fear of many others that their coverage could be lost in the event of job loss. In particular, insurance will probably be reformed so that there will be guaranteed availability and renewability, community rating, and prior existing conditions will be covered. This is likely to require additional spending, possibly of the order of $35 billion per year.[31] The exact amount of extra spending will be determined by the generosity of the basic package of benefits. It would include some coverage for preventive care and limited coverage for dental care, but whether there is any coverage for long-term care or prescription drugs is less clear. The Administration believes that the package should cost about $4 200 per year for a family of 4 ($1 800 for a single person). Part of the package can be paid for by administrative savings, estimated to be on the order of $40 to $50 billion per year.[32] The only tax increase required will be on cigarettes (up to $1 per pack). Employers will be mandated to pay 80 per cent of the premiums required, with a ceiling of about

8 per cent of the wage bill. However, subsidies will reduce that by at least half for small businesses. Some degree of flexibility will be offered to individual states to vary the contents of the package, as well as to manage the way in which plans and providers compete on price and quality. Cost containment is to be achieved through the discipline imposed on providers to maximise profits under the managed-competition approach, in addition to the incentives for individuals to minimise cost in their choice of plans (as they pay all costs at the margin). A backup system of overall budgets on alliances will also be put in place. The plan is intended to be deficit neutral in the short run (2 to 4 years) and expenditure saving thereafter.

"Investment proposals"

Besides spending cuts, the Administration also proposed $220 billion in gross spending increases and tax incentives (or about $203 billion excluding the direct and indirect effects of those parts of the stimulus package which failed to pass the Congress). The bulk of these increases are discretionary in nature, and all are intended to be investments, broadly defined (Table 9). Substantial amounts are to be made available for transportation infrastructure (see Chapter III), environmental protection, rural development, energy research and conservation, community development (including 9 so-called "empowerment zones" and 95 "enterprise communities" in depressed areas – with tax incentives for investment and job creation worth $3.5 billion over 5 years), technology and defence conversion (see Chapter III), housing (especially for those with low incomes), worker training and other "lifelong learning" initiatives (see Chapter III), reforms designed to make work more rewarding (primarily welfare reform – see below) and a variety of initiatives to improve public health by, for example, increasing childhood immunisation and expanding the Food Stamps programme.

As mentioned, the Administration has embarked on a redesign of the U.S. welfare system, which primarily consists of the Aid to Families with Dependent Children (AFDC) programme. There are currently 4.7 million beneficiaries, up from 3.5 million in 1976. The basic idea will be to place a time limit (of, perhaps, two years) on eligibility for benefits before some sort of education and/or training would become necessary. The required expansion in training, along with improved child-support collection, would cost about $3 billion per year, but the main additional incentive offered to welfare recipients to try to support

Table 9. **The Administration's "Investment Proposals"**

$ million

	1994	1995	1996	1997	1998	1994-98 Total
Rebuild America-infrastructure:						
Budget authority	8 100	14 183	16 550	18 123	18 772	75 728
Outlays	2 222	7 438	11 523	14 581	16 590	52 354
Tax incentives	1 845	2 819	3 589	4 426	5 218	17 897
Lifelong learning:						
Budget authority	6 148	10 339	13 594	16 365	17 802	64 248
Outlays	2 035	6 701	11 409	14 871	16 888	51 904
Tax incentives	627	815	906	1 024	1 169	4 541
Rewarding work: [1]						
Budget authority	668	4 188	7 719	8 008	8 308	28 891
Outlays	491	3 985	7 578	7 952	8 286	28 292
Tax incentives	68	924	1 039	1 063	1 099	4 193
Health care:						
Budget authority	3 297	6 386	7 676	9 129	10 554	37 042
Outlays	2 225	5 013	6 953	8 382	9 596	32 169
Tax incentives	313	–	–	–	–	313
Private sector incentives:						
Budget authority	295	321	341	362	384	1 703
Outlays	44	69	73	74	76	336
Tax incentives	9 215	7 820	4 379	2 826	3 499	27 739
Total investment proposals:						
Budget authority	18 508	35 417	45 880	51 987	55 820	20 612
Outlays	7 017	23 206	37 536	45 860	51 436	165 055
Tax incentives	12 068	12 378	9 913	9 339	10 985	54 683

1. The budget authority and outlay estimates exclude the revenue effect of the Earned Income Tax Credit expansion proposal included in tax incentives.

Source: Office Management and Budget (1993*c*).

themselves through gainful employment is the expansion in the EITC, set for $21 billion in 1994-98.[33] While the added incentive to work is clear for those not otherwise working, there is also an obvious disincentive to labour supply for those in the phase-out range of the EITC (Kosters, 1993).[34] This is a relatively dense part of the income distribution, and the number of those in the phase-out range increases as the range is extended.

Enforcement mechanisms

Some of the key elements to the final deficit-reduction legislation are the enforcement mechanisms it prescribes. Under the 1990 Budget Enforcement Act, discretionary spending caps were to be combined into a single category as from 1994 and would expire, along with pay-as-you-go enforcement, with the legislation after 1995. OBRA93 includes provisions which extend proposed combined discretionary spending caps and the pay-as-you-go requirement until 1998. The President also issued an executive order implementing a mechanism to limit entitlement spending as follows: if such spending exceeds OBRA93 levels, the President will have to call this to the attention of Congress and either recommend corrective action or argue why such action would not be appropriate. It is possible that this procedure will be hardened or that it will be enshrined in legislation in coming months.

These mechanisms are crucial, because a large part of the deficit reduction is not part of the 1994 Budget and will need to be approved in later Congressional sessions. Furthermore, without restraint on mandatory spending, deficit overshooting is quite likely, given limitations on the ability to raise taxes. For example, since 1980, Medicare and Medicaid have risen from 7.6 to 13.3 per cent of total federal spending in FY 1992 and, without reform, would reach a projected 27.3 per cent in 2003 (Congressional Budget Office, 1993*a*). Even after the deficit-reduction plan is implemented (but excluding the effect of any future health-care overhaul), prudent economic assumptions indicate that the deficit will begin to rise again as a share of GDP in 1998 and reach nearly 4 per cent of GDP within a decade. Federal debt held by the public (as opposed to that which is held by federal trust funds, such as social security), which is expected to reach 53 per cent of GDP at the end of September 1993 (the highest since 1955), would then keep on rising to 55 per cent by 1998 and about 59 per cent in 2003 (Diagram 9).

The macroeconomic impact

Once implemented, these changes will have far-reaching effects on the American economy. However, few of them are quantifiable over a medium-term horizon. Some, such as spending more on the Head Start programme, for example, might take decades before any measurable benefits could be realised. Nevertheless, the CBO (1993*c*) has estimated that the direct effects of deficit reduction should raise the growth rate of potential output by 0.1 per cent per year by 1998.

Diagram 9. **TRENDS IN FEDERAL DEBT HELD BY THE PUBLIC**

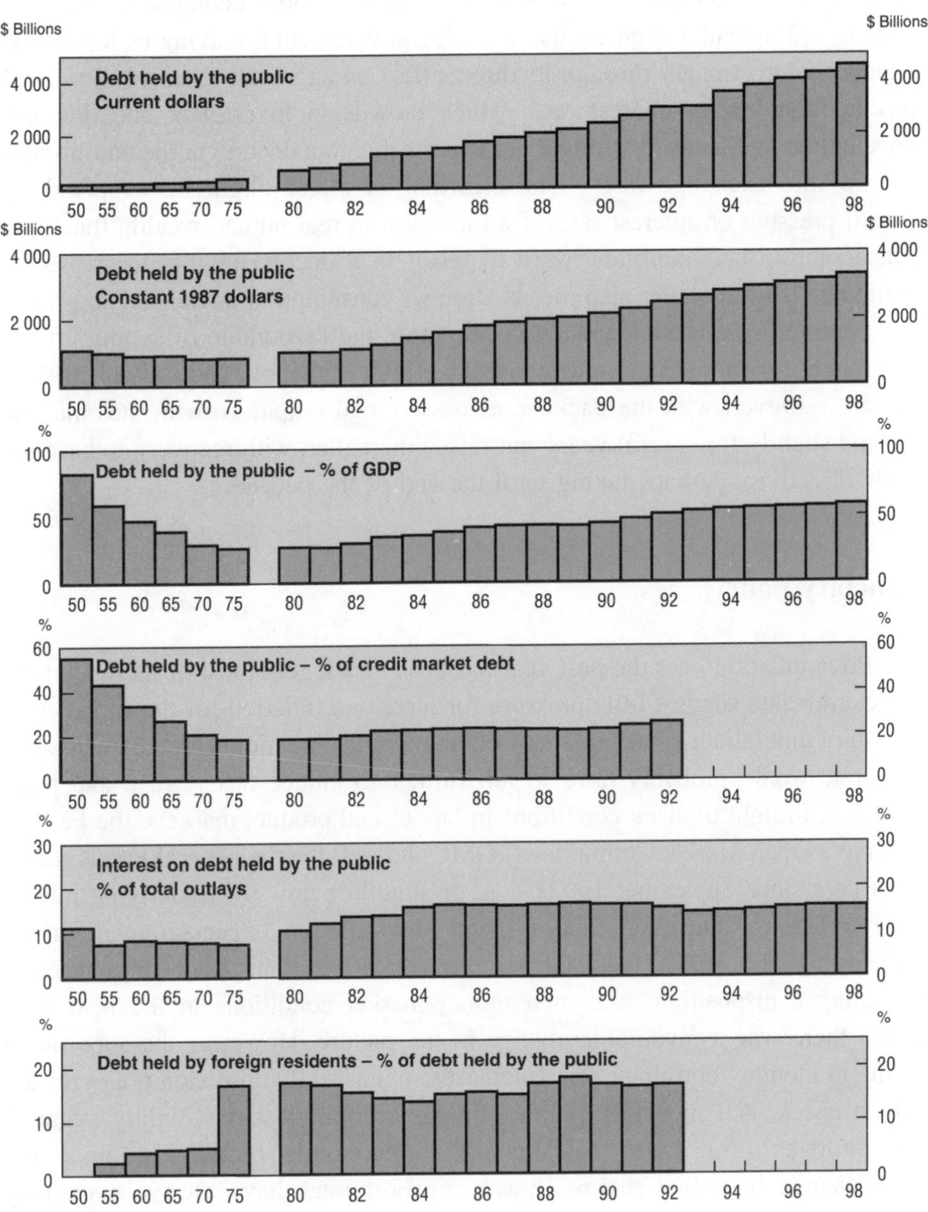

Source: Office of Management and Budget (1993*c*).

Also, some analysts have attempted to quantify the macroeconomic impact of deficit reduction on the U.S. economy using traditional econometric models. There is widespread agreement that reducing government dissaving is, in the first instance, contractionary through its direct effect on aggregate demand. But fiscal consolidation lowers interest rates which crowds in investment and durables consumption and leads to stronger net exports due to a decline in the equilibrium value of the exchange rate.[35] The crowding-in effect might be tempered by upward pressure on interest rates if an increase in real human wealth, thanks to reduced future tax liabilities, were to result in a decline in the private-sector saving rate. But the latter also means stronger consumption demand. The greater is the credibility of deficit reduction, the more the favourable offsetting effects are brought forward (Clark and Symansky, 1993; McKibbin and Bagnoli, 1993). Overall, however, with the package as passed, real output growth rates may be lowered slightly for several years and raised thereafter, with recovery to baseline levels of activity perhaps taking until the end of the decade.

Monetary policy

Price inflation over the past year has been erratic, but most of its fundamental determinants suggest little pressure for increased inflation for the time being: growth of unit labour costs remains well below price inflation, and the unemployment rate would probably have to fall further to induce faster wage and price increases. In light of slack conditions in labour and product markets, the Federal Reserve's Open Market Committee (FOMC) has left the the Federal Funds rate at 3 per cent since September 1992[36] – at or slightly below the underlying rate of price inflation. Concerned that inflation and inflation expectations might be intensifying, the FOMC adopted a policy directive at its May 1993 meeting indicating a disposition to tighten money-market conditions in the near term unless there was a favourable change in the picture. However, the subsequent easing in monthly consumer price increases suggested that inflation pressures are still in check, and monetary policy remains accommodative. Slightly negative real short-term rates are not unusual in economic recoveries; since the 1979 change in policy regime, however, short rates have always eventually returned to an average level near the rate of growth of nominal GDP. Also, real short-term rates have averaged about 1¼ per cent since 1960. Thus, even if inflation news is good over the next year, and even though the 1994 federal budget implements credible deficit reduction, by the time the recovery is complete the Secretariat projects that the Federal Funds rate is likely to have risen closer to 5 per cent than the current 3 per cent.

The yield curve continued to steepen until the spring of 1992, with 10-year Treasury notes yielding nearly 4 percentage points more than 3-month Treasury bills (Diagram 10). Thereafter, the available indicators suggested sluggish economic activity; thus, any increases in the Funds rate appeared likely to occur only slowly over the next few years, and medium- and long-term rates reached a trough in the early autumn. Leading up to the election, long-term rates rebounded, given indications of a stronger recovery, as well as fears of excessive fiscal stimulus and an earlier monetary tightening. Following the election, several factors suggested less need to tighten soon: evidence of weaker activity, signs of coming deficit reduction and the possibility of a shift in the federal debt's financing mix toward shorter maturities. Thus, long-term rates fell, in unison with their foreign counterparts. Even after the strong bond-market rally between December and February, however, long-term rates remained high relative to short-term rates – perhaps indicating the resilience of inflation expectations after the poor inflation performance in early 1993. But by the summer, the bond market rally had resumed, and by September real 10-year rates fell to about 2½ per cent, leaving the yield curve still steeper than its long-term historical average. Information contained in the yield curve in September 1993 (the yield on various Treasury notes less that on three-month Treasury bills) suggests that the market anticipates a tightening of 60-70 basis points in the first half of 1994 and another 140 basis points by March 1996 – leaving short-term rates in 1996 much closer to likely rates of growth in nominal activity.

The broad monetary aggregates have stagnated since late 1990, and growth in recent months continues to be sluggish. Despite a modest pick-up in the second quarter of 1992, M3 remains below its end-1990 level. Weak M3 growth can be traced to weak asset expansion at depository institutions and the use of non-deposit liabilities. The sluggishness of M2 growth has been less extreme – this aggregate has not actually declined (except in the first quarter of 1993), but nonetheless its velocity has continued the uptrend that began in early 1991. In marked contrast, growth of currency and checkable deposits (M1) has exceeded GDP growth by a wide margin every quarter since mid-1990. The steepness of

Diagram 10. **SHORT- AND LONG-TERM INTEREST RATES**

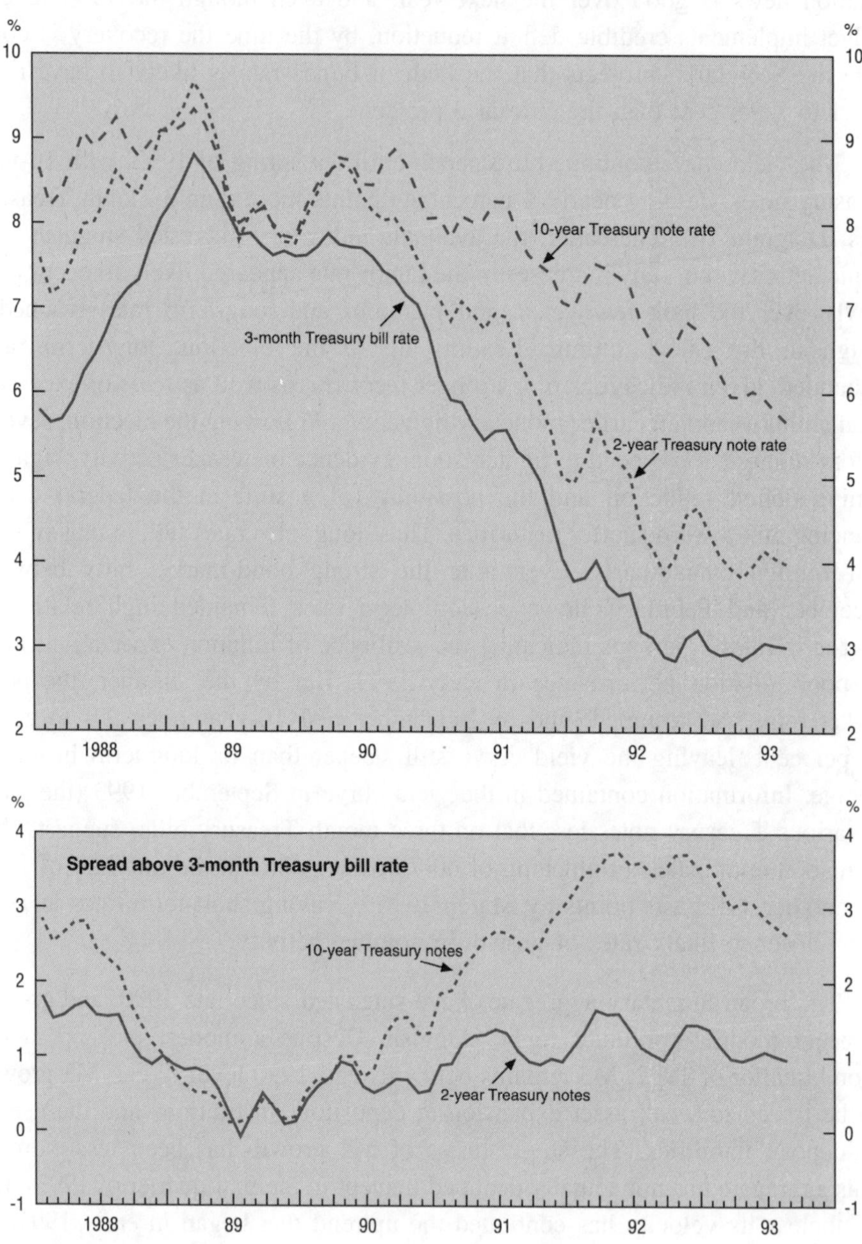

Source: Federal Reserve Board.

Diagram 11. **VELOCITY OF THE MONETARY AGGREGATES**[1]

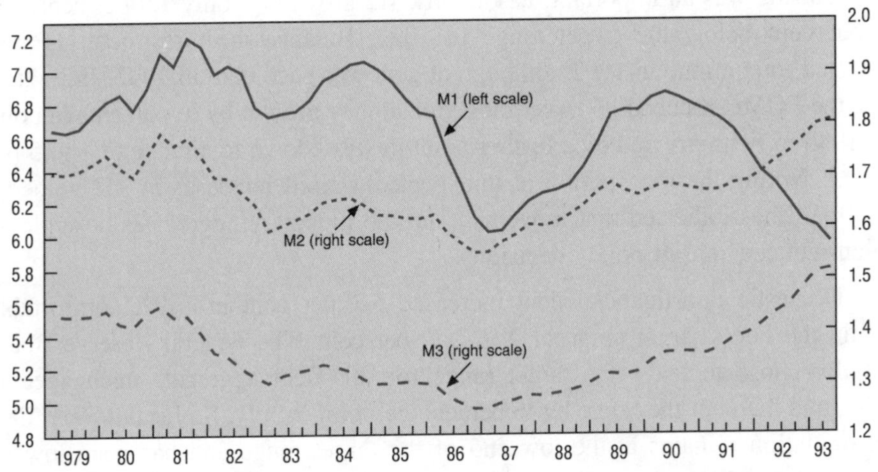

1. Defined as nominal GDP divided by the monetary aggregates M1, M2, and M3, respectively.
Source: OECD.

the yield curve explains much of this behaviour: the opportunity cost of shifting funds from Treasury bills to checking accounts is now relatively low,[37] while the cost of holding money-market funds or Eurodollars (large non-M1 components of M3) remains quite high relative to longer-term capital-market assets (especially bond and equity mutual funds), even after the declines in long-term rates and in dividend yields on stocks since the end of 1992.

The shift of funds from banks to capital markets, induced in part by the steep yield curve, is not the only reason for weak growth of broad money aggregates up to early 1993. Other factors have also played an important role: businesses continued to pay down their bank debts (though the "credit crunch" probably no longer plays much of a role[38]). In addition, more stringent bank supervision and regulation may also have led some banks to bid less vigorously for deposits and to offer fewer credit-financing instruments included in M3. Most of the above considerations can be grouped together under the rubric of "balance-sheet restructuring": an on-going process for businesses, households, banks and state governments.

In February 1993, Chairman Greenspan indicated that this balance-sheet restructuring was an important reason why M2 growth (at only 1.9 per cent) fell ½ per cent below the target range in 1992. Balance-sheet restructuring was expected to continue in 1993, although at a slower pace than in 1992. In light of this, the FOMC reduced its target range for money growth by ½ percentage point for 1993 in February and by a further point in July (down to a range of 1 to 5 per cent).[39] Noting the long period of unexpectedly rapid increases in M2 velocity, the Board has indicated that movements in the monetary aggregates now play a much-reduced role in policy decisions.

Domestic non-financial debt increased 5.1 per cent in 1992, comfortably within the Fed's target range of 4½ - 8½ per cent. The Federal Reserve Board initially chose to leave the target range for this debt aggregate unchanged in 1993, and then cut the range by ½ percentage point in July. So far this year, debt accumulation remains at the low end of the target range and has been low by historical standards. Increases in private debt slowed somewhat in the first quarter, while the federal deficit dropped off more noticeably with unexpectedly weak defence spending and high tax receipts.

The lack of sustained growth of bank loans to business to date probably has more to do with a lack of demand than tight supply conditions, especially given the substantial improvement in banks' financial situation over the last year or so. The supply of loans has apparently begun to ease: a Fed survey of bank loan officers found about 10 per cent reported easing in May 1993, the first such easing reported in many months. An even larger shift was reported in the August survey. Nonetheless, the regulatory agencies are taking steps to limit any regulatory impediments to lending. A recent study by the four bank regulatory agencies estimated the cost of the regulatory burden on banks at somewhere between $7.5 billion and $17 billion in 1991, with a disproportionately large burden on small banks. Concern that this burden was impeding credit supply led them to announce on 10 March 1993 several changes in lending rules. These changes are aimed at easing availability of credit to small business, where there had been some worry about a possible credit crunch (although much of the decline in credit to small business instead reflected a cyclical fall-off in demand and increase in risk due to the recession). Well-capitalised banks with a good supervisory rating are to be allowed to make character loans based on their judgement of the borrower rather than detailed documentation and collateral. The regulatory agencies also raised the threshold below which appraisals will not be required for collateral loans, and stopped the appraisal requirement when property is offered as additional collateral on business loans.

Exchange rates have not been a major concern of monetary policy recently. Between February and June public statements by several Administration officials, and by President Clinton, were interpreted by markets as suggesting encouragement for the yen to appreciate substantially. The result of this (along with two successive unfavourable merchandise trade reports) was an unexpected surge of about 12 per cent in the dollar value of the yen. Attempts to reverse direction through a statement of policy by Treasury officials, as well as a modest amount of intervention in late spring, stabilised the dollar-yen rate only briefly; however, the fall of the Japanese government in June temporarily reversed some of the earlier decline. In the summer the yen's rise against the dollar resumed. This was met by another modest round of intervention and a Treasury statement noting that excessive volatility in exchange rates can be counter-productive to growth. On the other hand, European interest rate declines and the relative cyclical strength of U.S. output growth have boosted the dollar relative to European currencies since the summer of 1992, and in effective terms the dollar has remained fairly stable.

Diagram 12. **EXCHANGE VALUE OF THE DOLLAR**

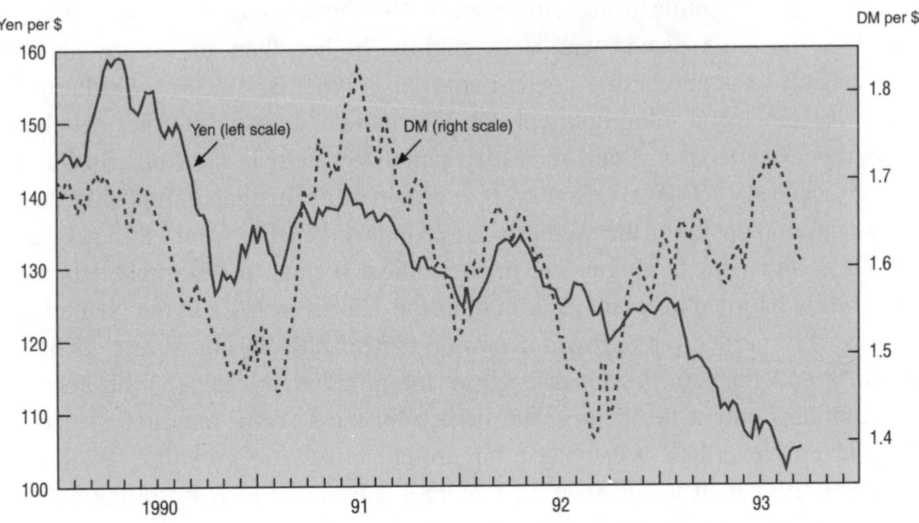

Source: OECD.

III. Issues in productivity and competitiveness and the new policy focus

Introduction

U.S. labour is the most productive in the world and enjoys its highest living standard, thanks to a rich resource base, an extensive stock of high-technology equipment, a highly skilled labour force and vigorous competition in domestic markets (Table 10). While measured U.S. productivity growth has slowed dramatically over the last three decades, and other OECD countries have made substantial strides in closing the productivity gap with the United States, U.S. productivity is still well above the OECD average and far above Japanese levels, even in manufacturing. However, in 1990, measured output per worker in the U.S. business sector was only slightly higher than in France and the Netherlands on a purchasing-power-parity basis (OECD, 1993*c*).[40] Furthermore, U.S. workers spend more hours on the job than do workers in other developed countries except Japan – thus measured output per hour in the Netherlands may already exceed U.S. levels. However, a large part of this gap is probably due to industrial composition: the Netherlands economy benefits from extremely high labour productivity in its gas and petrochemical sectors, for example.[41] In addition, while national accounts data in both the United States and the Netherlands assume zero productivity growth in several non-manufacturing sectors, including banking and finance, French data allow for productivity gains. With common assumptions, output per hour in the French business sector may not exceed the U.S. level. Nevertheless, barring a turnaround in relative growth rates of trend productivity, which would seem to require a substantial increase in the nation's saving and investment, the U.S. productivity standard is likely to be surpassed in the next decade or so by a number of countries.

Table 10. **International productivity comparisons**

United States = 100

	Japan	Europe	Germany	France	United Kingdom
I. GDP per person employed, 1990 (1990 PPP basis)	74		87	93	72
II. GDP per full-time equivalent in market economy, 1988 (1990 PPP basis)	61		80	84	72
III. GDP per hour worked in market economy, 1988 (1990 PPP basis)	52		92	98	77
IV. Manufacturing value added per hour worked, 1989 (PPP basis)	80		80	76	61
V. Labour productivity[1] – airlines, 1989	n.a.	72	n.a.	n.a.	n.a.
VI. Labour productivity[1] – retail banking, 1989	n.a.		68	n.a.	64
VII. Labour productivity[1] – general merchandise retailing, 1987	44		96	69	82
VIII. Labour productivity[1] – restaurants, 1987	n.a.		92	104	n.a.
IX. Labour productivity[1] – telecommunications, 1989					
i) Output measure: number of calls	41		28	28	22
ii) Output measure: ½ × number of calls + ½ × number of access lines	66		50	56	38
X. Total factor productivity – telecommunications, 1989					
i) Output measure: number of calls	46		26	27	30
ii) Output measure: ½ × number of calls + ½ × number of access lines	74		47	55	51
iii) Output measure: 0.15 × number of calls + 0.85 × number of access lines	77		52	62	54

1. Per full-time equivalent.

Sources: Baily (1993), McKinsey Global Institute (1992) and OECD.

This relatively poor U.S. productivity growth performance has received a great deal of public attention. Some of this concern is misplaced: the productivity slowdown is not occurring in all parts of the economy, by any means, and measurement problems are severe in sectors where productivity growth has apparently been slow. In addition, the slowdown in productivity growth is a world-wide phenomenon, not limited to the United States. Furthermore, in dollar terms U.S. unit labour costs remain well below those in Japan and most other competitors in world markets. Nonetheless, several disturbing trends have appeared in recent years – problems which, if not corrected, could undermine labour productivity, living standards and social harmony in the future. The nation has devoted a relatively small portion of its income to saving over the last three decades and has invested relatively little of its income in productive capital or in training for less skilled workers. This latter omission has contributed to the aggregate productivity slowdown, but also has other negative implications. In the late 1970s and through the 1980s, the productivity of U.S. workers has increased sharply relative to the unskilled, contributing to a widening gap between the incomes of rich and poor. And widening skill-based disparities in productivity and incomes have the makings of a social problem, given inadequate access to training for minorities and the non-college-bound.

The Clinton administration has proposed a variety of policy changes designed to speed overall productivity growth in coming years, including several programmes targeted at boosting the productivity of the unskilled. Later sections of this chapter will review in greater depth various issues affecting productivity growth and the policy proposals that have been formulated to date. Attention will be paid to the contributions of saving, investment and physical capital intensity; the adjustment costs of industrial restructuring and military downsizing; public infrastructure investment; education, training and human-capital intensity; research and development and the state of technology; and government regulation. In addition, consideration will be given to a number of other factors which have, as yet, not elicited any formal policy response: the corporate governance system and the litigiousness of American society. First, however, the broad outlines of the problem will be defined. The next section focuses on trends in productivity growth and competitiveness – comparing outcomes in the manufacturing and service sectors – and will review the reasons for superior foreign productivity growth performance.

The productivity and competitiveness record

Measured output per U.S. worker increased very rapidly in the two decades following the second world war but may have decelerated somewhat already in the years before the first oil price shock of 1973 (Diagram 13). Since then, productivity growth has been substantially slower. However, the strong productivity gains in 1991 and 1992 have led some to argue that trend growth rate of productivity may have picked up in the 1990s (Greenspan, 1993; Roach, 1993*b*). Several fundamental changes might have caused such an increase:

Diagram 13. **ESTIMATED TREND LABOUR PRODUCTIVITY GROWTH**

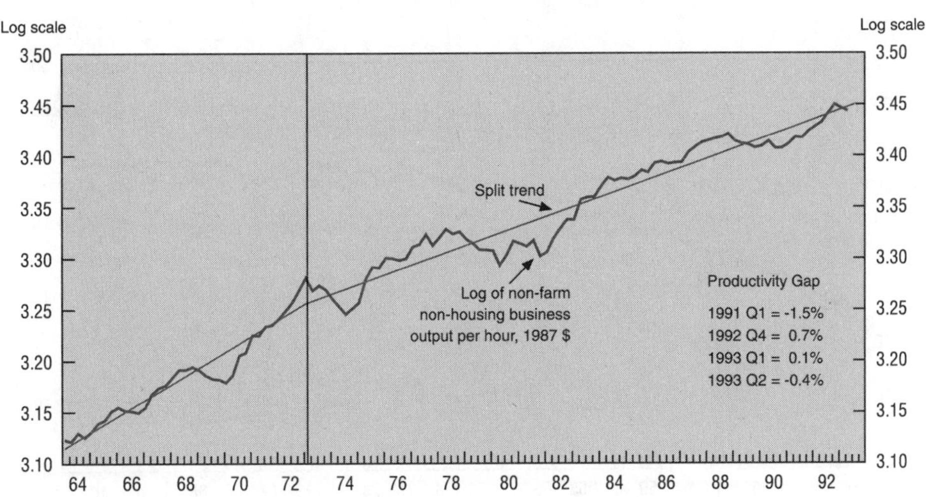

Source: OECD.

- an increase in expenditure on education in the 1980s,
- an increased maturity of the labour force,
- an increased focus in the 1980s on high-technology investment,
- the spreading popularity of "re-engineering" (Hammer, 1990),[42]
- the "information revolution", and
- a downtrend in underlying inflationary pressures since 1989, setting a more favourable macroeconomic environment for productivity improvement.

Unfortunately, the estimates of trend productivity in Diagram 13 give little indication that the 1990s to date have seen anything but a normal cyclical recovery in productivity. It would be discouraging if the trend growth in productivity were truly as low – 1 per cent a year – as Diagram 13 implies. However, close examination of the sectoral data reveals that the weakness may be less severe than casual observation would suggest.

Patterns of measured productivity growth have been very different in the industrial and service sectors of the economy. Diagram 14 shows that manufac-

Diagram 14. **SECTORAL PRODUCTIVITY DEVELOPMENTS**
Output per hour in 1987 dollars

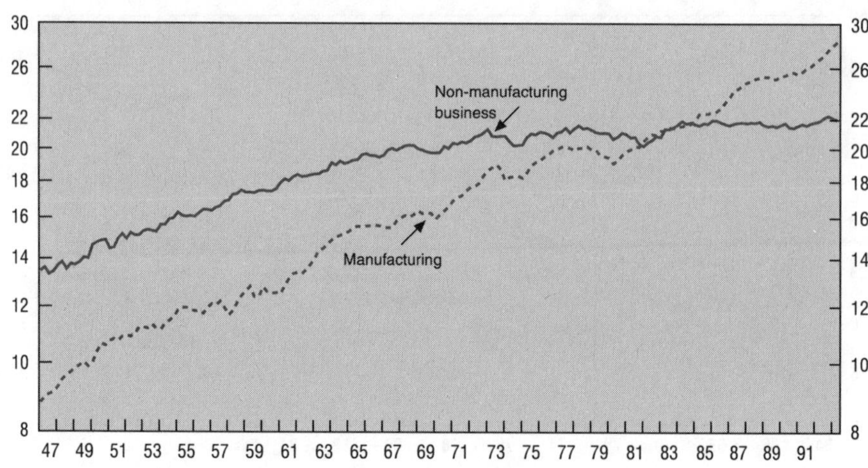

Source: OECD.

turing output per worker increased rapidly in the immediate post-war period, slowed following the 1973 oil shock and then recovered strongly in the 1980s. Remarkably, one-third of this growth in manufacturing productivity during the 1980s occurred in just one sub-sector – computer production (Gullickson, 1992). Even outside of computer production, however, manufacturing productivity growth recovered strongly.

In the service sector, growth of output per hour has always been slower than in manufacturing, and productivity gains in services decelerated steadily over the post-war period. Part of the slow measured growth in this sector is an artefact of measurement methods: in some service sectors, notably government and financial services, the Commerce Department assumes away productivity increases by setting the growth of real output originating in the sector equal to that of real labour input. In fact, regulatory and technological changes have probably boosted potential productivity in the financial sector substantially – and these changes have occurred faster in the 1980s than previously.[43] Excluding the financial sector, non-manufacturing productivity growth in the 1980s has fallen less dramatically relative to the 1960s.[44]

However, the weakness in productivity growth is very real in parts of the sector classified as ''general services'': there are inherent difficulties in increasing the output of workers in some personal services, medical and educational services and the arts. (An often-cited example is the number of labour-hours required to perform a string quartet.) This fundamental weakness in growth of

Diagram 15. **COMPARATIVE PRODUCTIVITY GROWTH**[1]

Average annual percentage change

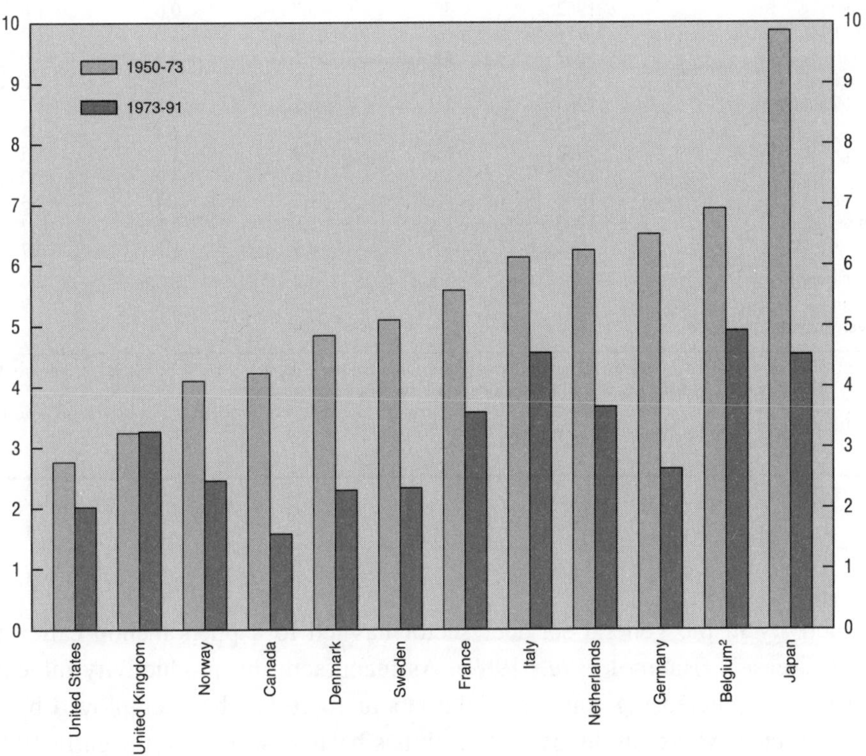

1. Output per hour in manufacturing.
2. The initial productivity growth rate for Belgium is for 1960-1973.

Source: Bureau of Labor Statistics, *Monthly Labor Review*.

Table 11. **Estimates of trend growth in labour productivity**

(Business sector)

Percentage change, annual rate

	First year	First year -1973	1974-79	1980-86	1987-92
United States	**1962**	**2.0**	**0.0**	**0.5**	**0.9**
Japan	1963	8.3	3.4	2.8	2.9
Germany	1962	4.5	3.1	1.5	1.9
France	1964	5.3	3.2	2.6	2.3
Italy	1962	6.1	2.7	1.9	2.1
United Kingdom	1962	3.3	2.0	2.6	1.8
Canada	1967	2.6	2.1	1.0	1.6
Austria	1962	5.7	3.4	1.8	1.9
Australia	1971	4.1	2.3	0.3	1.7
Belgium-Luxembourg	1971	4.7	2.7	2.5	2.3
Denmark	1962	4.2	2.6	1.8	2.9
Finland	1962	4.8	3.5	3.3	4.3
Greece	1962	8.7	3.7	0.6	1.6
Iceland	1974	..	4.0	1.0	1.8
Ireland	1962	4.6	2.5	4.9	4.0
Netherlands	1971	5.1	2.9	1.6	1.2
New Zealand	1963	1.3	–0.2	1.2	1.3
Norway	1963	4.0	0.1	1.3	1.5
Portugal	1962	6.7	1.9	1.8	1.5
Spain	1965	5.9	2.9	4.0	2.0
Sweden	1964	4.1	1.7	1.4	2.3
Switzerland	1962	3.1	1.0	0.7	1.7
Turkey	1973	..	4.5	1.7	3.7
Upper quartile		5.8	3.4	2.6	2.6
Median		4.6	2.7	1.8	1.9
Lower quartile		3.6	1.9	1.2	1.6

Notes: Estimates obtained by regressing productivity growth on a constant, dummy variables for each of the post 1973 periods and changes in capacity utilisation to take account of cyclical variation.
The capacity utilisation measure was defined as the per cent difference between GDP and its trend level, which was estimated using the Hodrick-Prescott filter.

Source: OECD.

productivity in the general services sector has led to a phenomenon called the ''cost disease'' (Baumol *et al.*, 1989). As manufacturing productivity increases over time, an increasing fraction of the labour force has been employed by the service sector, where productivity growth has been slower since the early 1980s. This shift has held down measured aggregate productivity growth – and would have done so even in the absence of any decline within manufacturing or within services.

The increase in the share of the service sector in overall employment is a phenomenon common to all OECD countries, perhaps contributing to the common slowdown in measured productivity in recent years. In the early post-war period, much of the more rapid productivity growth in Europe and Japan was attributable to catch-up and the later shift from agriculture (Denison, 1985; Helliwell *et al.*, 1986). Yet because productivity growth of most OECD countries has exceeded that of the United States across the entire post-war period (partly due to different statistical assumptions), other explanations are necessary, encompassing any productivity slowdown within U.S. manufacturing and services, and the faster overall productivity growth abroad.

Part of the reason for faster productivity growth in Europe and Japan has little to do with problems in the United States, but rather with progress abroad. When sufficient infrastructure and educational grounding exist, business opportunities and returns to investment tend to be greater in countries where productivity begins relatively low (the so-called "advantages of backwardness") (Diagram 16). Thus, technology transfer and more intensive capital investment lead to

Diagram 16. **THE ADVANTAGES OF BACKWARDNESS:**
Labour productivity growth 1960-1992, versus the levels of labour productivity in 1960

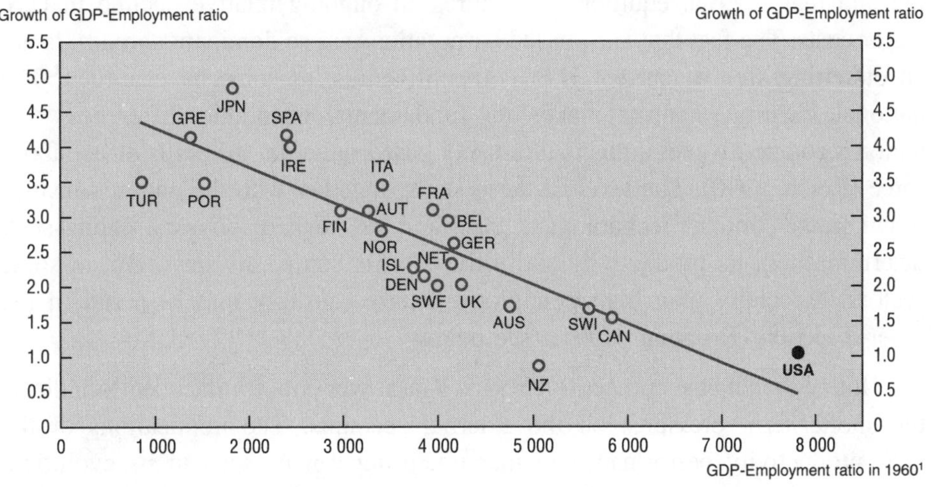

1. GDP per employed person at 1960 purchasing power parities for GDP.
Source : OECD.

faster growth of output per worker in these countries, and productivity converges internationally – as has occurred among OECD member countries since the second world war[45] (Baumol *et al.,* 1989).

This convergence phenomenon goes partway toward explaining the higher share of income devoted to investment in Europe and Japan than in the United States over the post-war period. More recently, however, U.S. relative investment trends have deteriorated in ways that are more difficult to explain away. Over the 1980s personal and government saving rates declined sharply in the United States, such that the overall national rate fell significantly (Diagram 17). During the mid-1980s, an inflow of foreign capital partially shielded national investment from the saving decline. However, since 1984 the share of investment in national income has fallen steadily, to levels well below even the low levels of the 1960s and 1970s. Even if productivity growth had not been a problem to this point, it would probably become one soon, unless saving and investment rates were to increase substantially.[46]

A nation's competitiveness is closely linked to its relative productivity outcomes. Competitiveness is a rather vague term, but most would agree that it is related to a nation's ability to provide sustainable increases in the real standard of living for the entire population. On this basis, the role of productivity growth is fairly clear, and one would have to conclude that U.S. competitiveness is declining and that external equilibrium requires an ongoing relative decline in U.S. factor costs. The fact that U.S.-based corporations are so dominant abroad[47] is not an offsetting sign of current U.S. competitiveness, as some have argued. The national identity of firms makes no fundamental economic difference to a nation's competitiveness; this is ultimately based rather on the skills of its labour force (Reich, 1990). The level of these skills, together with the nation's institutional framework, its technological base and its stock of physical capital will determine both its productivity and ultimately its competitiveness. But in some sectors, especially of a high-technology nature, causality may also run in the other direction (Krugman, 1991) (see below).

International cost competitiveness is a narrower concept intended to indicate the shorter-term pressures on the external accounts. The implications of the U.S. productivity performance in manufacturing can be seen in its evolution. Relative costs are also a function of relative wage outcomes as well as changes in the effective exchange rate. Despite the nation's meagre gains in productivity,

Diagram 17. **NATIONAL SAVINGS AND INVESTMENT RATES**

% of GDP

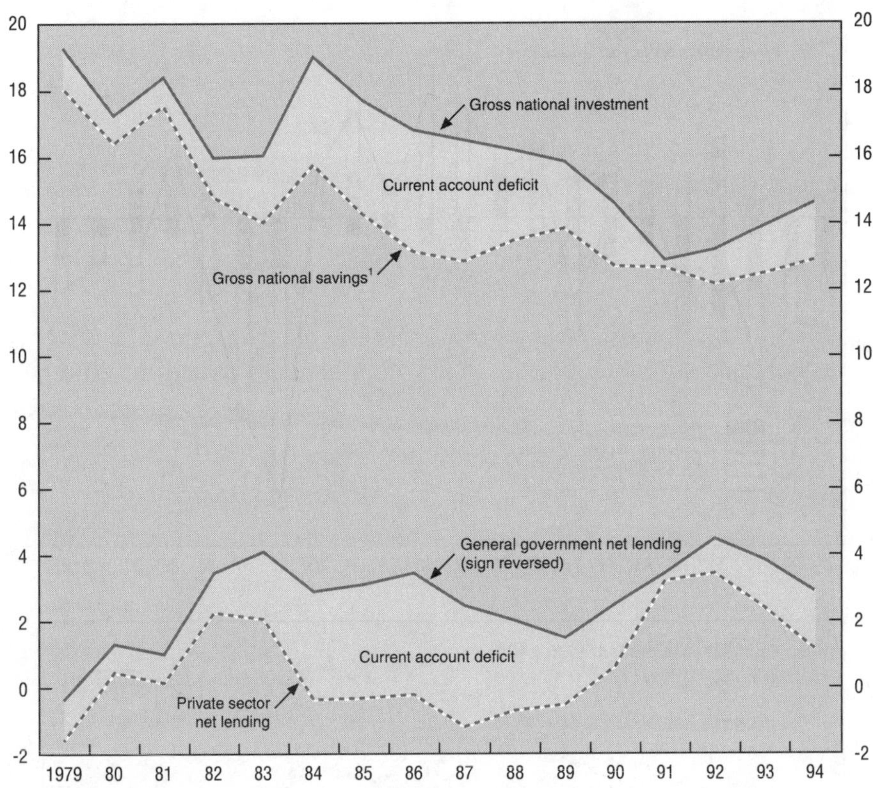

1. Including net transfers abroad.

Source: OECD.

cost competitiveness improved markedly through most of the 1970s, as increases in wages were even more modest by trading-partner standards and the dollar declined from 1970 to 1973 (Diagram 18). Since the beginning of the 1980s, productivity growth closely shadowed that of competitors, as have wages, and labour cost competitiveness has evolved in tandem with the exchange rate: in particular, the enormous appreciation of the first half of the decade was reversed by 1987, and limited further improvements since then are attributable to relative wage moderation and further depreciation.

Diagram 18. **THE DETERMINANTS OF U.S. COST COMPETITIVENESS IN MANUFACTURING**

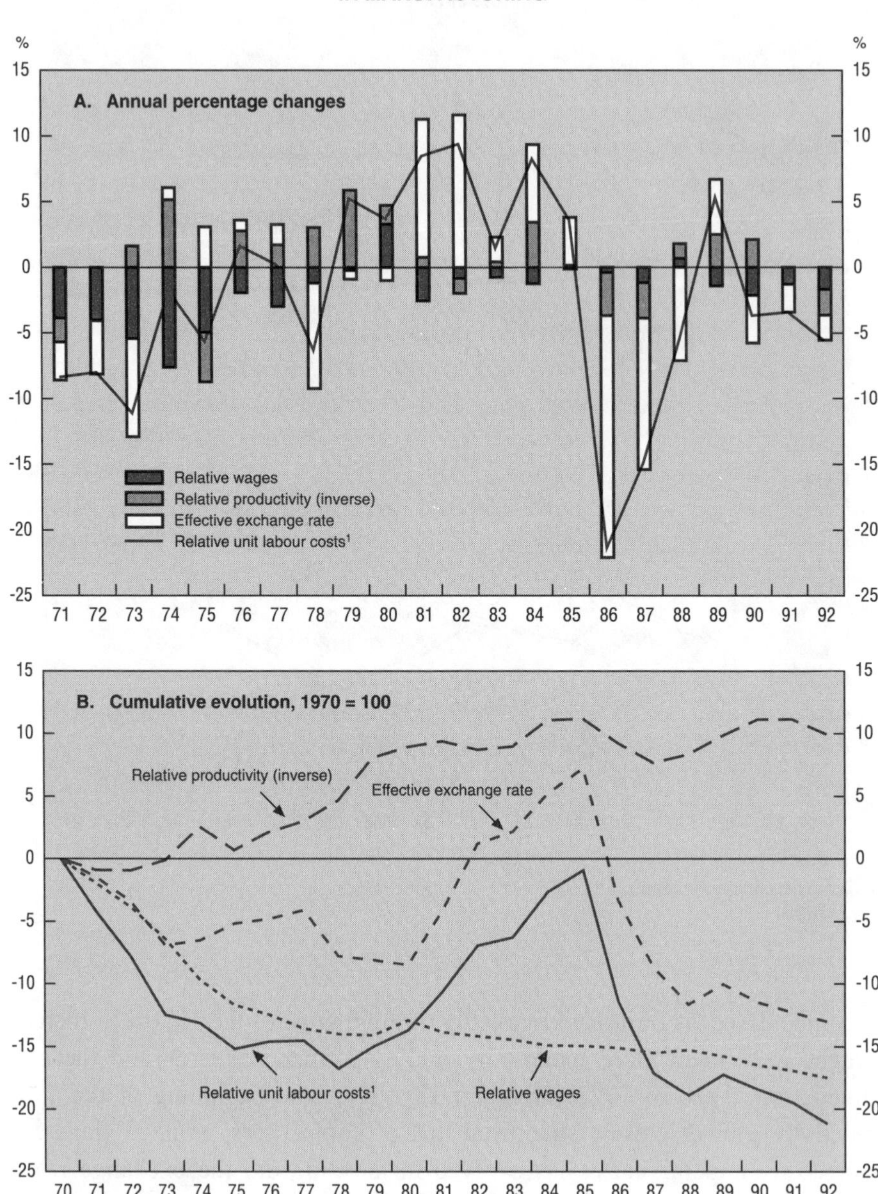

1. In a common currency.

Source: OECD

However, the discussion of cost competitiveness is incomplete to the extent that it fails to give any information regarding absolute levels. Preliminary results of a very recent investigation for the manufacturing sector[48] show that U.S. labour costs were very close to those of trading partners in 1973, remained below theirs until 1980, surged to a level 30 per cent above by 1985 and are currently some 30 per cent below the weighted average foreign level (Diagram 19). With that kind of absolute labour cost advantage, the question that then naturally arises is why U.S. manufacturers have not been more successful in defending domestic markets from import competition since 1987, in particular in the 1990s, and, to a lesser extent, in maintaining the pace of their gains in market shares abroad. A number of possible explanations suggest themselves. First, foreign exporters seem to have been able and willing to price to market in the United States, driving down their margins to very low levels (see Diagram 4 in Chapter I). Second, labour is but one component of total costs, and while energy is, if anything, cheaper than elsewhere, and materials are probably equally costly throughout the world, capital costs may have diverged. This latter possibility is explored below in the section on corporate governance.

The impact of inadequate saving and investment

Over the last decade or so, the United States has saved remarkably little of its national income. Between 1981 and 1991, net national saving was approximately 4½ per cent of national disposable income, *versus* 9 per cent for the OECD as a whole and 21 per cent in Japan.[49] Low U.S. saving rates are worrisome if the country is intent on increasing its living standard in future years.

The raw statistics on national saving may be slightly deceptive. U.S. personal saving rates, while low, would not have declined nearly as far in the 1980s if saving were defined to include additions to wealth from capital gains and increases in the value of the housing stock. However, government borrowing ballooned in the 1980s, reducing the overall national saving rate – changes in personal saving clearly did nothing to offset the government dissaving. Some argue that such government dissaving is not a problem: the general-government deficit may be small when proper account is taken of growth in government investment in physical and human capital (Eisner, 1993). However, the trend increase in the federal debt relative to GDP since the beginning of the 1980s is

Diagram 19. **ABSOLUTE LABOUR COST COMPETITIVENESS IN MANUFACTURING**

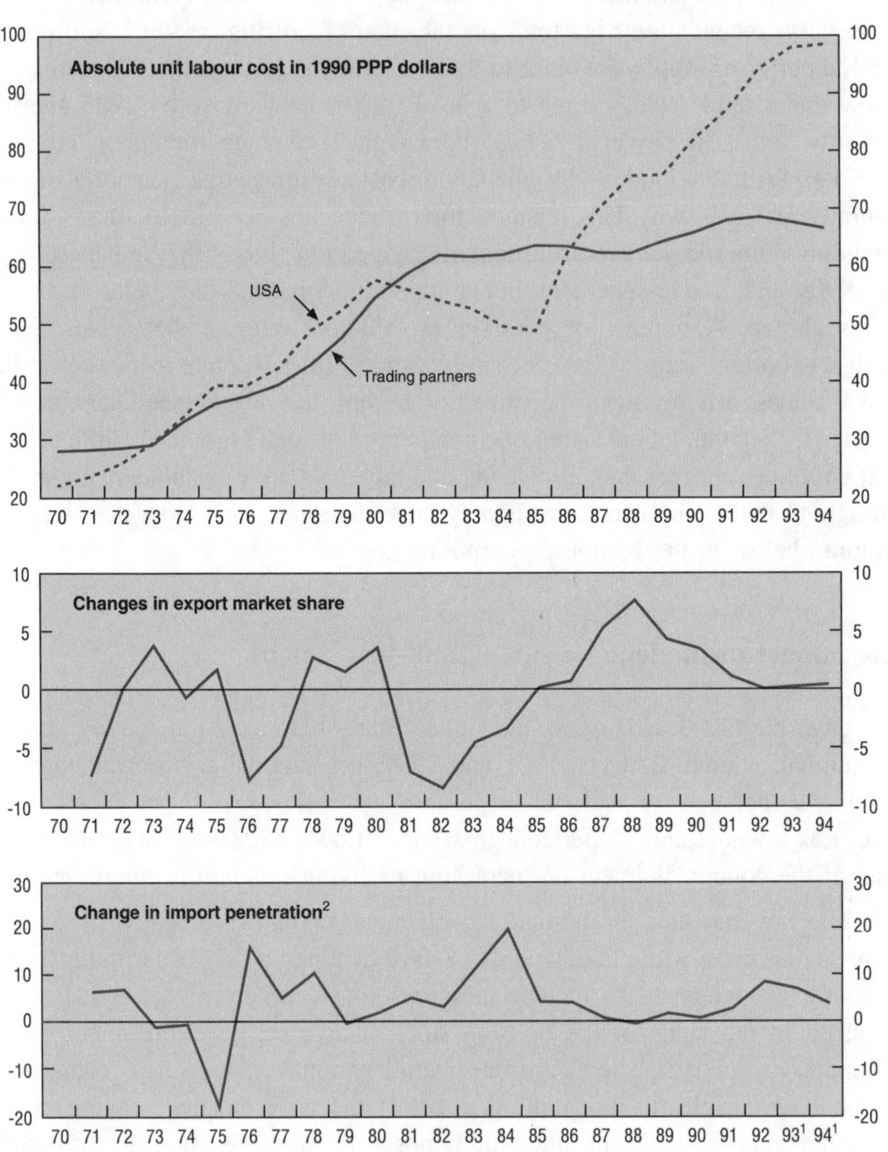

1. Projections.
2. Volume of manufactured imports divided by import weighted demand.

Source: OECD.

Table 12. **Saving and investment trends**

As a percentage of GDP

	1961-65	1966-70	1971-75	1976-80	1981-85	1986-92
Capital formation	15.6	15.9	16.4	18.1	17.4	15.1
Business investment	10.5	11.7	11.4	12.8	13.2	10.8
Residential investment	5.1	4.2	5.0	5.3	4.2	4.3
National saving	16.7	16.2	16.7	17.6	16.2	13.2
Government saving	–0.2	–0.5	–1.2	–0.8	–2.9	–2.9
Federal	–0.2	–0.5	–1.8	–1.8	–4.1	–3.6
State and local	0.0	0.1	0.6	1.1	1.2	0.7
Private saving	16.9	16.7	17.9	18.3	19.1	16.1
Business saving	12.3	11.6	11.9	13.3	13.5	12.7
Household saving	4.6	5.1	6.0	5.0	5.7	3.4
Statistical discrepancy	–0.2	0.0	0.2	0.5	–0.0	–0.0
Net foreign investment	0.9	0.4	0.5	0.0	–1.2	–1.8
Memo:						
Net capital formation	7.1	7.5	7.0	7.3	5.5	4.0
Net saving	8.2	7.8	7.3	6.8	4.3	2.2

Note: Data may not add due to rounding.
Source: U.S. Department of Commerce, *Survey of Current Business*.

clearly unsustainable. Either federal expenditures are insufficiently productive to boost GDP in line with spending (and thus government consumption and transfers must eventually be brought under tighter control), or taxes must increase at some point in the near future to control the growth of debt. Waiting before restraining the deficit increases the tax burden placed on future generations (Kotlikoff, 1992).[50]

To a certain extent, U.S. capital investment was sustained in the 1980s despite low national savings, through foreign borrowing. For the decade as a whole, the net national saving rate plunged 3½ percentage points relative to the 1970s average, while the net national investment rate fell only ½ percentage point, to 6½ per cent of national income. However, steadily increasing liabilities to foreigners seems unlikely to be a sustainable course. At some point, saving must increase; otherwise, national investment will ultimately fall to close the gap – a disturbing possibility, given current national saving of no more than 3 per cent of national disposable income, even adjusting for the cyclical weakness in the 1990s. The actual U.S. net investment rate over the past twelve years was already very low (about 3 percentage points below those of Germany and France, and 12 points below the Japanese rate). As a result, foreign capital intensity has been catching up.[51] A few OECD countries apparently passed the United States in capital intensity during the late 1980s: Heston (1993) suggests that Japan did so in 1989, and that three other countries – Australia, Norway and Sweden – also now appear to have more capital per worker. However, levels of U.S. investment and physical capital stock are underestimated in simple international comparisons, since capital goods are relatively cheaper in the United States than abroad. Correcting for this price difference sharply narrows the gap between investment per capita in the United States and other OECD countries[52] and suggests that the true aggregate stock of capital per capita may still be higher in the United States than in any other country. However, investment rates plunged in the late 1980s to such an extent that in a few years the United States may no longer enjoy that advantage – unless trend rates of national saving and investment pick up soon.

Historically, productivity growth in the United States and across OECD countries has been strongly correlated with capital deepening, that is, additions to the stock of capital per worker. In the United States, capital deepening was very rapid in the immediate post-war period and continued at a still healthy pace of 2.8 per cent per year from the early 1960s until the first oil-price shock in 1973. Over the same decade and a half, growth of output per hour in the business sector was also relatively strong, at about 2½ per cent annually. However, since the early 1970s capital deepening has slowed dramatically, to about 0.8 per cent per year.[53] It is probably no coincidence that growth of output per hour has also slowed, to about 0.8 per cent annually. Capital deepening in the rest of the OECD has also slowed in recent years, along with productivity growth, though both remain well above U.S. rates.[54]

To a large extent, new technology is embodied in capital equipment: there has, therefore, been a historical correlation between growth in total factor productivity and capital deepening (Englander and Mittelstadt, 1988). This might imply that a further boost to equipment investment would raise total factor productivity, with a very large social pay-off to the investment.[55] Some have argued, however, that it may not be possible to induce additional large productivity gains at low cost, if there is not sufficient unused new technology waiting in the wings. Past experience may reflect a pattern whereby new discoveries

Diagram 20. **CAPITAL DEEPENING AND TOTAL FACTOR PRODUCTIVITY GROWTH**

Average annual percentage change, 1950 to 1991

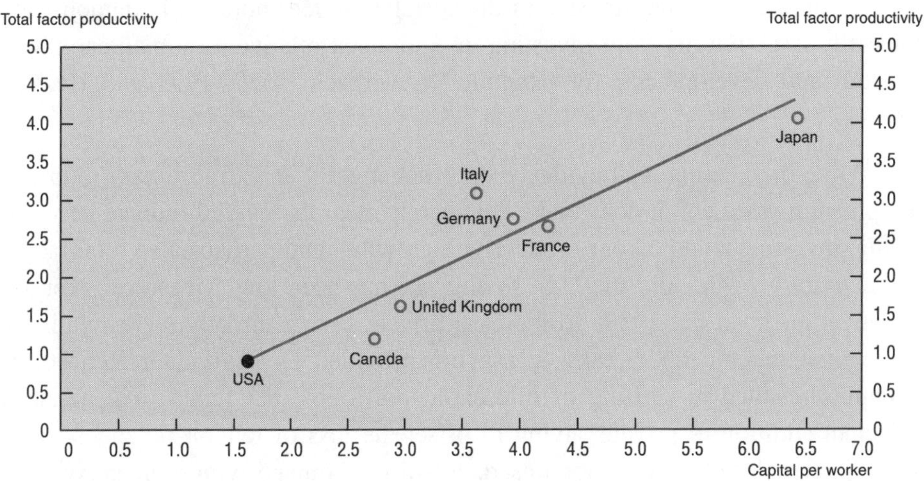

Source: OECD.

increase the returns to new investments that embody the discoveries – inducing additions to the capital stock.[56, 57]

Opinions differ on the direction and strength of causation between equipment investment and productivity growth; for the United States, however, it is suggestive that productivity growth is highly positively correlated with increases in the capital-output ratio over the previous two years, and no positive correlation is evident between growth in the capital-output ratio and current or past changes in labour productivity. This makes more plausible the claim that other things being equal, higher equipment investment might boost productivity growth. However, it is unclear whether the favourable externalities resulting from the added capital formation would be large enough to justify the cost of government support of such investment in the form, for example, of an investment tax credit. Some argue that the observed correlation between equipment investment and productivity growth is so strong that the cost to society of additional equipment investment is probably less than the social return; that is, there may be external benefits to the economy from investment in equipment (DeLong and Summers,

1991 and 1992). However, the evidence for such external benefits is controversial. Clearly, equipment and productivity growth are linked (though not so much since the mid-1970s), but the size of the correlation does not clearly demonstrate unusually large returns from investing in equipment relative to human capital or research and development, for example[58] (Auerbach *et al.*, 1993 and Heston, 1993).

While the international evidence does not suggest an extraordinary return to equipment investment, it does make abundantly clear the overall linkage between saving, investment and labour productivity growth – and perhaps also total factor productivity growth. And the U.S. saving rate has been low. Measures taken by the government in the 1980s to increase private saving directly were relatively ineffective: income tax breaks for saving provided by Individual Retirement Accounts resulted in shifting of household portfolios, but failed to generate a sufficient addition to private saving to offset the loss of federal revenues. As a result, national saving was not raised. Results of other savings incentive programmes were mixed (Baily *et al.,* 1993).

However, a good case can be made for reducing some existing distortions in the personal tax laws that reduce savings available for investment in equipment, research, etc. For example, mortgage interest deductibility encourages excess residential construction relative to other forms of investment.[59] While full elimination of this tax break would be very difficult politically, it may be possible to cap more tightly the deduction for mortgage interest in line with the limit on other deductions for high-income taxpayers.[60] In addition, the current tax deductibility of interest on home-equity loans (consumer loans disguised to generate mortgage interest charges) is an indirect incentive to borrow for consumption, and its restriction or elimination could be pursued. A number of other possible measures to stimulate private saving are more problematic, however. For example, taxpayers are now liable for the full extent of capital gains on equities, including the purely inflationary component. In principle, capital gains should be adjusted for inflation for the purposes of taxation. Under current tax law, inflation can reduce the incentive to save in the form of equities. However, correcting the problem might simply create new distortions: tax shelters could then exploit the lack of an inflation adjustment in deductibility of business borrowing costs. Introduction of a value-added tax might provide private saving incentives; however, the administrative expense would be a significant drawback. Personal tax increases might marginally reduce private saving, but would nonetheless boost national saving.

In addition to boosting national saving, the government could also attempt to encourage private investment directly. But given the recent studies on equipment spending mentioned above, it is not clear whether special incentives to increase business investment would yield significant social gains. Certainly a temporary incremental investment tax credit – as originally proposed by the Administration – would have had marginal benefits at best, given the difficulty in designing recapture rules that would adequately limit shifting investment forward into the tax-credit year.[61] Other investment initiatives in the 1994 Budget are small, but seem likely to be beneficial. Extending faster depreciation to firms under the alternative minimum tax may boost investment marginally. The temporary extension of the Research and Experimentation Tax credit (see below) and new rules confining its availability to domestic research may induce a marginal increase in equipment investment to incorporate the R&D output, a few years hence. Ultimately, however, the best way to boost U.S. investment is to reduce the drain on investment funds and lower real long-term interest rates – by reducing public dissaving through a cut in the federal deficit.

Adjustment costs: structural change and military downsizing

Another possible factor impeding growth in output and productivity is the cost of adjustment associated with structural change in production. As an economy is confronted with changes in the pattern of demand and eventually of supply, it must re-allocate its capital and labour inputs to match these new needs, and during the transition process, productivity growth can be temporarily slowed. Of course, such re-allocation is happening to all countries at all times. The question that needs to be answered is whether such shocks have been more important in the United States economy in the recent past than is usual. There is some empirical evidence that sectoral changes in value added in manufacturing industries in the 1980s were greater than in the 1970s (Table 13) and than in most other major countries. But since they were substantially greater still in Japan, it seems unlikely that such adjustment costs can have been too onerous. Furthermore, more up-to-date employment-based data reveal a definite reduction in

Table 13. **Indicators of structural change in manufacturing**

	USA	Japan	Germany	France	U.K.	Italy	Canada
A. Index of structural change[1]							
1970s	4.0	10.4	4.5	n.a.	5.1	n.a.	5.2
1980s	7.9	12.9	5.1	2.7	3.4	5.4	5.8
1970-89	11.1	22.3	9.6	n.a.	5.9	n.a.	9.9
B. Changes in share of manufacturing valued added in current prices 1980-89[2] (in percentage points)							
High technology	3.06	4.64	2.71	n.a.	2.80	1.54	0.88
Medium technology	1.13	1.66	4.92	n.a.	–1.51	0.09	3.87
Low technology	–4.19	–6.31	–7.63	n.a.	–1.28	–1.63	–4.75
Science based	2.36	1.66	0.67	n.a.	2.49	1.81	0.96
High wage	6.25	2.86	3.43	n.a.	2.04	0.92	5.69
Medium wage	–6.42	–1.67	0.74	n.a.	–0.66	–1.12	–2.94
Low wage	0.18	–1.18	–4.16	n.a.	–1.38	0.20	–2.76

1. Sum of the absolute value of sectoral changes in the share of manufacturing valued added.
2. Except the United Kingdom (1980-88) and Italy (1980-87). For definitions of industry groupings see footnotes to Table 16.
Source: OECD (1993*b*).

overall structural change during most of the 1980s in the United States, to a rate that was slower than elsewhere among the major OECD countries (Diagram 21).

One structural change which is significant enough to merit special attention in this context is the downsizing of the military (sometimes called the defence "build-down"). The real value of outlays for national defence has been falling since 1989, and their share of GDP since 1986 (Table 14). Despite a rather low level of labour intensity,[62] defence-related employment fell by nearly 900 000 in the five years to 1992. Similar changes have been happening abroad, with major declines in the world arms trade: according to Data Resources Incorporated, exports of major weapons systems have fallen by more than half since 1987. Both the previous and current Administrations have planned to take advantage of the new geopolitical environment to make further significant reductions in defence spending over the next four years (the so-called "peace dividend") and to shift the focus of federal R&D away from defence.[63] Under current proposals, less than a third of the employment shrinkage had occurred by end-1992,[64] with a further loss of nearly 1.9 million defence-related jobs expected by 1997 (Saunders, 1993), an average of over 30 000 per month. This compares with about 150 000 workers per month who were displaced by plant closings or relocation,

Diagram 21. **AN INDICATOR OF STRUCTURAL CHANGE: AN INTERNATIONAL COMPARISON**

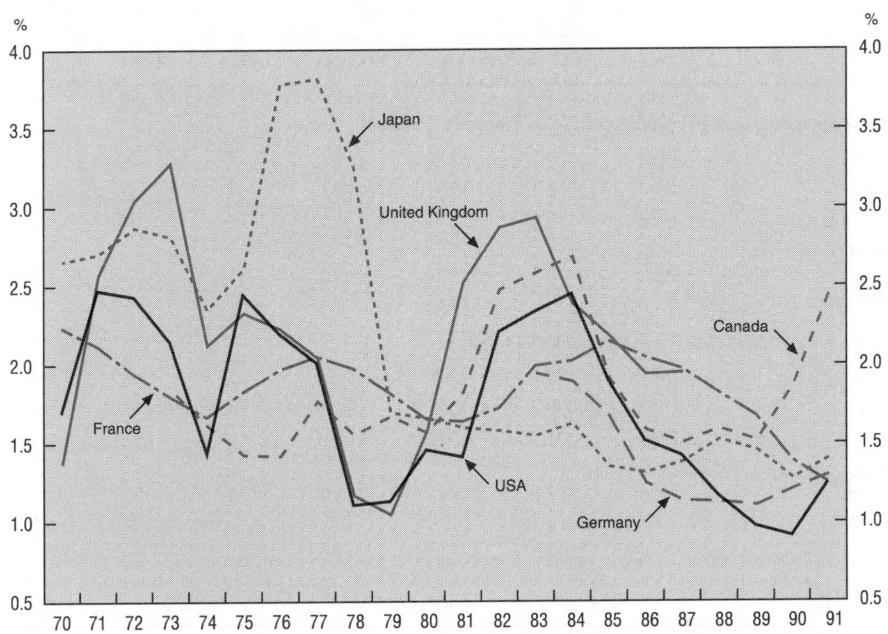

1. Three-year moving average of the weighted absolute difference between sectoral annual growth rates of employment and aggregate employment, both in per cent. Thus, the higher the value, the greater the structural change.

Source: OECD, *Annual Labour Force Statistics.*

elimination of a position or shift, or slack work in the five years 1985-89. And there is probably more to come: in 1992 an arm of the U.S. Congress made predictions that imply that employment will fall up to an additional 450 000 in the years 1997-2001 (U.S. Congress, Office of Technology Assessment, 1992*a*). The impact is proportionally more severe for the armed forces than for civilian defence-related employees, and particularly intense for occupations with low educational attainment.[65] In terms of timing, the peak impact is expected to be in 1993, with a projected decline in outlays of 9.2 per cent.

While the cuts are not going to be as severe as any of the other post-World War II drawdowns, previous military shrinkages were accomplished during peri-

Table 14. **Comparison of previous and current defense drawdowns**[1]

Era	Peak		Low point		Difference		Average change per year (Percentage)
	Year	GDP %	Year	GDP %	Years	GDP %	
Defense spending as a percentage of Gross Domestic Product							
WW II	1944	39.3	1948	3.7	4	35.6	8.09
Korea	1953	14.5	1956	10.2	3	4.3	1.43
Vietnam	1968	9.6	1978	4.8	10	4.8	0.48
Current							
Bush	1986	6.5	1997	3.6	11	2.9	0.26
Clinton				3.1		3.4	0.31
Outlays for national defense (billions of 1993 dollars)							
WW II	1945	885.7	1948	80.4	3	805.3	268.4
Korea	1953	390.7	1956	284.5	3	106.2	35.4
Vietnam	1968	371.2	1977	219.1	9	152.1	16.9
Current							
Bush	1989	353.6	1997	256.9	8	96.7	12.1
Clinton				223.1		130.5	16.3

1. Includes all national defense spending, including Department of Energy defense activities.

Sources: U.S. Department of Defense (1992) and Secretariat calculations based on Office of Management and Budget (1993*b*).

ods of strong overall growth and plentiful of alternative job creation, in possible contrast to the current episode. In addition, today's defence workers are probably more specialised than their predecessors. The inability of the economy to re-employ quickly and flexibly those who have been the victims of the drawdown even to this point in the adjustment process is illustrated by the fact that the unemployment rate in the four states most heavily impacted (Connecticut, Virginia, Massachusetts and California) rose 4.1 percentage points between 1988 and September 1992, while for the other 46 the rise was only 1.5 percentage points (U.S. Department of Commerce, 1993). Heavy regional concentration of defence-related employment (in 1991 eight states accounted for about half the total) makes the adjustment all the more burdensome.

What is the impact of military spending on growth and productivity? According to some, the cross-country correlation between the size of the military establishment and overall growth performance is no accident; it serves to explain longer-term fluctuations in national economic power (Kennedy, 1987). Bayoumi *et al.* (1993) argue that defence spending crowds out investment, thereby lowering long-run economic growth. Others have uncovered a negative impact of military spending on the rate of new-product innovation (Guellec and Ralle, 1991). Overall, it is hard to see how defence spending can be other than a burden in the first instance. The question is: to what extent is this burden mitigated by spillovers in R&D? There is now a fairly broad consensus that defence-related R&D spending has a lower social rate of return than private, non-defence spending (Lichtenberg, 1992), with fewer spillovers from military to civilian technology than in the first decades after World War II (Nelson and Wright, 1992). Indeed, in many areas, defence is now most likely a technology laggard. But some have argued that defence procurement exerts a powerful stimulus on private R&D investment (Cohen and Noll, 1992).[66]

In macroeconomic terms, even without any microeconomic gains, the defence cut-backs could have measurable effects. Assuming that the savings will be devoted either to cutting selected taxes, stimulating public investments (see the following section) or reducing the deficit, rather than increasing other non-defence purchases of a current-consumption nature, the long-term impact on investment and output should be positive,[67] although the timing of the expected turnaround is in dispute. A credibly announced reduction should "front-load" the initial contractionary adjustment and allow a more rapid entry into the recovery phase. But, over the next few years, all experts are agreed that, barring monetary-policy offsets, the growth of real GDP will be reduced by the defence cut-backs.[68]

The Administration has proposed the Defence Reinvestment and Conversion Initiative to ease the transition. It embodies 29 different programmes. A number are aimed at personnel (early retirement, health benefits, retraining, scholarships, employment services, counselling, relocation assistance); others are for the local communities worst hit by the closure of military or contractor installations. Last, there are a series which will try to set up partnerships between industry and the 726 national laboratories (that do some $23 billion or about 13 per cent of the nation's total R&D), especially for dual-use technology, and provide matching grants for industry-led R&D (see below). The total package is evaluated at some $20 billion over five years. For fiscal 1993 it includes $1.4 billion appropriated by Congress last year, but not spent, plus another $0.3 billion. The total is set to rise to $5.2 billion in FY 1997. While this sounds like a substantial fiscal effort, there is reason for scepticism as to the feasibility of conversion (Lundquist, 1993). The markets for typical conversion products are small when compared with the Defence Department's previous needs. And many defence contractors have a poor record of selling to the commercial market, given their specialised product development skills, lack of prior focus on cost minimisation and the legal as well as administrative separation of their defence and commercial divisions. In any case, if amounts as significant as this are to be spent effectively, it will be necessary to monitor the success of each programme through the development of explicit measures of progress toward well-defined goals. Other reforms that have been suggested (U.S. Department of Defence, 1992) would be to rely on the private sector to a greater degree for maintenance and repair and R&D and to encourage greater commercial-military integration by standardising Defence Department purchasing and accounting practices and standards and specifications.

Investment in public infrastructure

Public investment in physical infrastructure declined as a share of GDP from 3.1 per cent in the 1960s to 2.0 per cent in the 1970s and further to 1.4 per cent in the 1980s (Diagram 22).[69] Views differ as to how serious a problem this declining trend represents. Some argue that it largely reflects changing requirements and hence should not be a cause for concern. For example, the sharp fall in construction of school facilities after 1975 was simply a result of the post-baby-boom drop in school enrolments, and a virtual completion of the inter-state highway network in the early 1970s brought about a large cut-back in road construction spending. In contrast, those holding a less sanguine view, including the new Administration, doubt if existing facilities are adequate and point to a need for increased infrastructure spending to meet the demands for future growth in living standards. Oft-cited symptoms of inadequate public investment include insufficient capacity to deal with waste water and solid waste, poor conditions of roads and bridges, and increased urban freeway congestion and air-traffic delays.

The view that inadequate public infrastructure investment is a drag on economic performance was reinforced by the much-publicised study by Aschauer (1989) which suggested that public investment has a large impact on private

Diagram 22. **PUBLIC INFRASTRUCTURE CAPITAL STOCK AND INVESTMENT**

Per cent of GDP

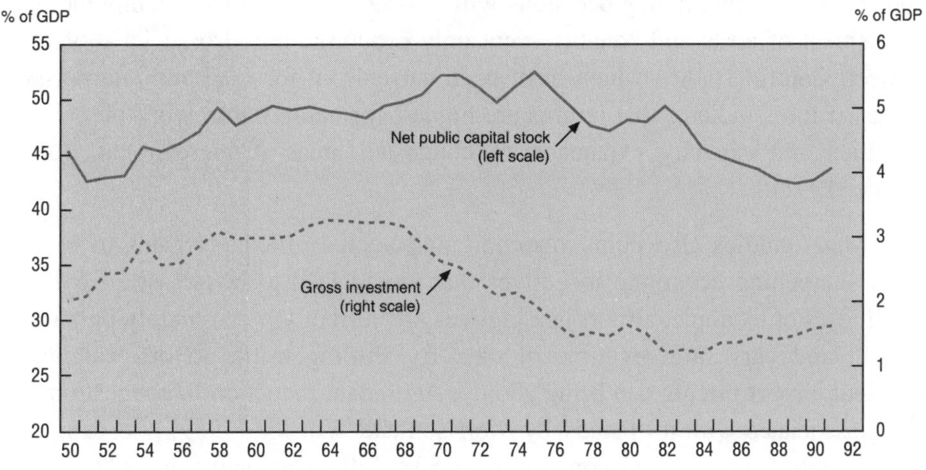

Source : Department of Commerce, Bureau of Economic Analysis.

output and productivity at an aggregate level; a given percentage increase in public capital would raise private output by the same proportion, implying a unitary elasticity between the two. Subsequent work, based also on aggregate time-series data, has tended to show much smaller effects, with elasticities ranging from 0.02 to 0.30.[70] More recently, most of these time-series-based estimates have been seriously challenged based on problems with their statistical foundations (Jorgenson, 1991). Cross-section studies, which do not suffer from this particular statistical problem, however, also report a positive association between the level of public capital stock and private output.[71] Judging from this and other scattered evidence, it would be reasonable to think that such a link does exist. However, the consensus of the literature in this area seems to be that the causal relation can run in either direction – although increased public investment leads to higher private output, the latter also both raises the need for additional infrastructure and generates public revenues to finance it.[72]

Estimates of aggregate elasticities are in any case of very limited help for policy makers in determining the appropriate level of infrastructure stock and resulting investment needs in a forward-looking context. Returns on public infrastructure investment typically vary widely across different investment categories and regions, so that policy decisions will have to be guided by a comprehensive assessment of costs and benefits – not only economic but also social – of each project. Careful studies which have been carried out for road and air transport infrastructures indicate that returns are highest for maintenance work on existing facilities and capacity expansion in congested areas (Congressional Budget Office, 1991).

Many studies also point to important potential efficiency gains to be had from sharpening economic incentives that would lead to better use of existing facilities. For example, airport landing fees are currently based mainly on aircraft weight and vary little by time of day. By shifting traffic to off-peak hours efficient airport pricing can bring about a significant reduction in congestion and costs associated with it (a study by Morrison and Winston (1989) puts estimated net benefits from reduced congestion at $3.8 billion annually in 1988 prices). Similarly, congestion pricing of road use could yield substantial economic benefits (as much as $5.7 billion in 1981 prices according to a study by Small *et al.* (1989)). An equally important potential source of efficiency gains is the reduced cost of road maintenance. Taxes on highway users are currently unrelated to the damage they cause to the pavement. Wear and tear of roads result largely from the weight per axle of the vehicle.[73] Adoption of fees based on weight per axle and distance driven could eventually lead to less need for highway maintenance (a study by Small *et al.* (1989)) gives an estimate of annual net saving of $5.4 billion at 1982 prices from optimal taxation of road damage). Introduction of optimal pricing for the use of roads and airports could, according to leading advocates (Winston, for example), even make capacity expansion unnecessary, at least for a time. Such pricing would also allow subsequent investment decisions to be made on a sounder basis.

The need for improvement in public physical infrastructure was already evident in the early 1980s. For example, the poor state of transport infrastructure was often highlighted by press reports of bumpy highways and collapsing bridges.[74] The share in GDP of public investment in physical infrastructure stabilised in the mid-1980s and has since been rising steadily, despite the tightening budgetary constraint. Judged by the level of funding and spending priority, the new Administration's policy does not appear to be substantially different from that of the previous Administration. The new Administration, however, attaches greater weight to enhancing public infrastructure as a way of improving productivity and living standards.

In its 1994 Budget, the new Administration proposed a modest increase in public infrastructure investment over the CBO baseline. Most of the proposed increase in funding seems to be money well-spent, that is in areas likely to promise high returns in economic and social terms. For example, expansion of the Federal-aid highway programme to the levels contained in the Intermodal Surface Transportation Efficiency Act (ISTEA) will contribute to maintaining conditions and performance of the National Highway System,[75] and emphasis given to water-quality improvement is consistent with the priority suggested by cost-benefit studies. As well, acceleration of the Intelligent Vehicle-Highways Initiative (IVHS) will not only improve traffic-control systems but also make the introduction of more innovative highway policy such as congestion pricing a reality. While the Administration's infrastructure investment proposals seem reasonable, in view of the tight budget constraint more energetic moves towards implementing policies to promote efficient use of existing facilities seem warranted. And indeed, this seems to be the path the Administration intends to follow in its infrastructure initiatives.

Education and human capital

Improvements in the education of the U.S. labour force were an important factor behind the boom in productivity between World War II and the early 1970s. There is an increasing premium on education and training: thus, a higher proportion of high-school graduates are going to college than ever before. Other OECD countries also made major gains in educational attainment; however, the overall U.S. labour force remains more highly educated – measured in terms of attainment – than that of any other developed country (OECD, 1992*a*) (Table 15).[76] However, the aggregate attainment statistics mask some disturbing problems that have appeared over the past decade or so. College graduates have seen healthy growth in their real incomes, but more than half of all working-age Americans have not attended college – and their real incomes have fallen over the same period.[77] Furthermore, the work-related skills of many American youths are now disturbingly poor, relative to those in other developed countries. Thus,

Table 15. **Educational attainment for the adult population in 1989**[1]

Shares in per cent

<table>
<tr><th></th><th>Pre-primary and primary</th><th>Lower-secondary</th><th>Upper-secondary</th><th>Non-university tertiary</th><th>University</th><th>Undistributed</th></tr>
<tr><td>Canada</td><td>14</td><td>14</td><td>41</td><td>15</td><td>15</td><td>0</td></tr>
<tr><td>United States</td><td>8</td><td>10</td><td>46</td><td>12</td><td>23</td><td>0</td></tr>
<tr><td>Australia</td><td>14</td><td>30</td><td>25</td><td>21</td><td>10</td><td>1</td></tr>
<tr><td>Japan</td><td colspan="2">30</td><td>48</td><td>8</td><td>13</td><td>1</td></tr>
<tr><td>New Zealand</td><td>33</td><td>10</td><td>25</td><td>22</td><td>9</td><td>1</td></tr>
<tr><td>Austria</td><td colspan="2">35</td><td>60</td><td colspan="2">5[2]</td><td>0</td></tr>
<tr><td>Belgium</td><td>33</td><td>30</td><td>20</td><td>10</td><td>7</td><td>0</td></tr>
<tr><td>France</td><td>24</td><td>26</td><td>33</td><td>7</td><td>7</td><td>3</td></tr>
<tr><td>Germany</td><td colspan="2">22</td><td>61</td><td>7</td><td>10</td><td>0</td></tr>
<tr><td>Ireland</td><td>37</td><td>25</td><td>23</td><td>7</td><td>7</td><td>1</td></tr>
<tr><td>Netherlands</td><td>19</td><td>26</td><td>36</td><td>13</td><td>6</td><td>0</td></tr>
<tr><td>Switzerland</td><td colspan="2">20</td><td>50</td><td>15</td><td>9</td><td>6</td></tr>
<tr><td>United Kingdom</td><td colspan="2">35</td><td>48</td><td>6</td><td>9</td><td>1</td></tr>
<tr><td>Italy</td><td>44</td><td>30</td><td>20</td><td colspan="2">6[2]</td><td>0</td></tr>
<tr><td>Portugal</td><td>89</td><td>4</td><td>2</td><td>2</td><td>4</td><td>0</td></tr>
<tr><td>Spain</td><td>67</td><td>13</td><td>10</td><td colspan="2">9[2]</td><td>0</td></tr>
<tr><td>Denmark</td><td colspan="2">43</td><td>40</td><td>7</td><td>10</td><td>0</td></tr>
<tr><td>Finland</td><td colspan="2">42</td><td>40</td><td>8</td><td>10</td><td>0</td></tr>
<tr><td>Sweden</td><td colspan="2">33</td><td>44</td><td>11</td><td>12</td><td>0</td></tr>
<tr><td>Norway</td><td colspan="2">35</td><td>42</td><td>10</td><td>11</td><td>2</td></tr>
<tr><td>Simple average of above countries</td><td colspan="2">45</td><td>36</td><td>9</td><td>10</td><td>1</td></tr>
<tr><td>Simple average of European countries</td><td colspan="2">49</td><td>35</td><td>7</td><td>8</td><td>1</td></tr>
</table>

1. Population aged 25-64 in 1989, except Japan (1987), Denmark (1988), New Zealand (1990), the Netherlands (1990) and Norway (1990).
2. All tertiary education, but virtually all are university.

Source: OECD, Centre for Education Research and Innovation, *Education at a Glance*, 1992.

the Administration has put in place several initiatives to deal with problems of school quality and upgrading the skills of the non-college-bound, as discussed below.

Human capital has been a major contributor to U.S. economic growth. Denison and Kendrick estimate that up to a quarter of income growth per worker since World War II has resulted from better education (Dean, 1984). Jorgenson estimated that growth of labour quality contributed nearly ½ per cent annually to post-war output growth. This healthy growth in educational attainment and productivity did not come at the expense of social equity – at least until the early

1970s: the gap between the incomes of the skilled and the unskilled actually narrowed somewhat over that period. However, increased research and development spending and the computer revolution have steadily boosted the demand for skilled labour, while inducing change in production technology that economises on unskilled labour. At the same time, the increasing openness of the U.S. economy has put unskilled U.S. labour into more direct competition with lower-cost labour in Mexico, China, and other developing countries – in firms' foreign outsourcing decisions, for example. In the 1970s, these shifts in relative labour demand were offset by a surge in the supply of relatively skilled young workers as the baby-boom generation finished college. The overall returns to education declined. However, in the last decade or so, the demographic factors have reversed, due to a slowdown in the supply of college graduates, and the gap between the incomes of skilled and unskilled workers has widened from about 15 per cent to almost 50 per cent.[78] Compounding the problem is high unemployment among the less skilled: an increasing fraction of unskilled men were unemployed or dropped out of the labour force in the 1970s, and the increase in non-employment has not been corrected in the intervening years.

The growing skill-based disparities in employment and earnings have the makings of a major social problem,[79] since public schools available to urban minorities are frequently underfunded, and a disproportionate share of the unskilled are members of minorities. The fraction of the black labour force without a high-school diploma is over 20 per cent, half again as large as the corresponding figure for whites. The high-school dropout rate for Hispanic Americans is a stunning 33 per cent.[80] These minority dropout rates have very disturbing long-term implications for the average skill level of the American workforce, bearing in mind that more than one-third of Americans born in the 1980s are black or Hispanic.

Internationally, per capita income growth in poorer countries tends to exceed that of higher-income countries – but this tendency toward convergence only occurs among countries with similar educational attainments (Baumol *et al.,* 1989; Barro, 1992). Domestically, the same may hold true for inner-city enclaves of blacks and Hispanics: increases in inner-city public works programmes and "enterprise zone" business investment will probably fail to narrow the income gap of these urban areas unless the education gap is narrowed sufficiently (Baumol *et al.,* 1989). Thus, efforts to improve the skills of the least-educated

Americans, especially among minorities in the inner cities, are badly needed for equity reasons. Furthermore, education initiatives may improve economic efficiency as well. Education contributes a variety of external benefits beyond the increased income accruing to the student: two such benefits which are measurable are a reduction in crime[81] and reduced costs for welfare payments. These two external benefits are more likely to be realised from education of the least skilled, suggesting that targeted education initiatives may yield especially high social benefits.

The federal government has typically played only a minor role in the financing of education and vocational training systems (it spent about $35 billion in 1992), with a much larger part played by state and local governments and private industry, respectively. However, since incomes vary substantially across school districts, significant imbalances arise in state and local educational spending per pupil. This in turn contributes to inefficiency in spending, in part because of the above-mentioned external benefits to education in poorer school districts. Thus, federal efforts have focused primarily on investing additional resources in education and skill-training for low-income groups, since they have tended to be underserved by state and local programmes. The government budget for fiscal 1994 proposes to increase sharply these federal efforts, as discussed below.

By far the largest spending increases in the budget package go toward education and related human-capital programmes. These are targeted at all levels – pre-school, elementary and high school, college, vocational education, and on-the-job training. At least eleven programmes are involved (proposed funding increases in 1997 in parentheses; the appropriations process is ongoing, so actual spending levels may change):

- extending availability of Head Start education programmes to all eligible poor children ($9 billion);
- public school reform ($420 million for 1994, $6.2 billion through 1997);
- expansion of education and training for disadvantaged youth (Job Corps and summer programmes $2.5 billion);
- math-science education research ($100-200 million in 1994);
- youth apprenticeships at school and work (eventually abandoned; $1.2 billion);
- increased funding of means-tested college tuition assistance ($2 billion);[82]

- financing college education in return for community-service work (National Service Trust Act, $6 billion);
- re-employment/retraining programmes for dislocated workers ($4.6 billion);
- one-stop retraining or job-change centres ($0.7 billion);
- tax incentives for on-the-job training ($1.9 billion).

So far, only one of these proposals has made significant progress through Congress: public-school reform. This re-authorisation of the Great Society programme to support the poorest public schools (the Elementary and Secondary Education Act of 1964) includes a new attempt to establish national standards for public schools, albeit voluntary ones with no required national testing to go along with the standards. The bill proposes substantial spending increases over the next five years, but only $420 million in outlays for fiscal 1994 – reverting to the spending levels of the first Bush education plan, which was then rejected by many in Congress as insufficient. Budget constraints have held proposed near-term spending in the new bill to levels below those in the second Bush education package of $690 million: that bill did not pass due to controversy over a clause allowing poor students the choice to attend private schools at public expense (Zuckman, 1993*a*). No such controversial clause appears in the new school reform bill.

There will be difficulty in getting consensus on re-allocation of federal funds to more needy public schools, but the current inefficiency of spending on public schools is well documented. The United States already spends large sums per student relative to other OECD countries, yet average test results for mathematics and science are poor – especially so for U.S. students living in poor neighbourhoods. Money is not the only problem underlying these sub-par results: nonetheless, federal as well as state and local governments do not adequately target funds on poor school districts.[83] Currently, the size of federal grants is tied to state outlays per student, which has had the effect of allocating more funds to wealthier states. One study estimates that more than half of all federal funds for elementary and secondary education go to students who are not from poor families (Zuckman, 1993*b*). Thus, total federal and local funding for schools in poor areas remains relatively low, despite an overall nation-wide level of education spending which compares favourably with other OECD countries. Given this inequity, and the external benefits from training of the least-educated, the national goals of equal opportunity and improved average performance will both be served by a re-allocation in federal education spending toward poorer public schools. Beginning next year, the shifts in federal funding based on the new 1990 census data will help marginally: many school districts will lose from the redistribution, but $235 million has been allocated to ease their transition. Even after the re-allocation, however, fundamental distributional inefficiencies will remain.

Most of the other human capital initiatives in the 1994 Budget simply increase spending for existing programmes or implement previous plans[84] – these spending initiatives appear worthwhile, given the training needs discussed above. However, several of the proposals are radically different from any programmes or proposals of the Bush and Reagan Administrations. One of these, mandated employer training programmes for large firms, apparently did not survive political opposition in Congress – and in any case similar experiments in France and Australia have not been entirely successful.[85] Much of the increased training expenditure in those countries was focused on more skilled employees, rather than the least-skilled workers who were the planned focus of the levies. And in the period the schemes have been in operation, there has been little evidence of noticeable gains in productivity growth due to increased on-the-job training. Two additional programmes were under consideration in the budget reconciliation process: youth apprenticeships, as in the German model, and a National Service Program, where students would receive federal funds for college tuition in exchange for one or two years of low-paid community-service work. The former was, however, abandoned.

All of these programmes are welcome attempts to address a serious social problem in the making. However, few clear results have been found in studies of the outcomes of existing federal human-capital programmes (Congressional Budget Office, 1991). Although an early study of Head Start's effectiveness found only transitory gains, more recent studies conclude that there is lasting effectiveness (Currie and Thomas, 1993). Suggestions have been made to extend the number of years of attendance for participating children, or to provide different forms of assistance instead.[86] In contrast, programmes like the Job Corps appear to help enough to pay for themselves, though mainly *via* a reduction in crime rather than major increases in earnings or reduced welfare payments.

Research and development and the state of U.S. technology

Technology is clearly a major factor in determining the competitiveness of individual firms as well as of their host countries. Modern production processes require fixed capital embodying the latest technological innovations, along with highly skilled manpower to operate it and effective management to combine these factors in a cost-efficient fashion. However, many questions remain as to the exact role of technology in the growth process. In recent years there have been increasingly frequent challenges to the by now traditional neo-classical growth model of Solow (1956) in which technological progress is exogenous. A first alternative view, initially suggested by Romer (1986), predicts that increases in total factor productivity and, therefore, the rate of growth are linearly related to the rate of capital accumulation,[87] implying the optimality of investment subsidies (see above). A second widely-held version of the endogeneity of technology is based on the influential role of R&D in determining the long-run growth rate, especially given observed spillovers.[88] Recent research has recognised that R&D intensity is by no means exogenous and has concentrated on the determinants of R&D or knowledge production more generally. Technological opportunities and appropriability conditions are key determining factors.

The link between improvements in technology and higher measured productivity has been tenuous in some sectors. Even in the manufacturing sector Steindel (1992) found only a limited impact of information processing equipment on labour productivity.[89] And for some time now, observers have wondered why the returns to computer investments were so difficult to discern in the non-manufacturing sector, at least until very recently (see, for example, Roach, 1988 and 1993). Some of the explanation no doubt lies with measurement problems, and some with investments which may have been made with goals other than improved productivity in mind (Baily and Gordon, 1988).

However, there is by now a great deal of evidence on the impact of R&D on productivity growth both at the micro- and macroeconomic levels. Cross-sectional approaches tend to give higher estimated sensitivities than those based on time-series data, but an overall consensus value for the elasticity of total factor productivity with respect to the stock of R&D capital is about 0.1 to 0.15 (Amable and Boyer, 1992), albeit less in the 1980s, at least cross-sectionally. This may be because of greater competition and therefore more rapid private obsolescence, as innovation may reduce the value of existing technological capital (Hall, 1993). For the manufacturing sector, time-series estimates yield substantially lower estimates for the United States than for Germany and Japan. Government-financed R&D is widely agreed to be less stimulative of productivity gains than firm-financed outlays, perhaps since so much of it is defence-related (Lichtenberg, 1992), and process-related efforts are more so than those designed with a new product in mind. Private (average rather than marginal) returns are believed to be in the range of 20 to 30 per cent per year, about equal with those of tangible capital, but given spillovers due to imperfect appropriability, social returns are believed to be at least double those rates (Bernstein and Nadiri, 1991). Indeed, in one extreme result (Lichtenberg, 1992), privately-funded R&D's social returns were found to be seven times those of fixed tangible investment.

Independent of the level of the national effort devoted to finding new technologies, the ability to exploit existing technology and harness it for commercial use is also vitally important. The United States is held to have a problem in downstream commercialisation, with a need to shift its focus from breakthroughs to leveraging such innovations for commercial advantage[90] and to faster dissemination of best-practice technology.

The United States was for a long time the undisputed leader in virtually all technologies, as it was in levels of labour and total factor productivity. It was able to see itself as technologically self-sufficient, with little need to seek contacts with foreign technology producers. But there has been a widely recognised process of convergence since about 1950, at least among OECD countries, as other nations have partially caught up to the United States through faster investment growth, both in tangible and intangible capital, the spreading availability of natural resources and the erosion of its market-size advantage through the reduction in transport costs and the elimination of trade barriers (Nelson and Wright, 1992). But to the extent that technology is imperfectly appropriable, it is cheaper to be a free rider, and absolute leadership may not be very important.

Many indicators are available to measure shorter-term trends in U.S. technological competitiveness. But all show that the United States is still the world's technological leader, even if its lead has clearly diminished in recent decades, primarily to the benefit of Japan.[91]

A first indicator, the "technological balance of payments", shows that the United States remains the world's largest exporter of intellectual property, earning about 4½ times what it pays abroad.[92] However, while the nation's net receipts of fees and royalties from abroad reversed their trend decline in relation to GDP in the mid-1980s, its share of total receipts by the major seven OECD countries had as yet shown no signs of recovery by the end of the decade (Diagram 23). External performance in terms of visible trade in high-technology manufactures has also waned, with very rapid increases in import penetration, combined with a narrowing lead in export markets (OECD, 1993*b*) (Table 16). Similarly, although U.S. manufacturers were doing more R&D in 1986-88 than they had a decade earlier, there was a noticeable decline from 1973 to 1990 in the U.S. share of manufacturing R&D performed by business among thirteen OECD countries, mainly at the expense of Japan (Diagram 24). The drop was evident in all categories: high-, medium- and low-technology manufactures. Yet the latest available data (1987) confirm that the United States still has the highest proportion of the labour force accounted for by scientists and engineers engaged in R&D and that its lead over other major OECD countries has widened somewhat since 1976. Furthermore, the relative position of the United States may be better than it seems for two reasons: first, R&D costs may be lower than elsewhere, given the availability of cheap instrumentation and a plentiful supply of doctoral students. Second, most software R&D is expensed, especially that which is undertaken by users, and the United States is the world leader in software.

Patent figures are also commonly used as indicators of technological change and inventive input and output over time (Griliches, 1990). Foreign residents have been granted a rising share of total patents granted in the United States at least through 1990, with particularly dynamic growth recorded for the Dynamic Asian Economies, Japan, Sweden and Switzerland. By 1990 Japanese residents represented 22 per cent of all U.S. patents, up from less than 10 per cent in 1977. But in third-country patenting, the United States continues to surpass Japan in all countries except Korea, and Germany everywhere except in France and Italy (Table 17). It also maintains a wide lead in terms of authorship of articles in more than 3 200 scientific and technical journals.

Leadership may be crucial if one believes that first-mover advantages lead to the earning of Schumpeterian rents and improved terms of trade over the medium term. Adherents to this view (Tyson, 1992) claim that not all industries

Diagram 23. **TECHNOLOGICAL BALANCE OF PAYMENTS**

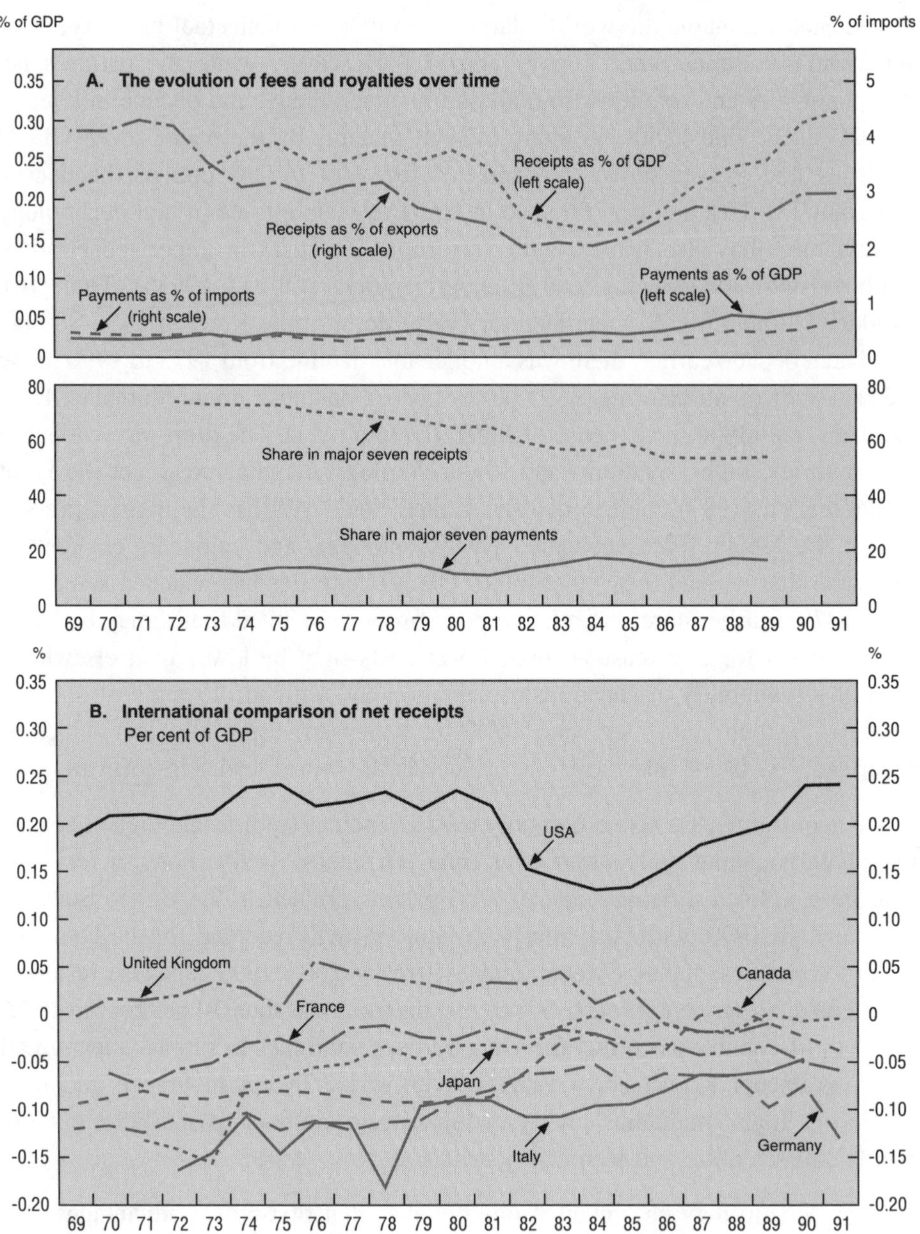

Source: OECD.

Table 16. **Sectoral structural trade indicators: an international comparison**

	USA		Japan		Germany		France		Italy		U.K.		EC 6[1]		Canada	
	1970	1990	1970	1990	1970	1990	1970	1990	1970	1990	1970	1990	1970	1990	1970	1990
A. Export shares of 13 OECD countries[2]																
High technology[3]	31.1	26.3	13.2	21.1	17.7	16.2	7.7	8.7	5.5	5.1	10.5	10.2	37.8	32.8	3.9	2.8
Medium technology[4]	21.7	15.4	8.5	16.9	23.1	24.7	8.5	10.0	7.1	7.7	11.9	8.5	45.3	43.7	8.9	5.9
Low technology[5]	13.4	13.3	13.2	7.1	15.0	17.9	10.7	12.1	8.5	12.8	8.9	8.5	40.8	48.5	7.0	6.1
B. Revealed comparative advantage[6]																
High technology	1.54	1.51	1.20	1.41	0.93	0.79	0.83	0.84	0.75	0.59	1.01	1.16	0.90	0.82	0.54	0.55
Medium technology	1.07	0.89	0.77	1.12	1.22	1.20	0.92	0.97	0.97	0.89	1.14	0.96	1.03	1.01	1.22	1.14
Low technology	0.66	0.76	1.19	0.47	0.79	0.87	1.15	1.18	1.16	1.49	0.85	0.95	1.01	1.13	0.96	1.19
Science based[7]	2.00	1.87	0.65	0.91	0.82	0.72	0.86	0.91	0.70	0.54	1.11	1.39	0.85	0.85	0.62	0.55
High wage[8]	1.30	1.17	0.61	1.06	1.11	1.03	0.99	1.03	0.88	0.60	1.04	1.04	1.01	0.95	1.00	0.94
Medium wage[9]	0.95	0.91	1.22	1.14	1.07	1.02	0.86	0.85	0.88	1.00	0.98	1.00	0.94	0.95	1.00	0.94
Low wage[10]	0.68	0.87	1.09	0.58	0.74	0.89	1.26	1.24	1.43	1.72	1.02	0.96	1.12	1.18	0.68	0.77
C. Import penetration[11]																
High technology	4.2	18.4	5.2	5.4	14.9	37.0	21.6	31.6	16.2	22.8	17.4	42.4	n.a.	n.a.	42.2	63.4
Medium technology	5.6	18.5	4.5	5.9	17.2	29.5	19.7	34.1	23.6	28.9	n.a.	39.4	n.a.	n.a.	42.9	53.3
Low technology	3.8	8.8	3.0	6.6	11.1	20.9	10.7	21.4	11.6	15.7	12.4	19.8	n.a.	n.a.	12.1	16.8
Science based	3.1	13.3	14.1	9.4	32.9	68.7	29.5	36.9	15.1	27.5	28.8	50.3	n.a.	n.a.	65.0	72.5

1. Germany, France, Italy, United Kingdom, the Netherlands, Denmark.
2. As in 1 plus USA, Japan, Canada, Australia, Finland, Norway, Sweden.
3. Drugs and medicines; electrical machinery; radio, TV and communication equipment; aircraft; professional goods; office and computing equipment.
4. Chemicals excluding drugs; rubber and plastic products; non-ferrous metals; non-electrical machinery; other transport equipment; motor vehicles; other manufacturing.
5. Food, beverages and tobacco; textiles, apparel and leather; wood products and furniture; paper products and printing, petroleum refineries and products; non-metallic mineral products; iron and steel; metal products; shipbuilding and repairing.
6. Country's (area's) export in an industry divided by its total exports normalised by the same ratio for the 13 OECD countries considered.
7. As in 3 except excludes electrical machinery and radio and TV and communication equipment.
8. Chemicals excluding drugs; drugs and medicines; petroleum refineries and products; office and computing equipment; motor vehicles; aircraft.
9. Paper products and printing; rubber and plastic products; non-metallic mineral products; iron and steel; non-ferrous metals; metal products; non-electrical machinery; radio, TV and communication equipment; shipbuilding and repairing; professional goods.
10. Food, beverages and tobacco; textiles, apparel and leather; wood products and furniture; electrical machinery excluding communication equipment; other transport equipment; other manufacturing.
11. Imports divided by total domestic demand (production plus imports less exports). Note that the 1990 data are, for the most part, from an earlier year in the late 1980s.

Source: OECD (1993*b*).

Diagram 24. **R&D SHARES AND INTENSITY RATIOS**

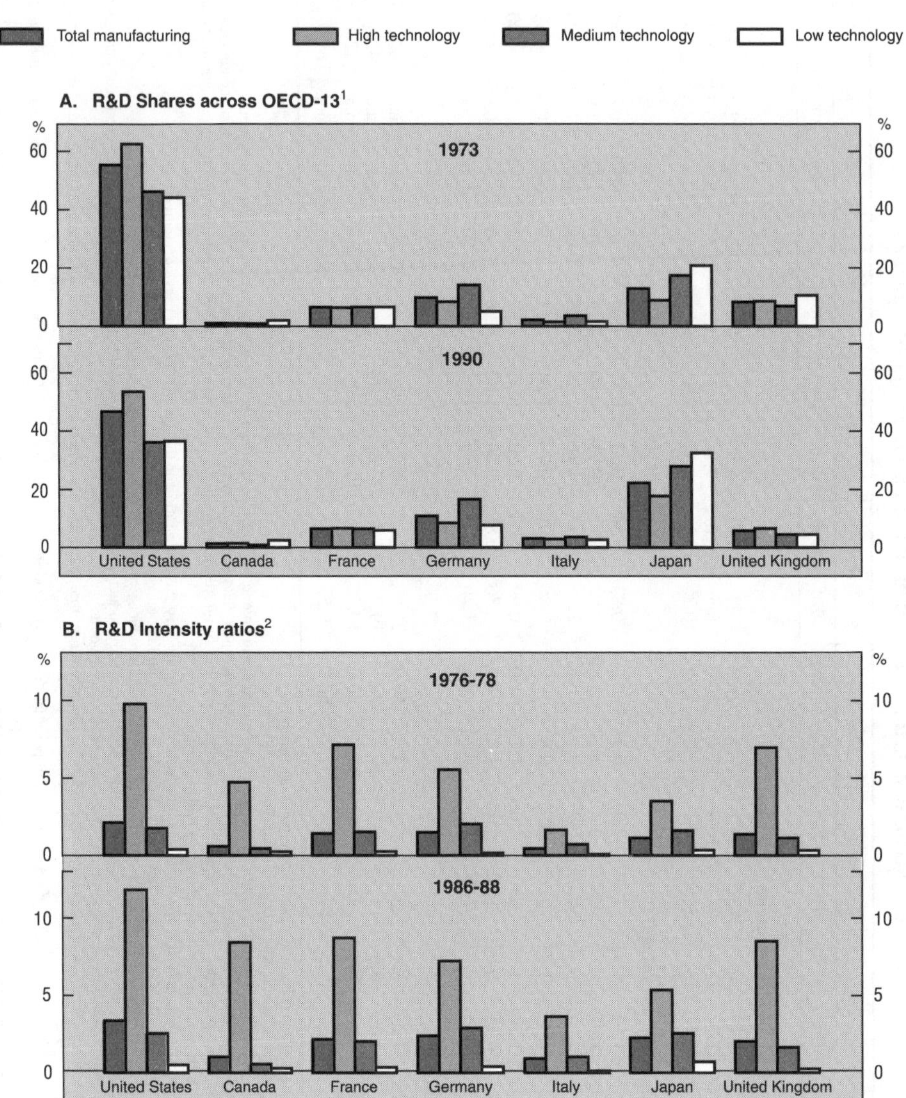

1. R&D performed by business as a proportion of business enterprise R&D for this industry of 13 OECD countries aggregated using purchasing power exchange rates for GDP.
2. Ratio of R&D performed by business to gross output.

Source: OECD (1993*b*).

Table 17. **Patenting shares by country of residence, 1989**

Granting country	Total patents	Patents to non-residents as percentage of total	Residence of inventor (share of non-resident patents in per cent)							
			United States	Japan	West Germany	France	United Kingdom	Italy	Sweden	Other non-residents
United States	**95 262**	**47.5**	**0.0**	**44.4**	**18.3**	**6.8**	**6.8**	**1.8**	**2.9**	**19.0**
Japan	63 301	13.5	44.4	0.0	21.2	7.6	5.0	2.2	2.3	17.3
West Germany	42 233	60.0	28.2	27.2	0.0	10.0	6.5	3.5	2.8	20.9
France	32 879	74.8	24.9	17.5	27.8	0.0	6.0	4.4	2.2	17.2
United Kingdom	30 897	86.3	25.7	20.4	23.2	9.1	0.0	3.2	2.1	16.3
Italy	15 832	98.7	22.8	9.1	29.4	12.9	6.7	0.0	2.4	16.7
Canada	16 299	93.4	52.9	13.7	8.6	6.1	5.7	1.8	1.7	9.6
Mexico	2 268	91.0	63.1	4.5	7.8	6.0	2.8	3.5	1.4	11.0
Brazil	3 510	86.5	41.2	5.2	16.2	9.1	10.0	4.3	2.2	11.7
South Korea	3 972	70.3	30.7	50.6	5.1	3.0	3.0	0.9	0.8	6.0
Soviet Union	84 577	1.5	13.6	8.3	19.5	7.0	4.1	4.8	1.9	40.8
India	1 986	78.0	35.4	6.8	14.0	7.2	7.3	2.8	1.7	24.6
Total	393 016	43.8	23.1	24.5	17.6	7.3	5.3	2.6	2.4	17.2

Sources: National Science Board (1991) and OECD.

and technologies are equally important. Some may have "positive feedback loops" of interaction between the knowledge base and skilled labour and suppliers and may be vital for the future competitiveness of the nation (Krugman, 1992). According to the U.S. Department of Commerce, the United States was the world leader in five of twelve such emerging technologies in 1990 and behind both Japan and the European Community (EC) in only one (digital imaging). But a trend analysis painted a more ominous picture: the United States was holding its position against Japan in only two and gaining in none, while against the EC it was holding in six and gaining in three.

Some have argued that this relative decline is the result of the heretofore rather hands-off U.S. approach to technology policy which, other than for defence, has traditionally been rather market-driven, even if direct government R&D spending is sizeable by international standards. Such spending, the bulk of which funds research performed in the private sector, amounts to nearly $70 billion per year, with heavy albeit declining concentration on military and basic (often health-related) research. The new Administration has recognised that the United States still has a high share of defence-related R&D (a peak of nearly two-thirds of U.S. federal government R&D outlays in 1988 and almost 29 per cent of total R&D, compared with as little as 1 per cent of the total in Japan) which, it is acknowledged, now yields little in the way of civilian spin-offs. Henceforth, federally-funded mission-oriented R&D will be used to try to improve the productivity of private R&D. Accordingly, the share of purely military R&D is being cut back, and resources are being directed to civilian and "dual-use" technologies by reforming existing agencies (national laboratories and the former Defense Advanced Research Projects Agency). Furthermore, these agencies are being directed to boost their R&D co-operation with industry through so-called CRADAs (co-operative agreements). These actually began in 1986 for agencies and 1989 for laboratories and had numbered over 1 500 already by 1992 with a value of $323 million.

The new Administration has also indicated a willingness to move toward greater activism by proposing a major budgetary increase ($535 million in FY 1994, nearly double this year's allocation) for the National Institute of Standards and Technology to proceed with its Advanced Technology Program to develop high-risk generic technologies. Such support is most easily justified, assuming partial funding is provided by the private sector, for pre-commercial/

pre-competitive generic R&D where social returns most likely exceed their private equivalents. Opposition is voiced because governments often do not make good decisions about what to support, they tend to be inflexible and unadaptive in the conduct of their R&D programmes, and there is always the risk of meddling and political influence (Cohen and Noll, 1992).[93] Most research into the productivity impact of federal contract R&D, using a production-function approach, has found little effect, except in the area of agricultural research. However, measurement problems abound, and it is likely that public support stimulates private research efforts which themselves generate significant returns. Cost-benefit analysis also shows positive net yields for medical research as well as academic research in the fields of science and engineering. Nevertheless, there has been a worrisome increase in Congressional intervention in the allocation of academic research funding which, along with the megaproject vogue, could undermine the current peer-review system.

A second key component of U.S. policy is the support provided by the temporary Research and Experimentation tax credit established in 1981.[94] Initially a tax credit of 25 per cent was offered on all incremental[95] R&D undertaken by the end of 1985, but it was extended, the rate was modified and conditions were changed seven times in subsequent years. Its temporary nature and the frequency of changes have been criticised for causing a bias away from long-term projects and its lack of refundability for diminishing its effectiveness. Overall, the credit has been equivalent to over $1½ billion per year in government expenditure. Yet initial research showed the incentive had little impact on the amount of R&D undertaken (1 or 2 per cent) – as in Canada and Sweden where tax incentives have also been tried – rather than merely a redefinition of what constitutes R&D. This research claimed that the credit yielded only an extra $0.35 of R&D for each dollar of tax expenditure (Mansfield, 1986). But more recent analysis has shown a much more substantial impact, in part because the short-run tax/price elasticity of R&D spending appears to be at least unity, rather than the 0.3 or so previously believed and because the average effective credit rate rose sharply in 1990-91 (Hall, 1992; Hines, 1991). The Administration proposed to make the credit permanent which would have served to enhance its effectiveness, but Congress extended it only through June 1995. Others have suggested that it should be made available to commercialisation expenditures as well.[96] However, while a credit can be justified based on the spillovers engendered by R&D, it is a rather crude device, since such spillovers inevitably differ substantially among different firms, industries and types of R&D outputs.

Thirdly, the Administration intends to promote ''Regional Technology Alliances'' and ''Agile Manufacturing Programs'' in order to assist in the exploitation of network externalities, and technology outreach or extension centres to stimulate technology transfer and ensure diffusion of innovations. It will also increase the emphasis on joint ventures. Support for R&D consortia is justified in order to help overcome the incentive problems associated with non-appropriability of R&D output, to avoid duplication and exploit scale economies more fully and to speed diffusion throughout the industry, especially in cases where firms suffer from the so-called ''not-invented-here'' syndrome (neglect of innovations achieved elsewhere). But besides the obvious antitrust risks,[97] such institutions inherently lack the advantages of multiple independent research approaches which are often thought to enhance technological progress. There is also a temptation for the political process to tend to support large, highly visible consortia at the expense of smaller, possibly more promising projects.[98] The antitrust laws were also amended in June 1993 to allow joint production ventures in order to pool risks. The justification for this is rather less clear.

The new Administration has advocated a large number of other technology-policy initiatives (see Clinton and Gore, 1993), including the following. First, it supported and Congress approved the idea of creating ''empowerment'' zones and/or enterprise communities in areas of high structural unemployment in order to attract new investment and enhance employment opportunities. However, one recent look at the results of existing programmes in the state of Indiana concluded that the economic well-being of enterprise zone residents was ''not appreciably improved'' (Papke, 1993). Nevertheless, the Administration proposals differ significantly from previous enterprise zone programmes.[99] Second, the government will assume a co-ordinating role in establishing a national information infrastructure (''information superhighways'') where economies of scope are indeed likely to exist. It will also provide funding for pilot projects in the education and health-care spheres as well as $784 million over the next four years for related ''cross-cutting high performance computing''. Third, the automobile industry will benefit from targeted assistance with a view to developing technologies to enhance environmental friendliness of vehicle use. Fourth, support will be given to the development of new equipment and software to facilitate education in both formal and informal settings.

The impact of government regulation

There is little doubt that the amount of government regulation exploded in the 1960s and 1970s with little analysis of the impact of such constraints on economic welfare. Much progress has been made since the days when regulators were trying to force regulated industries to raise their prices. Airlines, trucking, rail, oil and natural gas were deregulated; and there was a major effort to slow the imposition of new regulation during the 1980s. In 1981, the incoming Administration ordered that no regulatory action be taken without the completion of an analysis of the costs entailed. By 1990, that required analysis became full-blown cost-benefit analysis. In 1992, the Bush Administration instituted a moratorium on new regulation, during which time substantial regulatory savings were implemented.

Recent research has focused on improving the crude tools used for estimating the costs of regulation, which seem to be significant in both static and dynamic terms. The role of regulatory uncertainty in investment and new product development can be important. Excluding redistributional aspects (which might involve as much as another $130 billion per year and which undoubtedly entail efficiency costs through rent-seeking behaviour), the gross costs of all federal regulation have been estimated to have been as much as $412 billion in 1991 (7¼ per cent of GDP) (Hopkins, 1992) and are set to rise substantially by the year 2000[100] (Diagram 25). Therefore, the "regulatory budget" is nearly half as large as its traditional counterpart, that is taxpayers pay half again as much in regulatory costs as their narrowly defined tax burden. Environmental regulations alone are officially estimated to have imposed direct costs (excluding those resulting from changes in the cost of capital) of 2.1 per cent of GNP in 1990 (prior to the imposition of the 1990 Clean Air Act changes),[101] up from 0.9 per cent in 1972 (U.S. Environmental Protection Agency, 1990), and such costs are expected to continue to rise in the 1990s, reaching 2.8 per cent by the end of the decade (OECD, 1991*b*). Indications are that they have had a measurable impact on long-term growth over the period – possibly as much as 0.2 percentage point per year.[102] Such costs are much higher than those borne by other OECD

Some examples of the costs of regulation

The text refers to a figure of 7 1/4 per cent of GDP as the compliance cost of all federal regulation in 1991. Such a significant burden may surprise some readers. Accordingly, it might be useful to list the 15 costliest regulations which the Bush Administration expected to be implemented in 1992 (taken from Hopkins, 1992). They represent the overwhelming majority of the cost of the 57 new regulations issued in final form during that year. Virtually all such regulations are intended to safeguard the environment or protect occupational health and safety.

	Annual costs in $ million
Environmental Protection Agency	
Acid rain emissions/electric utilities	3 000
On-board diagnostics/motor vehicles	1 600
Reformulated gasoline/motor vehicles	1 000
Clean Air Act Title V permits	650
Used oil management/motor vehicles	610
Oxygenated fuels/motor vehicles	430
Municipal waste combustors emissions standards	390
Air emissions from hazardous waste tanks	360
Air emissions from municipal solid waste landfills	320
Nitrogen oxide limits/electric utilities	200-400
Carbon monoxide winter warm-up auto emissions	280
Occupational Safety and Health Administration	
Hazardous materials handling standards	711
Scaffolding and stairway standards	462
Food and Drug Administration	
Clinical laboratory practices	1 600
Department of Transportation	
Double-hull standards for ocean oil tankers	349
Total cost	12 062

While many regulations appear to impose heavy costs, their benefits may likewise be substantial. One measure of the cost effectiveness of health and safety regulation is the cost per premature death averted. The most recent *Regulatory Program of the United States Government* provides a list of estimates of such costs for selected regulations issued since 1967. They range from modest sums of some $100 000 (in 1990 prices) for aircraft fire protection standards and automobile seat-belt requirements to many billions for the ban on hazardous waste land disposal, municipal solid waste landfill standards, formaldehyde occupational exposure limits and the atrazine/alachlor drinking water standard.

Diagram 25. **THE GROSS PRIVATE COSTS OF FEDERAL REGULATION**
Billions of 1991 dollars

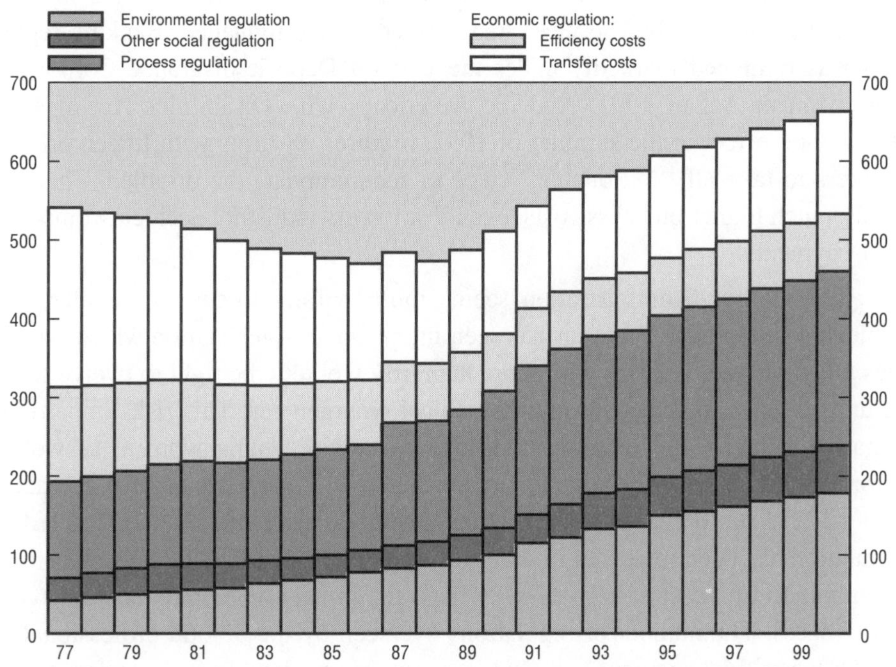

Note: Data for 1992 to 2000 are the author's projections.
Source: Hopkins (1992).

countries (OECD, 1991*b*, Table 23), with obvious implications for competitiveness.[103] In addition, even these costs are generally only private compliance costs, that is the engineering costs of installed capital and related operating and maintenance expenses, whereas the social costs of regulation (as measured by the willingness to pay in order to avoid its imposition) may very well be much higher.[104] However, again there are obvious benefits that cannot be ignored, and on a net-cost basis regulation may not be quite so burdensome.[105]

Recently there has been a tendency to question the benefits and recognise the limits of deregulation. And fiscal pressures have given legislators tremendous incentives to use social regulation as an alternative to direct spending to achieve their political objectives. The 1990 Clean Air Act is an example of increased private compliance costs. While cable television was not re-regulated in 1992, competition and ''public service'' requirements were tightened. Banking regulation was tightened markedly under the Federal Deposit Insurance Corporation Improvement Act of 1991. And the Americans with Disabilities Act of 1990, which took effect in the summer of 1992, requires all firms with fifteen or more workers to take all ''reasonable'' steps to accommodate the disabled. This may imply much higher business costs, even if it lowers industrial accident compensation payments.

The Clinton Administration seems more willing to turn to regulation to achieve social goals. This year has seen the passage of legislation which guarantees all employees of firms with more than fifty workers the right to twelve weeks of unpaid leave to deal with family medical emergencies. This risks imparting a negative influence on employer willingness to hire young women, as well as efforts to cut out other benefits to pay for the costs of such leave. Also, Executive Order 12291 of 20 February 1981 which governs presidential oversight of federal regulation has been reviewed in order to supplement cost-benefit analysis with an examination of ''cost effectiveness''[106] and the impact on employment and competitiveness. The number of regulations overseen by the 30-odd professionals in the Office of Management and Budget who are responsible for carrying out the Order may decline from the current level of about 2 000 per year, and better inter-agency co-ordination may be sought.

Corporate governance, short-termism and employee compensation

It has become fashionable of late to point to the system of corporate governance in general and the short-termism it allegedly engenders in particular as key factors holding back U.S. competitiveness. Despite the strengths of the U.S. system of capital allocation – specifically, its flexibility, responsiveness, openness and average profitability – many believe it to be in need of fundamental reform:

> The American system creates a divergence of interests among shareholders, corporations, and their managers that impedes the flow of capital to those corporate investments that offer the greatest pay-offs. Just as significant, it

fails to align the interests of individual investors and corporations with those of the economy and the nation as a whole (Porter, 1992).

While the corporate governance structure includes the relationships between all the stakeholders in the firm (shareholders, managers, employees, creditors, suppliers and customers), this section will focus on those involving the first two, before finishing with some thoughts relating to employee compensation.

Questions of corporate governance are at the centre of allegations of the failings of the system. Adherents to this view make the following arguments. Echoing ideas first voiced sixty years ago by Berle and Means (1932), modern theory has developed a literature on the "principal-agent problem" inherent in business organisations. Managers (the agents) are little constrained in their behaviour to act in the best interests of the owners of the firm (the principals). In the United States there is an unusually and increasingly antagonistic relationship between the users (managers) and the providers of capital (shareholders and lenders, especially institutional investors) – as there was in earlier decades between labour and management.[107] In the absence of a relationship involving sufficient dialogue, oversight and control, shareholders lack an effective voice in the running of the firm and a means to ensure management accountability, and, if dissatisfied, merely liquidate their positions. According to these critics, they have become short-term traders relying on quarterly results, rather than true long-term owners, and, with the demise of relationship banking,[108] capital has become nothing more than a financial commodity.[109] This outcome has been encouraged by management who have succeeded in recent years in dominating the board of directors[110] and in weakening disciplines stemming from the market for corporate control through the widespread passage of state anti-takeover statutes, given the absence of federal legislation in this domain (Roe, 1991). The result is: 1) greater investor uncertainty as to how efficiently capital is being used and, therefore, a higher required rate of return[111] and lower capital formation, especially for investment projects without visible returns for long periods of time; and 2) higher costs of co-ordination, with resulting limits on specialisation and, therefore, on productivity (see Becker and Murphy, 1992).

Numerous studies have shown the cost of capital to have indeed been higher in the United States over the past twenty years or so than elsewhere in the OECD (Fukao, 1993), although substantial convergence has occurred in recent years (McCauley and Zimmer, 1992) (Diagram 26). Most of the attention has focused on bilateral comparisons with Japan (Poterba, 1991), where, for example, Japanese subsidiaries of U.S. firms obtain higher stockmarket valuations than their parents (Fikre, 1991). In this case the consensus view has been challenged by Kester and Luehrman (1991) who argue that riskless real interest rates have been the same in both countries, as has the price of risk, although they admit there may be systematic differences in the final component of capital costs: the quantity of risk.

According to some observers, with capital providers having limited long-term interests, managers too have taken an increasingly short-term focus in their business decisions, as evidenced by low rates of tangible investment. Supporters of the present corporate-governance system point to the system of managerial compensation as the means to bridge the gap between investors and management. But executive compensation is often largely insensitive to performance or, if not, excessively sensitive to profitability at the time of the executive's retirement: a 1991 study of the 1 000 largest U.S. firms showed that only 4 per cent of the variance in executive compensation was traceable to differences in shareholder returns (Baily *et al.,* 1993).[112] Also, American chief executive officers (CEOs) are paid much more generously than their foreign counterparts (8 to 10 times more than Japanese CEOs, according to Jacobs (1991)) and own an average of only 1/4 of 1 per cent of their firm's equity (less than two years' pay), which may reduce their incentive to act in the interest of their shareholders.[113] Furthermore, even granting stock options may not be successful, as it may induce excessive retention of earnings because option holders are not entitled to receive dividends. The 1994 Budget withdraws corporate tax deductibility for all executive salaries in excess of $1 million per year per person unless tied to performance.

Whether there is any need for a wide-ranging policy response to these problems is by no means clear. For example, in recent years there have been signs that, at least in part, the problems may be solved endogenously through increasing shareholder activism, especially on the part of institutional investors.[114] Despite the opposing entrenched interests of those benefiting from high rates of turnover (brokers, analysts and, to a lesser extent, money managers), newly emboldened boards of directors have decided to take firm action by forcing the departure of chief executive officers at even the largest U.S. corporations and by seeking to give more weight to non-executive directors. These are just two signs of an apparently broader trend to what has been termed ''relation-

Diagram 26. **THE U.S. COST OF CAPITAL DISADVANTAGE**

Gap between U.S. and competitor country in percentage points

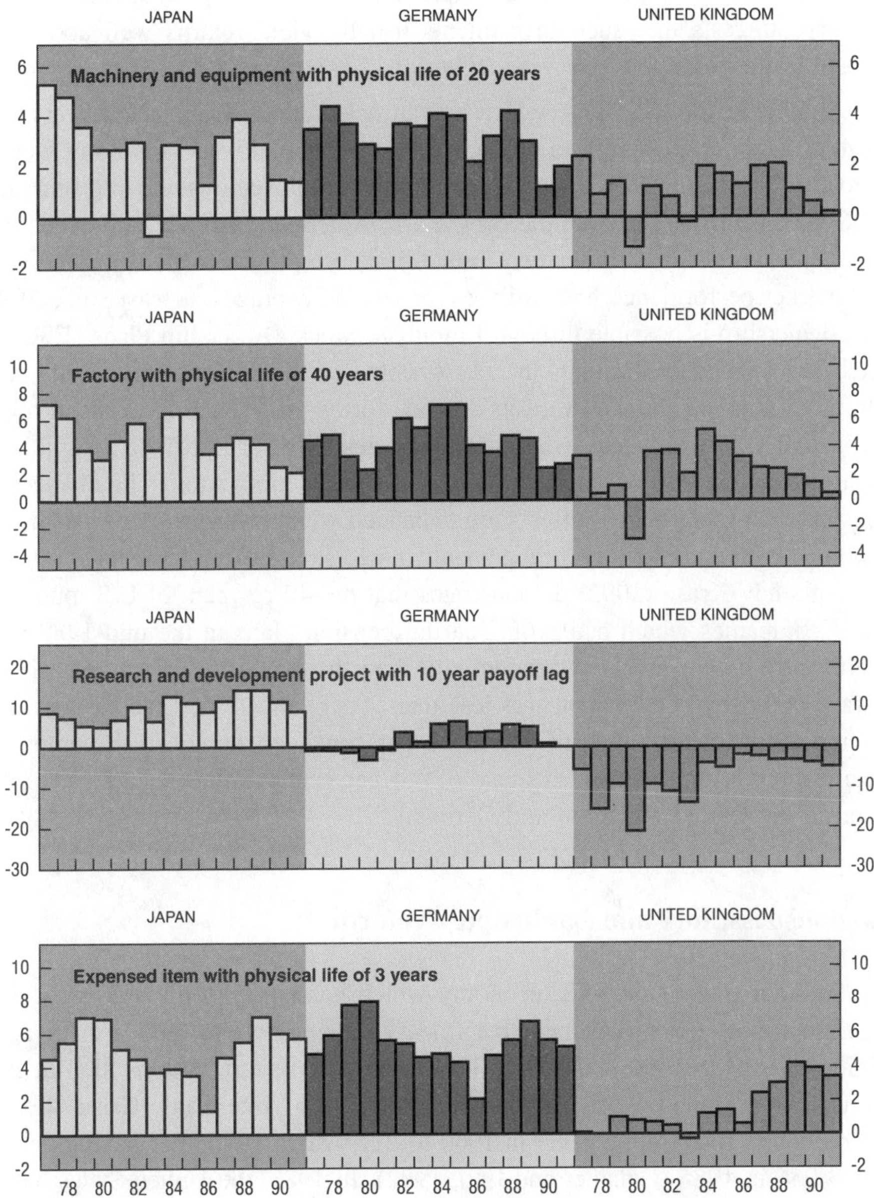

Source: McCauley and Zimmer (1992).

ship investing'' in which assertive shareholders contribute to the formulation of corporate policy with or without an explicit agreement with management. Some evidence suggests that such investments usually yield returns well above the average in the following few years (Gordon, 1993).

Another workplace issue which has attracted attention in recent years as a potential factor contributing to productivity and competitiveness is tying worker compensation to company performance through employee ownership/profit-sharing. Some 355 firms listed on the New York, American or NASDAQ exchanges currently have at least 10 per cent broad-based employee ownership, and their stockmarket performance has easily exceeded the averages at least since 1991. Such ownership is possible through Employee Stock Ownership Plans (ESOPs), which are subsidised through the tax system, or through the spread of stock options to non-executives. In all its various forms profit-sharing exists at about one in five U.S. firms, and, when optimally designed, can provide a significant boost to productivity by inspiring enhanced worker motivation. The chances of realising such motivational effects are enhanced when reformed pay systems are combined with participatory arrangements in decision making (Blinder, 1990). In a recent study Kruse (1992) demonstrates that the 40 per cent of U.S. publicly-traded companies which had profit-sharing pension plans in the mid-1980s had significantly higher levels of productivity than those which did not, even if the average company contribution was less than 2 per cent of total labour cost. The difference fell in the range of 2½ to 11 per cent, depending on the empirical specification, with a median estimate of 4.4 per cent. Similar results have been found in the United Kingdom and Germany.

Litigiousness, tort and bankruptcy reform

Another trait of the U.S. economy which has come in for a good deal of criticism for its potentially negative impact on productivity and growth is its litigiousness.[115] In 1990, there were 18.4 million civil (tort) actions filed in state courts in the United States, or one for every 13.6 Americans. Cases filed in federal courts rose from 51 063 in 1960 to 217 421 in 1990 after having peaked at 273 056 in 1985 (Galanter and Epp, 1992). In 1983, the United States had as many as one-third of the world's lawyers, a much higher concentration than anywhere else in the world.[116] (To some degree, however, these cross-country comparisons may be misleading due to greater use of informal dispute resolution mechanisms outside the United States.) Since 1970, the share of the population trained as lawyers has more than doubled. In 1980, direct and indirect costs of tort actions amounted to some 1.5 per cent of GDP, but by 1987 they had surged to an estimated 2.7 per cent of GDP (Baily *et al.,* 1993). Elsewhere in the OECD, such costs are believed to be in the range of 0.5 to 0.7 per cent of GDP.

It must be noted that there are undoubtedly corresponding benefits in the form of enhanced consumer and employee safety, and that there had been some signs of improvement in recent years (for example, declining product liability claims and fewer punitive damage awards). But the lack of predictability of future levels of liability and the high level of awards are apparently having an indirect depressing effect on output and innovative activity (Huber and Litan, 1991; Viscusi and Moore, 1993), and 1992 saw a significant increase in the scale of punitive awards (eight over $100 million, up from 2 in 1991). The Supreme Court has just refused to hear an appeal of a West Virginia case in which punitive damages of over 500 times compensatory damages were awarded, implicitly demanding the legislators decide the issue. Some states have reformed some of the relevant legislation, but no overarching federal legislation has been passed with a view to calming these tendencies in the areas of private antitrust, product liability, medical malpractice, or mergers and acquisitions. Perhaps, financial incentives could be rebalanced by requiring losing parties to pay the costs of winning parties. Or alternative means of dispute resolution could be sought, as the expenditure of scarce entrepreneurial talent on such unproductive or even destructive pursuits (Baumol, 1990) cannot but impede the progress of the economy.

Another costly aspect of the liability system is the fall-out from wrongful-dismissal suits against employers. While 95 per cent of all cases are resolved without going to trial and the direct legal costs of such suits is estimated to be rather small (about 0.1 per cent of the nation's total wage bill according to Dertouzos *et al.,* 1988), states' judicial decisions in the 1980s and several legislative changes such as the 1988 Worker Adjustment and Retraining Notification Act have expanded the reach of the courts. Furthermore, there is some empirical evidence from cross-state data that where states have adopted tough new legal doctrines, employers, either due to misinformation or extreme risk aversion, have reduced their long-run levels of employment by up to 5 per cent, equivalent to a wage rise of about 10 per cent or 100 times the direct legal costs (Dertouzos and Karoly, 1992).[117] Again, there are clear benefits to such liability in the form of reduced uncertainty about the enforcement of the implicit contract (leading to a greater willingness to invest in firm-specific human capital on both sides) and possibly lower wages in return for enhanced job security. But they would be unlikely to measure up to the costs, if they have not been over-estimated here.

The U.S. bankruptcy system is also the object of increasing criticism. Most critics allege that it has favoured debtors at the expense of creditors since the last time it was reformed in 1978. When combined with the associated legal costs and years of delay faced by creditors going through the courts due to the nearly 1 million individuals and companies seeking bankruptcy protection each year, many seek to reach out-of-court settlements. The central problem is probably with Chapter 11 of the code, which allows firms to reorganise free from creditor pressure (Jensen, 1991). While this is a laudable objective, it allows the existing management to remain in place, despite the business problems it has created. Critics argue that in some sectors, firms operating under bankruptcy protection adopt unusually aggressive business strategies, putting their rivals under extreme stress.

IV. Trade policy and other structural reforms

Besides budget deficit reduction, health-care reform and all the proposed policy changes designed to boost productivity growth and enhance competitiveness, the new Administration has taken a new tack on trade policy and on a number of other structural policies. This chapter is an attempt to fulfil the Committee's surveillance responsibilities in this regard.

New directions in trade policy

The new Administration has voiced continued strong support for a successful conclusion to the Uruguay Round which has been dragging on now for some seven years. After the expiry of the previous fast-track authority at end-May 1993, the Administration requested its renewal, and Congress passed the required legislation at end-June. Negotiations must be completed by 15 December, and the agreement must be signed (in Geneva) by 16 April 1994. Earlier this year, it seemed that the bottleneck had shifted from U.S.-European Community differences over farm subsidies (resolved in late 1992 in the so-called Blair House accord) to the nature of the deal on market access. Recently, however, questions have been raised in Europe as to the acceptability of the Blair House accord. Other remaining important differences include the outcomes in the textiles, wood, paper, non-ferrous metals and cultural goods sectors.

The Administration has also stated its support for the North American Free Trade Area (NAFTA) Agreement, signed in December 1992 by President Bush and the leaders of Mexico and Canada,[118] supplemented by side agreements in the areas of labour, the environment and import surges. These were seen to be necessary for two main reasons. First, enforcement of health and safety standards as well as of environmental laws in Mexico has allegedly been lax (U.S. Congress, Office of Technology Assessment, 1992*b*), thereby allowing lower regulatory costs and the risk of job displacement for U.S. workers. Second, there is a fear that U.S. manufacturers may be attracted by Mexican wage levels, thereby eliminating U.S. jobs. However, a large part of the relative factor price shock which results from freer trade with Mexico may already have occurred. U.S. barriers to Mexican imports are already low, and there is anecdotal evidence that several firms might repatriate some operations (in the auto industry, for example), primarily because of the high costs of Mexico's remote location (relative to the heartland of U.S. markets) (Leamer and Medberry, 1993). Negotiation of the supplemental agreements was completed in August 1993. The labour and environmental agreements establish Commissions, set forth principles and objectives concerning the development, implementation and enforcement of environmental and labour laws and provide for public participation. The agreements also provide dispute settlement procedures, but, critics argue, without real guarantees. The agreement on import surges establishes a consultative mechanism to monitor and review NAFTA's safeguard provisions. The Administration is expected to submit NAFTA for Congressional approval in the fall of 1993 so that it could come into effect on 1 January 1994.

Both of these trade initiatives are important to the well-being of the U.S. economy, as well as that of its trading partners. Recent evidence has suggested that a cut of one-third in the world's tariff and non-tariff barriers with a ten-year phase-in – an approximation of the Uruguay Round goal – could raise GDP in both the United States and the other major OECD countries by over 3 per cent and employment by nearly 1 per cent (DRI/McGraw-Hill, 1993).[119] Also, based on expectations of closer economic integration, the Mexican economy has already undergone substantial restructuring, and, since 1987, Mexico has moved past the United Kingdom into the number three position as a destination for U.S. exports and past the United Kingdom, Korea, Taiwan and Germany into third place among exporters to the United States. Despite fears to the contrary, the International Trade Commission (ITC) predicted that implementation of the NAFTA would be a mild boon to the United States, with between 35 and 94 thousand extra jobs created.[120] Last year, the ITC hosted a conference of professional modellers who had simulated the effects of such an agreement, and the results were unanimously favourable for overall U.S. output, employment, wages and welfare (Table 18).

Table 18. **Predicted aggregate results for the United States from a NAFTA**[1]

Percentage changes

	Welfare	Real GDP	Employment	Wage Rate	Return to Capital	Trade Balance
Static models						
Bachrach and Mizrahi[2]	n.a.	+0.04	n.c.	+0.03	+0.07	+0.07
Brown *et al.*[3]	+0.3	n.a.	n.c.	+0.2	+0.2	n.c.
Hinojosa and Robinson[4]	n.a.	+0.1	0.0	RW –0.4 UU +0.7 UW +0.1 WC +0.3	+1.2	n.c.
Robinson *et al.*[5]	n.a.	+0.23	n.a.	RW –1.3 UU –1.7 US +0.1 P +0.1	+0.1	n.c.
Roland-Holst *et al.*						
Constant returns to scale	+1.67	+1.34	+1.88	n.c.	+2.43	n.c.
Increasing returns to scale[6]	+2.55	+2.07	+2.47	n.c.	+3.40	n.c.
Dynamic models						
Almon	n.a.	+0.17	+0.05	+0.28	+1.64	+18.4
McCleery[7]	n.a.	+0.51	n.c.	n.a.	n.a.	n.a.

n.a. Not available.
n.c. Unchanged by assumption.
1. Assuming liberalisation of non-tariff barriers as well.
2. With additional capital in Mexico; free trade area.
3. Including direct foreign investment.
4. Including capital flows but excluding migration. Wage changes are: rural workers (RW), urban unskilled (UU), union workers (UW) and white collar (WC).
5. Wage changes are as in 4 and urban skilled (US) and professional (P).
6. Assuming contestable markets.
7. With increased investor confidence and dynamic gains.
Source: U.S. International Trade Commission (1992).

While consistent with the GATT, the United States continues to make frequent use of anti-dumping and countervailing duties, to the dismay of its trading partners.[121] In January 1993 the Commerce Department provisionally determined that steel of a value of $3.2 billion from 19 foreign countries had been dumped in the U.S. market and that anti-dumping duties were called for. Much of the steel was also found to be subsidised and was, therefore, subject to countervailing duties as well. In July, these decisions were confirmed, and indeed the estimated dumping margins were increased in many cases, ranging from less than 5 to over 109 per cent. In August 1993, the ITC made its final decision as to whether the duties would be made permanent and found that the domestic industry had been harmed[122] by the foreign trade practices in only 32 of the 72 cases.[123] Other important dumping decisions include the initial estimates of dumping margins of as much as 87 per cent on semiconductors from Korea in October 1992 (later reduced to a maximum of 7 per cent) and final imposition of duties of 112 per cent on steel wire rope from Mexico in February 1993.

U.S. procedures for determining dumping and subsidisation are quasi-judicial, and the Administration maintains that outcomes are not indicative of Administration trade policy.[124] However, several of the procedures are controversial. The most contentious is probably the determination of dumping margins by comparing foreign producers' export prices with their costs rather than with their domestic prices, especially since costs are arbitrarily required to include mark-ups over estimates of average cost of 10 per cent for overhead and 8 per cent for profits. In addition, the average cost estimations are sometimes based on "best information available" which consists at times of competitor allegations.

The Administration has been clear in its determination to open foreign markets, particularly so with Japan. Perceiving the 1990 semiconductor arrangement to have been a success, and, following an explicitly results-oriented approach, it has negotiated the *Japan-United States Framework for a New Economic Partnership* with a combination of macroeconomic and microeconomic goals. The *Framework* is an agreement designed in part to replace the Structural Impediments Initiative. On the macroeconomic side, Japan refused a specific target for its current-account surplus. But it agreed to promote strong and sustainable domestic-demand-led growth and to increase the market access of competitive foreign goods and services, thereby achieving "a highly significant decrease" in its current-account surplus over an undefined medium term. The two sides seem to have different interpretations of what constitutes such a decrease and of what exactly is the horizon over which it is to be achieved. For its part, the United States committed itself to a substantial reduction in its fiscal deficit, greater domestic saving and strengthened international competitiveness.

In addition, sectoral and structural consultations are to be undertaken in five areas:

– In the area of *Government Procurement,* Japan is to aim at significant expansion of government purchases of competitive foreign items. Computers, supercomputers, satellites, medical technology and telecommunications are explicitly mentioned. The United States is to encourage U.S. firms to take advantage of new opportunities in Japan and to adhere to the GATT Agreement on Government Procurement.

- With regard to *Regulatory Reform and Competitiveness,* the two countries are to address the issue of reforming relevant laws, regulations and government guidance where they restrict market access. Financial services, insurance, competition policy, transparent government procedures and distribution are cited. The United States is to promote exports to Japan through measures to facilitate business and enhance competitiveness.
- Under the heading *Other Major Sectors,* efforts will be made to achieve a significant expansion of Japanese automobile producers' purchases of foreign parts and to encourage imports of foreign cars and parts to Japan. The United States is to promote such exports.
- A basket of topics entitled *Economic Harmonisation* is to deal with issues affecting foreign direct investment, intellectual property rights, access to technology and long-term vertical inter-firm relationships in both countries.
- A discussion group will monitor the *Implementation of Existing Arrangements and Measures.*

All liberalisations being sought are on a most-favoured-nation basis: no explicit preference for U.S. producers is being solicited, in contrast to the announcement in January 1992 that Japanese car producers would make global purchases of U.S. parts at an annual rate of $19 billion in 1994.

It is the U.S. demand for "objective criteria, either qualitative, quantitative or both" that has been the most controversial element of the *Framework.* Such criteria are to be used in assessing the progress achieved in implementing the measures and policies in each sectoral and structural area. But again interpretations of the nature of such criteria seem to differ between the two parties. Looking forward, if these criteria were to become precisely fixed numerical targets, this would seem to entail the risk of cartelisation of Japanese industry in order to achieve particular targets. Despite the inclusion of a statement that consultations are limited to "matters within the scope and responsibility of government", it is conceivable that trade could become bureaucratised, with sectoral trade outcomes determined more by political influence of interest groups than by market-based competitive advantage.

Even if these risks are avoided, it is unlikely that reductions in Japanese trade barriers and improvements in the particular sectors mentioned would be matched by corresponding changes in the overall external balance of Japan or the United States. For the U.S. deficit is a macroeconomic phenomenon, reflecting its low rate of saving and the resulting need for foreign capital inflows to finance domestic investment.

As with the sectoral negotiations, if a rigid quantitative target for the overall Japanese current-account surplus were to be set, it would require knowledge of the optimal value for this endogenous variable, not only at present, but in the future when the verification will occur. This is an ambitious task, given the many unobservable shocks to which the determining factors are continuously subject. Even if it were widely agreed that the value of the Japanese external surplus is excessive today,[125] it cannot be known whether this value might become optimal in a few years if, for example, U.S. (and others') investment rates pick up, without a corresponding increase in global savings.

Other structural policy developments

The new Administration has been quite ambitious in its *labour-market reform* goals, as seen in Chapter III. However, despite much talk in the early days of the new Administration, it seems unlikely that there will be any increase in the national minimum wage in the immediate future. It is recognised that mandated cost increases might become excessive and that tax-based policies are a better way to deal with the problems of the working poor.[126] The House of Representatives has again passed legislation which would prevent firms from hiring permanent replacements for union members who strike. While the Administration supports the bill, it is unclear whether the Senate will pass it. However, legislation was passed in February 1993 granting workers of all firms with 50 or more employees as well as all government employees up to 12 weeks a year of unpaid leave to deal with family medical emergencies.

In the domain of *competition policy* the Supreme Court again refused to place limits on punitive damages awarded in civil lawsuits in 1993. In

April 1992, the Justice Department and the Federal Trade Commission jointly issued new guidelines to be used in merger and acquisition investigations. They should enhance the level of economic analysis in such investigations.

What is known as the National Performance Review was published in September. Its goal is, in the words of Osborne and Gaebler (1992), to ''reinvent government'' in order to enhance *public-sector efficiency.* The thrust of the idea seems to be quite similar to approaches followed by New Zealand in recent years. Highlights include:

- changing hiring and firing as well as procurement procedures to provide government managers greater authority and discretion;
- reducing federal employment by an additional 152 000 beyond the 100 000 to be cut as part of the deficit-reduction package and bringing the ratio of managers to employees from one in seven to one in fifteen;
- eliminating certain government offices and the monopoly position of others and privatising some heretofore public functions such as air-traffic control; and
- adopting a two-year federal budget cycle.

The Administration claims that enacting the Review's recommendations will save $108 billion over the next five years. However, while nearly half of the Review's 800 recommendations can be implemented by executive order, others will require Congressional approval which may prove difficult. Additional obstacles will no doubt arise from bureaucratic intransigence as well as opposition from public-employee unions. A long line of similar attempts to reform the operations of the federal government – most recently in the form of a Commission headed by Peter Grace during the Reagan Administration – have brought little change. The Administration has also decided not to extend beyond 1997 operating *subsidies* to ships flying the U.S. flag.

The overall level of *agricultural* protection, as measured by the average producer subsidy equivalent (PSE), reversed direction and rose slightly in 1992. The PSE increased from 27 to 28 per cent or $34 billion (up 7.7 per cent), while the consumer subsidy equivalent edged up from 18 to 19 per cent ($19 billion, up 5.2 per cent). Because the increase is entirely attributable to a jump in the quantities produced, it is the opinion of the Secretariat that there has been little change in the degree of market orientation of U.S. agricultural policy (OECD,

1993*a*). But, at $20 000, the amount of PSE per farmer is still well above the OECD average, even though the levels of the PSE and CSE remain well below OECD averages of 44 and 37 per cent, respectively. Nevertheless, the U.S. Export Enhancement Program of subsidies for exports of farm products has been extended to cover more importing countries and a greater volume of exports. Budgetary outlays have been nearly $1 billion per year of late.

On the *environmental* front, in June 1993 the Administration signed the biodiversity treaty negotiated at Rio de Janeiro in 1992 and has affirmed its commitment to reducing its greenhouse-gas emissions to their 1990 levels by the year 2000 through a cost-effective set of policies addressing energy, transportation, agriculture and forestry. On 30 March 1993, trading began in air-pollution allowances for sulphur dioxide, granted by the Environmental Protection Agency; this is part of its plan to cut such emissions in half by the year 2000 as laid out in the 1990 Clean Air Act. In July 1993, the Administration announced a substantial reduction in allowed harvests of old-growth timber in the Pacific North-west, along with a commitment of $1.2 billion per year in community assistance and river and watershed restoration. In August it announced a package of reforms to address the controversial question of wetlands by reaffirming the goal of ''no net loss''.

U.S. *banks* continue to earn record profits due, in part, to the steepness of the yield curve and a restructuring of their portfolios. As a result, the Federal Deposit Insurance Corporation was able to leave unchanged and make permanent the level of premiums temporarily put into effect in January 1993 (23 to 31 cents per $100 of domestic deposits depending on capitalisation). Debate is continuing on whether the derivatives market needs tighter regulation. The ''credit equivalent exposure'' for all U.S. banks reached $140 billion at the end of the first quarter of 1993, but regulators point to significant favourable developments in terms of risk reduction and management. While some Congressional committees have expressed concern, U.S. regulators think this is manageable and do not favour increased regulation. In a separate matter, in November 1992 the Securities and Exchange Commission voted to increase brokerage firms' net capital requirements for the first time since the mid-1970s, in order to protect customers against default.

V. Conclusions

The economic recovery has now entered its third year. While it remains far weaker than its historical predecessors, its pace has nonetheless picked up sufficiently to bring the unemployment rate down by about 1 percentage point since the June 1992 peak – a favourable performance given the difficult global environment. Low short-term interest rates and continuing declines in long-term rates have remained the main factors promoting recovery by generating robust growth in most types of investment. However, the expansion has been held back by a number of factors which were, by and large, foreseen. Defence downsizing is a response to the end of the Cold War and to the need for budgetary consolidation, given the continuing rise in federal indebtedness. Modest increases in state and local purchases are a reaction to their fragile financial condition. Dwindling investment in non-residential construction is a result of persistently high vacancy rates in commercial office buildings in a number of urban areas. Cautious hiring behaviour is caused by the high fixed costs of permanent employees, continued restructuring by major employers and the perceived uncertainty of demand. Hesitant consumer demand is the fall-out of a sustained desire to limit increases in debt and worries about the risk of unemployment. And slow growth in exports follows from the recessions in a number of other OECD countries. Thus, outcomes have conformed to previous expectations of a moderate recovery.

Along with the moderate pace of the expansion and an absence of any major supply shocks prior to the recent flooding, there has been a widely held view that excess capacity remains in both labour and product markets, making for falling inflation. However, while price rises have resumed a downward trend since the spring, wage increases have proved resistant to any further slowing.

It is likely that many of the same factors which have determined the nature of the recovery thus far will continue to play an important role. However, fiscal policy is beginning to tighten more noticeably already this year, and Secretariat projections are that short-term rates will probably rise in the near future, in spite of continuing moderation in the growth rates of the monetary aggregates. Also, policy-related uncertainty resulting from health-care reform may drag on for some time. Nevertheless, with further modest declines in long-term interest rates – already at 25-year lows – and a gradual pick-up in export markets, combined with both household and business balance-sheet restructuring improving and non-residential construction bottoming out, demand may on balance strengthen. Accordingly, the Secretariat believes that real GDP growth will pick up from a 2.6 per cent pace in 1992 to 2¾ per cent this year and 3 per cent in 1994. While this conforms quite closely to the consensus view, the Secretariat's central projection is more optimistic than many others with respect to inflation. With unemployment trending down only slowly to about 6½ per cent by end-1994, still somewhat above the point at which wages normally begin to accelerate, labour costs are unlikely to be much of a source of inflation pressure. And mark-ups are already showing signs of easing in a number of sectors after the rapid increases seen earlier this year. There is therefore good reason to expect inflation to remain below 3 per cent, even if the most recent monthly increases prove unsustainably modest. Finally, with continuing strength in import volumes outpacing rebounding demand for exports, declining net investment income and shrinking gains in export market shares, the current-account deficit is expected to widen slightly, reaching some 2 per cent of GDP in 1994.

Despite slow growth in the monetary aggregates, the basic stance of monetary policy has hardly changed over the last year; reserve conditions and the Federal Funds rate have not been modified since September 1992. But the monetary authorities have already had to consider the appropriate time to begin to tighten in order to make further progress towards their ultimate goal of achieving recorded inflation low enough that it does not affect economic behaviour. The current near-zero level of real short-term interest rates is not unusual for a period early in a business cycle expansion, but it is clearly unsustainable. In recent decades such rates have averaged about 1¼ per cent. An early monetary tightening would be called for if inflation has indeed bottomed out and is now beginning a sustained, even limited, upswing, since inflation of 3 per cent is seen by the Committee to be still excessive. Tightening could also be justified if expectations need a jolt and the Federal Reserve's credibility is endangered. Since few professional forecasters expect the inflation downtrend to resume, and there is a widespread belief that consumer price increases have reached a floor in the 3 per cent range, adverse expectational developments cannot be ruled out, especially after two consecutive quarters of sizeable increases in unit labour costs. Were scepticism about further disinflation to persevere, the costs for the economy would be felt in greater wage resistance by employees and investor reluctance to ease long-term interest rates any further. However, while the yield curve is still quite steep, long-term rates weathered quite well the inflation fears of the spring of 1993 and have since resumed their downtrend. Also, on an effective basis the dollar has remained quite firm, even if it has fallen sharply against the yen.

1993 has seen the inauguration of a new President, anxious to try to lift the economy's performance over the medium term. The new Administration's economic strategy is built on the view that government can do much to improve on market outcomes. Thus, while also clearly committed to "getting its own house in order" by bringing down the government budget deficit so as to ease the drain on national savings, it has shown willingness to pursue actively such objectives as countering the trend rise in income inequality, securing faster job creation and supporting higher rates of tangible and intangible investment in order to strengthen productivity outcomes and enhance the growth of real incomes. However, it does seem aware that governments are also capable of failure in their interventions, and that public-sector efficiency is a goal which is often difficult to attain.

The new Administration, to its credit, wasted little time in turning to the problem of the federal deficit. Its original proposals, along with the alternative deficit-reduction plan ultimately signed into law, go a long way to alleviating the fiscal imbalance. The magnitude of deficit reduction is, however, exaggerated by measuring the cuts relative to a single baseline, and many of the important details have yet to be worked out. Furthermore, it is important to note that, even after enactment, the federal deficit is still projected to be disappointingly large, at over 2½ per cent of GDP in 1997 (and that at virtually full employment), and the debt-to-GDP ratio would still be on an uptrend. And state and local governments' operating budgets remain stuck in deficit positions as well. This is a far worse outcome than would have been considered acceptable prior to the 1980s. It has been less than 3 years since the previous major deficit-reduction package was passed, and another might be required by 1998. The main problem is in the uncontrolled growth in so-called "entitlement spending", especially on medical care. The Administration has also devoted a great deal of its initial attention to a draft reform of the health-care system, keenly awaited by the public.

A number of the details of the fiscal plan are noteworthy. At the outset, however, it should be said that the split between tax increases and spending cuts in the final legislation is not of paramount importance: it is the size of deficit reduction which is decisive, especially given the difficulties in characterising many budgetary changes as tax increases or spending cuts. But big increases in marginal personal tax rates for high-income individuals, while justified on income-distribution grounds, may generate intensified tax-avoidance behaviour and therefore yield less additional revenue than set out in the plan. Second, looking to Social Security recipients to share in the burden of deficit reduction has not proven the political non-starter many had supposed. Perhaps it indicates that other parts of the tax system previously regarded as sacrosanct, such as mortgage-interest deductibility, are really not untouchable either. Third, the OECD has often recommended higher energy taxation as a means to combine deficit reduction, energy conservation and environmental improvement, and the proposed BTU tax was a good hybrid with those goals in mind. Its abandonment was regrettable. Fourth, the decision to modify debt management with a view to shortening the average maturity of outstanding debt may, on balance, be a good one, even if it might not reduce interest payments as much as is hoped. But with a still rising ratio of federal debt to GDP and sporadic Congressional attacks on the independence of the central bank, there are significant risks that this could lead to an increase in political pressures on the Federal Reserve to keep short-term interest rates low.

Employment growth has strengthened, despite the moderate nature of the recovery, reflecting the relatively flexible labour market. However, the pace of employment expansion and the trend level of unemployment as well as its demographic distribution remain a concern. Ensuring the availability of sufficient credit to smaller firms – in which, on net, all job creation is found – by easing the regulatory burden was a welcome step in this regard. Yet the balance between low-paying versus high-skilled positions is unsatisfactory; furthermore, too many Americans, especially in the minorities, are stuck in a kind of poverty trap. The proper way of dealing with the former problem is to upgrade human capital and skills, not to yield to protectionist pressures. The proposed expansion of the Earned Income Tax Credit and time-limitation of welfare payments are bold and worthy moves to confront the latter problem, but care should be taken not to raise marginal income tax rates to prohibitive levels in the phase-out range for any anti-poverty initiatives.

The new Administration brings with it a new policy focus on investment in all its forms, both tangible and intangible, physical and human, public and private. It is seeking substantial reforms in a wide variety of areas on account of their intended impact on the nation's productivity and competitiveness. Even though there are important measurement difficulties, and adjustment costs – at least from the ongoing downsizing of the defence establishment – may have been burdensome in recent years, productivity performance can only be judged to have been sub-par. Even in manufacturing, where productivity gains have been the fastest, they have, at least until recently, failed to enhance cost competitiveness, which, over the past decade, has been maintained primarily by exchange-rate depreciation. This poor productivity performance can be attributed to both macroeconomic and microeconomic factors.

The core macroeconomic problem is the lack of saving and investment. While there is broad agreement that direct tax incentives have not been successful in boosting private saving, the tax code could be purged of some of its anti-saving biases, especially the ability for households to deduct interest payments on what amounts to consumer debt through the use of home equity loans. Cutting the budget deficit is the surest way to boost national saving and – by bringing down interest rates – promote investment. Government measures of direct support for capital formation have less certain outcomes and risk widening the external deficit, at least in the short run.

Among the main factors alleged to be limiting productivity growth is a lack of public infrastructure capital. Infrastructure investment has indeed been much lower over the past decade than in the 1960s, for example, but to some extent that is ascribable to demographic factors and the satiation of certain transportation needs. The Administration believes, nonetheless, that there is an urgent need for more infrastructure which may generate favourable spillovers on private-sector productivity. Here too the statistical evidence is mixed, and, in any case, a proper evaluation requires a close look at individual projects. More generally, greater efficiency should be sought in the use of existing infrastructure through the introduction of proper pricing mechanisms: that might well avoid unnecessary public expenditures and could offer a clearer measure of exactly where additional investment would have the highest pay-off.

There is fairly strong evidence that the U.S. education system is delivering rather poor outcomes in many areas, and aggregate human capital and productivity is suffering as a result. Except for the elite, high school graduates are falling behind those in other developed countries in work-related skills, and the gap is especially pronounced for the least educated. The situation is all the more serious, since so many of those affected belong to minorities. A re-allocation of spending towards those most in need, combined with some increase in the overall level of resources devoted to education, would seem to offer the best approach on both equity and productivity-enhancement grounds. The Administration is clearly keenly concerned with equality of opportunity, and its efforts in this area are welcome, but pay-offs may take a very long time. Furthermore, efficiency throughout the system could be boosted by sharpening incentives: for students and teachers by implementing standardised tests, and for institutions by allowing students (and their parents) a degree of choice in where they enrol.

Technology policy is another focal point of Administration concerns. While the United States is still the world's largest producer and exporter of intellectual property and has its highest share of scientists and engineers in total employment, it is no longer the undisputed leader in all high technology manufacturing industries. This is seen to be a problem by those who believe that such industries generate rents, and those rents are slipping away. To this point too much of the nation's R&D spending has been devoted to defence-related projects, and direct federal outlays are set to shift to civilian and dual-use technologies. Also worthwhile is the closer co-operation between the national laboratories and private industry. The problems of exploiting and diffusing existing technology could be alleviated by the proposed setting-up of technology outreach or extension centres. Permanent extension of the Research and Experimentation Tax Credit would have increased its efficiency by reducing uncertainty, but it should probably not be made more generous, since not all R&D output is inappropriable. Greater federal involvement in pre-competitive generic R&D is legitimate, so long as there is substantial private-sector financial participation and care is taken to avoid political influence in project selection and location decisions.

The new Administration sees greater scope for government in correcting market failures than did the preceding Administration. The zeal for deregulation has clearly waned since the mid-1980's, and the government, even more than its predecessor, seems willing to turn to new regulation to achieve its social objectives in an environment of budgetary stringency, despite evidence of burgeoning regulatory costs imposed on the private sector in recent years, especially in the areas of the environment and occupational health and safety. As these costs are not as transparent as direct public outlays, the risk is that the pace of new regulation could accelerate, with harmful consequences for output, employment, productivity and cost competitiveness.

The greater willingness to intervene can also be seen, in part, in the new Administration's trade-policy approach. On the one hand, it is commendably pushing forward to reach a Uruguay Round settlement, to the benefit of all the world's trading nations, by asking Congress for an extension of the fast-track negotiating authority which expired earlier this year. It has also completed the side agreements for the North American Free Trade Area (NAFTA) agreement. The NAFTA will probably have a modest beneficial effect on the economies of the United States and Canada which already trade at world prices in most cases, but it is almost certainly crucial to Mexico's future rapid development. Yet on the other hand, the United States continues to resort to complex and costly investigative procedures in anti-dumping and countervailing duty cases. Most importantly, it has also moved to convince Japan to undertake what might be termed ''voluntary import expansions''. Building in part on the perceived success of the 1990 semiconductor arrangement, as well as disillusionment with the results of the Structural Impediments Initiative, in July 1993 the Administration completed negotiation of the *Japan-United States Framework for a New Economic Partnership.* Concerning the United States, the *Framework* is aimed at the medium-term objectives of substantially reducing its fiscal deficit, increasing domestic saving and strenghtening its international competitiveness. And, concerning Japan, it is aimed at ''the medium-term objectives of... strong and sustainable domestic demand-led growth and increasing the market access of competitive foreign goods and services, intended to achieve, over the medium term, a highly significant decrease in its (Japan's) current account surplus, and to promote a significant increase in global imports of goods and services, including from the United States''. The two governments will assess the implementation of measures and policies in a range of structural and sectoral trade concerns through ''objective criteria, either qualitative or quantitative or both as appropriate''. While the

Framework avoids any reference to precise, numerical targets, they are not excluded under its terms. But the Committee is concerned that sectoral quantitative targets, if adopted, might risk a bureaucratisation of trade: they would achieve no change to macroeconomic variables such as the U.S. current-account deficit and might undermine the free multilateral trading system. And precisely fixed optimal values for the size of current account surpluses or deficits are impossible to calculate, given all the factors which enter into their determination. Finally, while the *Framework* addresses only the concerns of the two parties, it does include a joint commitment to make any benefits accruing from it available to other countries on a most-favoured-nation basis.

The United States' system of corporate governance has come in for a great deal of criticism for the short-termism it allegedly engenders and for its failure to align the interests of the users and providers of capital. This is an exceedingly complex issue which deserves more research, but even if the charges are true, possible solutions may come from the market place, without the need for any wide-ranging policy response. On the other hand, action would seem to be called for to reform the bankruptcy system and to limit the nation's litigious tendencies. For example, legislated restraint in the area of wrongful-dismissal suits would appear likely to yield valuable dividends.

To sum up, despite its rather uneven pace, the recovery has continued to strengthen, and prospects are for a further acceleration in economic growth with fairly stable or possibly even declining inflation. The policy mix has appropriately shifted, with a credible plan to reduce the structural budget deficit permitting much lower long-term interest rates, even allowing for the continuing accommodative monetary policy stance. Many valuable structural reforms have been proposed by the new Administration, but the most important – dealing with the costly health-care system – is still eagerly awaited. If these reforms can be successfully implemented, the nation will be well on its way to better economic outcomes in the future.

Notes

1. The data in the establishment survey suggest net job creation has been a bit slower than normal, even given weak output growth, while the household survey suggests employment growth has been a little bit higher than normal. However, in another sense the recovery has been "jobless". When a recovery is relatively strong, employment gains usually make up a healthy fraction of total output growth, and both employment growth and productivity growth are robust. But when a recovery is relatively weak, the typical cyclical pickup in productivity implies modest employment growth – as in the period since 1991.
2. Multi-family construction has continued the plunge which began after the overbuilding of the the mid-1980s. However, this type of investment is small in magnitude relative to single-family construction: thus, movements in single-family construction dominate the multi-family figures in aggregate residential investment.
3. Estimates are that such temporary-agency workers have risen by 425 000 since the trough of the 1990-91 recession.
4. One regional example: high state taxation and stringent regulatory costs have encouraged flight of many businesses out of California and into the neighbouring Rocky Mountain states, where employment growth has been the fastest in the nation.
5. Some of these ex-manufacturing workers may have dropped out of the labour force, but overall labour force participation rates are higher now than at the 1991 cyclical trough.
6. The mean duration declined similarly. The number of those unemployed for more than six months declined from 2.1 million in December 1992 to 1.7 million in August 1993.
7. In the twelve months through December 1992, the CPI for energy rose 1.9 per cent, while the CPI for food increased 1.5 per cent.
8. The personal consumption deflator, excluding food and energy, increased at a 3.6 per cent rate over the four quarters of 1992 – but in contrast to the core CPI, inflation as measured by the core consumption deflator fell to a 3.2 per cent rate in the first quarter of 1993.
9. One category where price inflation has slowed noticeably is medical care. Medical care prices increased only 6.0 per cent in the twelve months through August 1993, down from a recent peak rate of 9.6 per cent in 1990.
10. The deflator actually declined 1 per cent, but this figure is distorted by the rising share of computers. The Commerce Department's preliminary estimates of fixed-weight and chain-weight indexes for equipment showed changes of 0.5 per cent and –0.2 per cent, respectively.

11. The Commerce Department assumes price growth for services purchased by the government (*i.e.* for work by federal employees) is identical to federal wage growth – in effect productivity changes are assumed to be zero. Employee compensation makes up nearly half of federal purchases. Thus, if growth in productivity of federal employees in fact averaged 1 per cent per annum, as in the overall economy, growth in the measured federal deflator would be overstated by almost ½ per cent per year.

12. Net government transfers abroad were $43 billion lower than normal in 1991, as Gulf War contributions were paid by the Allies. The unadjusted balance showed a deficit of $8 billion.

13. Weakened activity in 1991 held down foreign direct investment in the United States, reversing the shortfall of outward relative to inward direct investment seen since 1981. In 1992, recession abroad may have further discouraged foreign investment in the United States, and the excess of outward over inward direct investment widened from $16 billion in 1991 to $32 billion. In the first half of 1993, foreign investment in the United States picked up a bit, but the excess of outward over inward direct investment continued, although at a much-reduced $4 billion annual rate.

14. Compared with 4.6 per cent in 1992. This reduction is similar to the official estimate, though the Administration assumed less economic growth and less personal tax avoidance.

15. A significant part of this is due to the return to normal of net transfers to foreigners after the temporary decline in 1991 associated with the Gulf war.

16. Thus, there is a trend increase in the number of beneficiaries of means-tested transfers at any given level of unemployment. For example, the ratio of the number of food-stamp recipients to the number of unemployed trended up from 1.0 in the early 1980s to nearly 1.5 in 1989 where it remains to this day.

17. Projections are that the state-and-local surplus on a national-accounts basis may continue to shrink very slightly in 1993, as such governments continue to try to deal with burgeoning health-care costs and an acceleration in the benefit costs of their workers by raising property and sales taxes, in part offset by personal tax reductions.

18. The largest single reason for the discrepancy is the fact that the CBO chose to consider the $42 billion of discretionary spending cuts that would have been required in 1994 and 1995 under the terms of the Budget Enforcement Act of 1990 (part of OBRA90) as part of the baseline, whereas the Administration wished to take credit for implementing those cuts.

19. The most important component which was passed in April 1993 was a continuation in the availability of ''extended'' unemployment benefits for as many as 1.8 million unemployed through 2 October 1993 (a period when the unemployment rate is likely to average only about one percentage point above Secretariat estimates of full-employment levels) at a cost of some $4 billion. Besides the fiscal implications of such a large outlay, the extension is likely to boost the unemployment rate somewhat by reducing its cost and discouraging job search. A wide variety of international evidence is available to support this claim: for the United States, see Katz and Meyer (1990), and, for other OECD countries, see OECD (1991*a*, pp. 206-207).

20. The $496 billion figure is from the Congress and includes the $42 billion referred to in footnote 18 Later scorekeeping by the CBO (1993*f*) cut the projected deficit reduction by a further $21 billion, largely due to lower estimates of interest savings from changes in debt

management (see below). Independently, the Office of Management and Budget (1993*d*) also undertook a scorekeeping exercise for OBRA93 and concluded that deficit reduction therein amounts to $505 billion. In what follows, Congressional figures are cited for the impact of individual components of OBRA93 on the five-year cumulative deficit.

21. According to the CBO (1993*c*), the top 1 per cent of the income distribution would bear nearly 57 per cent of the burden of changes in taxes and transfers under the Administration proposals. The top 20 per cent would bear over 86 per cent. Another proposed tax change aimed at the wealthy is a restoration of the 53 and 55 per cent estate-tax brackets which had been in effect in 1992. This would generate over half a billion dollars a year by official estimates, but they are contested by some who maintain that estate taxes actually lose revenues – compared with the taxation of capital gains at death – because of tax-avoiding estate-planning behaviour.

22. Increases in marginal rates on high income earners may also have negative job-creation effects, as many of them are small business owners. In 1990, taxpayers with more than $200 000 in income had $69.3 billion in Sub-chapter S income (which is largely, though not entirely, small-business income) and $25.5 billion in professional and unincorporated business (Schedule C) income, compared with only $64.8 billion in dividends and taxable interest.

23. Indeed, there was a noticeable widening in the yield differential between municipal bonds and AAA corporate bonds, for example, from just before the 1992 election (145 basis points) through early March 1993 (209 basis points). All of that has, however, since been reversed.

24. Other than those mentioned in the text, the package includes business tax changes which: *i)* reduce the deductible portion of meals and entertainment expense from 80 to 50 per cent; *ii)* reduce the alternative minimum corporate tax; *iii)* allow small businesses to write off up to $17 500 in equipment purchases, up from the current level of $10 000; *iv)* deny deductibility for executive compensation in excess of $1 million per person, unless linked to performance; *v)* diminish the generosity of the tax incentives provided for investment in Puerto Rico; and *vi)* improve compliance, especially for multinational corporations that attempt to shift profits abroad through transfer pricing abuses. These and other miscellaneous tax increases on business would raise about $50 billion in extra revenues over the years 1994-98. Also, the Research and Experimentation Tax Credit would be extended through June 1995, at a five-year cost of $4.9 billion (see Chapter III), and capital-gains tax relief would be provided for investors in certain small businesses when shares are held at least five years.

25. Whether this will result in any true budgetary savings is unclear. The claimed savings are boosted by the accounting rules adopted in the 1990 reform which allowed the complete neglect of administrative costs in such calculations.

26. Also included are an increase in sugar and peanut assessments; reductions in producer payment limitations for honey and wool; domestic tobacco content requirements for cigarettes and a levy on imports of tobacco; reductions in the authorised funding for the Market Promotion Programme; the extension of certain land conservation programmes; and crop insurance reform.

27. The CBO (1993*e*) and others have done sensitivity analyses to examine the risk of interest rates moving in such a way as to actually raise interest costs. Such Monte Carlo studies show only a 1 per cent chance over a five-year horizon and 3 per cent over a ten-year horizon.

28. It was for this reason that a committee of bond-market participants opposed the change, calling the current mix ''broadly appropriate''.

29. A number of factors peculiar to this programme have combined to push its cost up at a rapid pace. First, state and local governments have successfully shifted various schemes (such as mental health) into Medicaid in order to qualify for federal matching payments. Second, there has been a rapid increase in applications for benefits by the disabled poor. Third, payments to providers have had to be increased to comply with a 1980 law that they be ''reasonable and adequate'' (CBO, 1993*a*).

30. To what extent these changes borrow from the revenues that might have otherwise been available to cover the increased costs resulting from the imminent overall health-care reform (discussed below) is unclear. In effect, many will ultimately have tax-like effects, as providers, especially hospitals, attempt to compensate for these revenue reductions by raising prices to private-sector payers.

31. This amount is gross of the spending which is currently required to provide uncompensated care for those without coverage, often in emergency rooms of public hospitals and at a late stage of illness.

32. This estimate is consistent with a figure of $31 billion in 1990 published by the U.S. General Accounting Office (1991).

33. The EITC was initially instituted in the mid-1970s, and the most recent expansion, enacted in 1990, has not yet been fully phased in. For those with more than one dependent, the maximum refundable credit in 1993 is $1 513 with $7 760 to $12 210 in earned income, and then the credit is phased out over a range up to $23 070. The Administration proposal was to boost the maximum credit to $3 371 at $8 500 to $11 000, with a phase-out range to $28 000, but the $28 billion cost was pared by a quarter in the final reconciliation bill largely by shortening the phase-out ceiling to $27 000 (1994 prices) and lengthening the period over which the reform will be implemented.

34. Kosters suggests that it might, therefore, be better to increase the standard deduction or personal tax exemptions as an alternative to enhancing the EITC. However, these alternatives would provide more benefits to those with higher incomes and, therefore, higher marginal tax rates.

35. Indeed, long-term interest rates have been falling since the election in November 1992, and the dollar interrupted its positive trend in March and April 1993, despite the continuing favourable relative cyclical position of the United States.

36. Similarly, the discount rate has been set at 3 per cent since July 1992.

37. This low opportunity cost was one important reason for rapid M1 growth; in addition, mortgage refinancings and prepayment of mortgage-backed securities induced a further, albeit temporary, shift into M1.

38. Business deleveraging in general is probably better explained by the unusually wide gap between the after-tax cost of debt and the yield on small time deposits, which induces weakness in demand for loans.

39. The range for M3 was also shifted downward by ½ percentage point in both February and July (to 0 to 4 per cent).

40. The international comparisons of levels of productivity made in this chapter are undertaken using 1990 purchasing-power-parity (PPP) data. Using the previous 1985 data and then extrapolating for relative inflation differences would give somewhat different outcomes for reasons that are not fully understood. In particular, relative U.S. productivity levels would be higher on a 1985 PPP basis, primarily in relation to European levels.

41. Also, high unemployment in the Netherlands and elsewhere in Europe may tend to inflate their measured productivity, as their least productive workers are less likely to be employed than in the United States.

42. Re-engineering denotes the radical re-design of business processes away from the organisation of work as a sequence of separate, narrowly defined tasks. It entails empowering individual workers to handle a wider variety of functions, thereby eliminating the need for as many layers of management.

43. However, labour productivity growth in the U.S. financial sector, as measured by official data, might be underestimated due to mismeasurement of the price-volume split in that sector. Certainly the number and value of transactions carried out per employee has increased substantially. It is less clear whether the underlying intermediation function of banking was truly carried out more efficiently in the 1980s, given the loan-loss problems of U.S. banks in that decade.

44. Another likely measurement problem exists in the construction sector, where measured labour productivity fell 20 per cent between 1967 and 1972, and another 20 per cent between 1977 and 1986. This struck Baily and Gordon (1988) as implausible, given a 15 per cent increase in materials handled per hour by construction labour over those two decades, as well as given a substantial increase in the capital-labour ratio for the construction sector.

45. DeLong (1988) argues that a grouping of industrial countries (such as the OECD) is not representative in testing for the existence of convergence. He suggests that industrial countries such as the OECD members are "an ex-post sample of countries that are now rich and have successfully developed... convergence is thus all but guaranteed in Baumol's regression...". DeLong further states that development outcomes are more diverse than suggested by the simplest convergence model. More recently, however, Barro and Lee (1993), among others, have shown that conditional on levels of educational attainment, this catch-up process was significant in a broad sample of 116 countries over recent decades.

46. There is by now widespread agreement on this point. Some observers are extremely ambitious as to a reasonable target: for example, the Committee for Economic Development (1992) called for policy to aim for a unified federal budget surplus of 1 per cent of GDP in order to return the net national saving rate to 8 per cent of national income, as it was prior to the 1980s.

47. Despite the excess of foreign direct investment in the United States over U.S. investment abroad from 1981 to 1990, official flow of funds data show that the current stock of

U.S. foreign direct investment abroad is still well above the stock of corresponding investment in the United States ($705 billion compared with $490 billion at end-1992).

48. The OECD Secretariat has begun to exploit the purchasing-power-parity data base by extracting the prices of manufactured goods, extending them over time and making international comparisons.

49. Harris and Steindel (1991) discuss the longer-term negative implications of these figures.

50. Parents could in principle boost savings and provide larger bequests to compensate, but inheritance taxes would siphon off part of the increased private saving, leaving each individual's gain from his efforts lower than the social gain (that is, inheritance taxes imply a free rider problem).

51. The relatively slow rate of U.S. capital deepening, probably reflecting the substantial degree of real wage flexibility in U.S. labour markets, has made it easier for business to meet demand growth with labour that would otherwise go unemployed, as in the European case. Furthermore, keeping these workers employed maintains and improves human capital. However, the investment slowdown is troublesome in its implications for future income growth – especially given the tendency for new technology to be embodied in new capital equipment.

52. If this price difference is allowed for, and investment is more broadly defined to include research and development, U.S. investment per capita was no lower than in other OECD countries, at least through 1980 (Lipsey and Kravis, 1988).

53. The slowdown in capital deepening is qualitatively clear, though the precise extent is not, since the measured capital stock data are far from perfect. The U.S. Bureau of Labor Statistics has constructed an alternative rental-price-weighted estimate of the capital stock, and that series shows capital deepening since the first oil shock of about 1.6 per cent per year – a more moderate slowdown. However, this series may overstate the growth of utilised capital since the first oil shock. Rapid oil price changes made some of the capital stock effectively obsolete: growth of utilised capital most likely averaged less than 1.6 per cent per year.

54. A similar correlation between capital deepening and growth appears within the U.S. business sector: deepening slowed more in non-manufacturing business, and correspondingly productivity growth slowed more outside of manufacturing. Between the 1950-73 period and the 1973-91 period, net additions of capital per worker outside of manufacturing dropped from 1.9 per cent annually to 0.5 per cent. Likewise, average growth of output per hour outside of manufacturing fell from 1.5 per cent annually to zero. In manufacturing, however, capital deepening continued unabated after 1973, at nearly 3 per cent per year. Correspondingly, average growth of manufacturing output per hour has fallen relatively little (only about 0.6 percentage point).

55. This argument has usually been applied to equipment, since the cross-country correlation between productivity and structures investment was not as great.

56. Even if new technology were not embodied in capital, one could make a similar argument. In periods where total factor productivity increases rapidly – for whatever reason – rapid growth in income will tend to boost saving rates (in line with the permanent income model

or because of slow adjustment in consumption habits), boosting funds available for investment.

57. DeLong and Summers (1991) argue that if higher savings and increased demand for capital goods are the causes of capital deepening, equipment prices should be relatively high in fast-growing countries – and no such pattern is visible in equipment prices internationally. Heston (1993) suggests that for many countries, capital goods are imported to a large extent, and the price of these imports is affected very little by increased demand.

58. Auerbach *et al.* (1993) show that excess returns to equipment investment have not been evident for the OECD countries as a group. The very strong relationship between equipment and growth found by DeLong and Summers depend critically on the inclusion of Korea and Argentina in their broader sample. DeLong and Summers argue that Korea and Argentina provide legitimate information about likely effects of increased equipment investment in the OECD countries. Auerbach *et al.* argue that equipment investment may yield excess returns when aggregate demand growth is extraordinarily rapid during the "take-off" process (as in the Korean case), or when capital markets have been heavily restricted (the Argentinian case): however, they dispute the relevance of these cases to the United States and most OECD countries.

59. Overbuilding has driven down the social return on investment in housing to a rate well below that of other forms of investment (Mills, 1987).

60. While the U.S. ceiling is $1 000 000, the limit in the United Kingdom, for example, is £30 000.

61. Apparently the 1986 corporate tax law change that eliminated the investment tax credit and lowered the corporate income tax rate, had only marginal effects (Goulder and Thalmann, 1990). The incremental credit plus the corporate tax increase originally proposed by the Administration looked in some ways like a mirror image of this 1986 change.

62. According to the Congressional Research Service, there are fewer than 3 800 employees per billion dollars of defence procurement, compared with nearly 8 000 for each billion dollars of typical purchases by state and local governments, for example.

63. According to the 1994 Budget, the defence share of federal R&D spending is set to fall slightly from 59 per cent in 1992 to 58 per cent in 1994 and then more swiftly, reaching less than half by 1998. See the section on R&D below.

64. Not surprisingly, a similar fraction of the downsizing has occurred in budget outlay terms. However, on a budget-authority basis, the adjustment is more than half over.

65. The military will be hiring about 100 000 fewer high school graduates per year (nearly 4 per cent of the total) over the next four years than it did in the Reagan military expansion.

66. The Reagan defence build-up may have been responsible for as much as one-half of the total increase in industrial R&D expenditures at the time, with each dollar of purchases eliciting 9 cents of added private R&D.

67. There is at least one possible output-depressing effect of lower defence outlays, if it results in a lower deficit in the long run (Ireland and Otrok, 1992): labour supply may be reduced due to the favourable wealth effect associated with the fall in the present discounted value of lower tax liabilities. Those authors estimate a vector autoregression and find a permanent

loss of 1.9 per cent of GNP resulting from the Bush proposals. This is in contrast to the gains approaching 1 per cent claimed by the Congressional Budget Office (1992) in simulations of two different widely used macroeconometric models.

68. According to the Congressional Budget Office (1992), the 1991 Bush proposals would have cut the level of GDP by 0.6 to 0.7 per cent by the mid-1990s. Larger cut-backs resembling the Clinton plan would put the decline in the 1 per cent range.

69. Public investment in physical infrastructure discussed here includes all non-defence capital spending on structures and equipment by Federal, state and local governments. It excludes investments made by public utilities.

70. These are summarised in, for example, Congressional Budget Office (1991) and Munnell (1993).

71. See, for example, Ford and Poret (1991) for cross-country estimates, and Nadiri and Mamuneas (1991) for cross-state results for manufacturing industry.

72. Statistical tests of causation based on data from 40 metropolitan areas showed that in 40 per cent of the cases examined changes in public investment caused changes in private investment, the opposite was the case in another 40 per cent, and elsewhere the results were indeterminate (Eberts and Fogarty, 1987).

73. The problem of wear and tear of roads in the United States is exacerbated by the fact that they have not been made thick enough and that the introduction of improved pavement materials has been lagging.

74. Since around 1983, however, the percentage of total highway mileage in poor conditions has fallen sharply: for urban inter-state highways, for example, it fell from 18 per cent in 1983 to 8 per cent in 1991, though the share of inter-state bridges that are deficient began to fall only in 1990 (The Report of the Secretary of Transportation to the Congress, 1993).

75. Full funding of the 1994 authorisations contained in the ISTEA was also proposed by the previous Administration.

76. American workers also work longer hours each year than workers in any other OECD nation except Japan. Furthermore, the relatively slow trend decline in hours worked each year by Americans has favourably affected output per worker in the United States relative to that in other OECD countries.

77. On a measured basis. However, official consumer price statistics tend to overstate the true rate of price inflation (Lebow *et al.,* 1992), and thus estimated growth of real incomes may be understated. Nevertheless, both the absolute and relative weakness of income growth of the unskilled remains a serious problem.

78. Tax changes played a role in this increased inequality in take-home pay, but the main culprit was the increasing penalty for lack of marketable skills (see Berman *et al.,* 1993). An additional factor driving up the skill premium is the so-called ''cost disease''. There may be inherent limits holding down the growth of productivity in teaching, yet real wages of professors rise in line with the faster productivity growth nation-wide. Thus, the real cost of education has risen steadily, driving down the demand for education on the part of those who would have gained only marginally: at the margin, the productivity of education will thereby increase, boosting the skill premium.

79. Inequality has also increased *within* groups with similar educational attainments. However, this form of inequality is probably less of a concern: the social goal is equality of opportunity, not necessarily equality of outcomes. And equal access to quality education is not available to all Americans.

80. Though the Hispanic high-school dropout rate has been at about this level for many years, the dropout rate has trended downward for blacks. Also, skills of blacks planning to attend college may have improved: their SAT (Scholastic Aptitude Test) scores have trended upward steadily since the mid-1970s, while those of whites have drifted downward. However, educational achievement of students in poor school districts lags well behind those in wealthy districts: A-average students in low-income areas typically score similarly to C-students in wealthy school districts on standardised tests (Zuckman, 1993*b*, citing ABT Associates). Furthermore, black males in their early twenties who went to urban high schools earn 9 per cent less than comparable black workers who went to suburban schools (Levy and Murnane, 1992).

81. For example, the Congressional Budget Office (1991) reports on a study of participants in the Job Corps programme in 1977 – showing a reduction in the cost of crime-related activities of $5 840 per person in 1990 prices in present value terms, almost as much as the value of participants' increased output.

82. The 1994 Budget also proposes direct administration of college student loans. Direct administration would ultimately involve no change in resources actually made available for education – simply possible cost reduction.

83. Over the past two decades, several court decisions *have* addressed the basis for school financing. More recently, the courts have forced many states to re-allocate educational funds from wealthier to less wealthy counties – but large inequities remain across school districts. ''Chapter One'' of the Elementary and Secondary Education Act attempts to address these inequities: this programme makes up the bulk of federal spending on public schools.

84. For example, one-stop shopping for job retraining and relocation amounts to a merger of several existing programmes, without much additional spending. It may nonetheless be a useful way to increase the effectiveness of existing active income-support programmes, given the incomplete information among the newly-unemployed about the variety of existing services. Likewise, the national goals outlined in the school reform bill are exactly those developed by the National Education Goals Panel initiated in the Bush Administration – but developing national goals, standards and tests is no less important simply because it is not a new idea.

85. While the Australian programme is still very new, the programme in France began more than twenty years ago. Its results are discussed in OECD (1992*b*, pp. 105-109).

86. The Cato institute, a conservative think tank, recommended replacing Head Start with a voucher system for poor children to use, allowing them the ''choice'' to attend private schools at public expense (Hood, 1992). This Bush Administration proposal might increase incentives for schools to deliver better training, but it was widely opposed in Congress on grounds that it might increase inequities, and it was noted that the average edge in private-school achievement is far smaller than the variation within the public school system or among private schools (Levy and Murnane, 1992). An ''incentive-school'' programme, with

bonuses for staffs of schools with rapidly improving outcomes, is one Administration proposal to overcome the lack of market incentives in the public school system.

87. However, others have pointed out that over the past century there has been little tendency for periods of high total factor productivity growth to coincide with those of rapid capital accumulation (Baily and Schultze, 1990), although the historical correlation with capital deepening has been stronger.

88. Jones (1992) has demonstrated declining returns in the long run, implying subsidies to R&D may only raise per capita growth during the transition to the steady-state growth path.

89. Similarly, Morrison and Berndt (1991) found that the rate of return on office automation equipment was no higher than on other forms of capital. However, using article counts in scientific papers, Adams (1990) argues that basic knowledge is a major contributor to productivity growth in manufacturing, with a lag of about twenty years from its creation to its effect on industrial productivity.

90. Mansfield (1988) showed that U.S. firms devote more R&D effort to inventing new products and production processes relative to making marginal improvements to existing products and processes in a bilateral comparison with Japan.

91. Leadership can be attributed to the quality of its advanced technical education and the resulting pool of available technical talent, the spirit of individual creativity and initiative cultivated by the nation's social values and the scale, homogeneity and openness of its market (Lee and Reid, 1991). For example, in 1986 the United States represented 44 per cent of the world market for high-technology manufactures, compared with 27 per cent for Japan and 17 per cent for Germany, France and the United Kingdom combined.

92. A note of caution should be made, however: a very high proportion of all such payments are made to related parties, that is they are internal to the firm and, therefore, subject to manipulation to minimise global tax liabilities. Furthermore, such royalties are paid only if the proprietor chooses not to exploit the advantage abroad through exporting but rather to licence the knowledge to a foreign subsidiary or another arms-length foreign firm.

93. These authors have pointed to the waste involved in the past in alluring large projects such as the breeder reactor, synfuels and the supersonic transport. The current group of such projects includes the space station, the superconducting super collider, the Earth Observation Satellite System and the National Aerospace Plane. Other countries' experiences with activist R&D policies have not been encouraging.

94. Corporations have been allowed to treat outlays on labour and materials used in R&D as an expense since 1954, implying a more generous treatment than one would base on economic depreciation which has been traditionally held to be about 15 per cent per year. This has been estimated to entail a revenue cost of some $1.4 billion per year (Congressional Budget Office, 1991).

95. Given the incremental nature of the credit as well as limits on carry-forward and -backward provisions, the effective rate was in the range of 5 per cent through most of the 1980s.

96. However, domestic R&D might possibly be restrained by a recently enacted small tax change. Recent research has pointed to the perverse incentives for U.S. multinational corporations to transfer R&D operations abroad resulting from the allocation of such

expenses against foreign-source income for U.S. tax purposes. As of now, the automatic allocation will be 50 rather than the previous 36 per cent.

97. These are purely social risks, as the private risks of triple damages were eliminated by the 1984 National Co-operative Research Act. After a slow start, the latest count shows that over 300 R&D joint ventures have been registered under the Act, with concentration in information technology, biotechnology and new materials. The question is whether it is possible for rivals to collaborate on research and compete on production.

98. The most publicised case is that of the $200 million Semiconductor Manufacturing Technology (Sematech), launched in 1987 and funded jointly by the industry and the Department of Defence. Its major success has been to improve communications between its chip-making members and equipment producers (Congressional Budget Office, 1990).

99. Enterprise zones provide incentives to invest in depressed areas. Empowerment zones give wage subsidies for workers resident and employed in the zone.

100. Hopkins' estimates are based on data provided by regulatory agencies and may, therefore, be downbiased; for example, the resulting litigation costs are probably excluded. Also excluded are those compliance costs which are paid for by the federal government itself which amount to about $14 billion per year, mostly in the environmental area. There are at least two other indicators of the importance of federal regulation. First, staffing levels in regulatory agencies rose steadily from 70 000 in 1970 to a peak of 122 000 in 1980, fell to 102 000 in 1985 and then climbed to 126 500 in 1993. Second, the number of pages in the *Federal Register* shows a slow uptrend until 1970, a sharp rise through the following decade, a precipitous decline through 1986 and a renewed moderate increase until the 1992 moratorium.

101. Jorgenson and Wilcoxen (1990) estimate such costs at 2.6 per cent of GNP using a multi-sectoral applied general equilibrium model. This is composed of 1.3 per cent of GNP attributable to the capital costs of pollution-control equipment, 0.8 per cent from motor-vehicle-emissions controls and 0.7 per cent from the opportunity costs of pollution abatement (the total is less than the sum of the parts due to the overlapping nature of some regulation).

102. While estimates range up to as much as ½ percentage point per year (William Niskanen of the Cato Institute, as reported in *The Economist* (1992)), Jorgenson and Wilcoxen (1990) attribute a growth-reducing effect of 0.19 per cent per year to overall regulation. Earlier growth-accounting estimates by Denison (1985) were only 0.07 per cent per year for the period 1973-82. Very recent research, using plant-level data for manufacturing (Gray and Shadbegian, 1993), has shown that environmental regulatory compliance costs have cut average total factor productivity levels by 3.1 per cent in oil refineries, 5.3 per cent in pulp and paper mills and 7.6 per cent in steel mills. A dollar increase in compliance costs reduces output by between three and four dollars (compared to a one-for-one ratio assumed in growth-accounting exercises). There is also some less direct evidence that the regulations promulgated by the Occupational Safety and Health Administration were even more instrumental in the post-1973 slowdown in productivity growth in U.S. manufacturing than those dealing with pollution control (Gray, 1987). Together, they may have been responsible for over 30 per cent of that slowdown.

103. In a general-equilibrium context the result is a decline in the foreign exchange value of the dollar. See, for example, Jorgenson and Wilcoxen (1990).

104. According to Hazilla and Kopp (1990), the compliance costs of regulation mandated by the Clean Air and Clean Water Acts alone amounted to 2.43 per cent of GNP prior to the 1990 revisions, but the social costs reached 5.85 per cent. Furthermore, regulation requires substantial administrative outlays by the public sector. According to one estimate, these amounted to over $13 billion in 1992, more than triple 1970 levels in inflation-adjusted terms (*The Economist,* 1992).

105. According to Hahn and Hird (1991), social regulation yields tiny net benefits, while economic regulation imposes net static costs which are less than 1 per cent of GDP.

106. Even if a regulation yields positive net benefits, it may not be the optimal way of changing economic behaviour.

107. Jacobs (1991) points out that today's contested take-overs are like strikes in as much as when workers lack trust in management they demand rigid work rules which raise labour costs, just as shareholders who are distrustful of managers demand higher rates of return, raising capital costs. However, U.S. shareholders probably have more control over management than do their counterparts in most other countries.

108. Regulation and judicial doctrine are said to have resulted in a fragmented financial-services industry offering a narrow range of services, with banks prevented from owning equity in their clients. As a result, lenders tend not to make as great an effort to work with their debtors in difficult times as in other OECD countries.

109. Witness the decline of the individual investor (institutional holdings rose from 27 per cent of NYSE-listed firms' equity in 1970 to 54 per cent in 1989) and the development of index-related investing which may reduce shareholder surveillance of management performance. Turnover is so rapid (in 1987, the average holding period on all NYSE stocks was less than a year, compared with eight years in the mid-1960s) that the nation's trading costs are now non-trivial – 13 per cent of total after-tax corporate profits in 1987, according to calculations based on data presented in Jacobs (1991). Only one-third of the capital of the 300 largest manufacturing corporations in the United States in January 1988 was provided by relationship-oriented investors, compared to over three-quarters in Japan.

110. CEOs are often exclusively charged with the selection of the board of directors (subject to shareholder ratification), members of which are rarely compensated in the form of stock or stock options. So little is expected of outside directors that corporations routinely provide them with liability insurance in case they are sued by dissatisfied shareholders. Premiums on such policies average over $1.3 million per firm per year (Jacobs, 1991).

111. There is some evidence that firms with legal takeover protection are valued systematically lower by the stock market than others and that firms incorporated in states with such statutes also have lower stock-market valuations. For example, Szewczyk and Tsetsekos (1992) show that listed firms incorporated in Pennsylvania lost over 9 per cent of their value, about $4 billion, as a result of 1990 legislation which limits shareholder proxy power and eliminates the fiduciary obligations of the board of directors to promote shareholder interests. And Schranz (1993) finds that when takeovers are restricted in the banking industry, other mechanisms come into play to provide incentives to maximise firm value, but that

they do not completely compensate for the the lack of an active takeover market. However, Comment and Schwert (1993) find that anti-takeover measures have provided little in the way of deterrence.

112. However, while vast majority of chief executive officers at large firms receive bonuses based on accounting profits rather than stockmarket performance, they are apparently not dissuaded from making investments in R&D, advertising and physical capital (Gibbons and Murphy, 1992).

113. Increases in management's ownership stake in the case of leveraged buy-outs (LBOs) tend to raise productivity growth: Lichtenberg and Siegel (1989) showed that 1 100 manufacturing plants involved in LBOs in the early 1980s had 14 per cent greater total factor productivity growth in the following five years than others in the same industry.

114. The Securities and Exchange Commission also assisted in this process in October 1992 by changing proxy rules and by forcing firms to disclose executive pay practices more fully. Earlier, in 1988, the Labor Department also contributed by requiring pension funds to vote the shares in their portfolios for the exclusive benefit of plan participants. However, while public pension funds are relatively free to engage in activist investing, private funds have been clearly less ambitious, possibly due to host company dissuasion.

115. For example, lawsuits cost the average family in New York City $120 per year in taxes to cover the city's liabilities, more than it pays for parks or libraries. Legal activities are an important part of what has been termed "transaction activities", that is those that are necessary to allocate resources. According to some estimates, the costs of such activities have risen substantially faster than non-transaction output which is what truly contributes to social welfare. This latter concept has grown about ¼ percentage point per year less than traditionally measured output since 1950 (*The Economist,* 1992).

116. According to research by Stephen Magee, there is a negative cross-country correlation between output growth and the share of the population who are lawyers. Lawyers are often the instrument of rent-seeking activities. For example, there were some 23 000 national trade associations in 1989, up from 4 900 in 1956; and while there were 365 paid lobbyists registered with the Senate in 1960, today there are 40 111, although "only" 7 566 are currently "active". In May 1993 the Senate passed the Lobby Disclosure Act, requiring more complete registration of lobbyists and disclosure of their gifts. The negative role of interest groups in the growth process has been emphasised by Olson – see, for example, Olson (1988).

117. Other possible indirect effects are that firms may not terminate poor performers, may expend more resources in the hiring process, may pay more severance payments than is necessary and may make greater recourse to overtime and temporary-agency staff in times of high demand.

118. The highlights of the final deal include: *i)* elimination of all Mexican tariffs and most non-tariff barriers within 10-15 years; *ii)* immediate elimination of tariffs on over $3 billion of agricultural trade and completely free trade in farm products within 15 years; *iii)* substantial easing of Mexican restrictions on entry into the financial services sector by the end of the decade or soon thereafter; *iv)* a guarantee of national treatment on all inward investment in Mexico; and *v)* the possibility of tariff snapbacks to pre-NAFTA levels for the first three

years for most products and four years for certain sensitive items, in the case of serious injury from imports from a NAFTA-partner country, plus special safeguards in agriculture and textile and clothing products.

119. These estimates include substantial dynamic gains from trade. The U.S. International Trade Commission (1991) estimates that the static losses from all U.S. import restraints on manufactures and agricultural products amount to $9.5 billion at 1988 prices. Feenstra (1992) pegs them at $15 to $30 billion and estimates the losses to world welfare from the elimination of half the world's inter-regional trade in a trade war at 2 to 8 per cent.

120. Hufbauer and Schott (1993) are even more optimistic, predicting a net gain of 171 000 jobs by 1995. They are particularly impressed with the NAFTA deal as it applies to the agriculture sector, intellectual property rights and the dispute settlement mechanism.

121. Recourse to such remedies is spreading internationally: among the 25 members of the GATT Anti-dumping Code there were 237 new investigations in the year to mid-1992, compared to 175 in the previous year. Japan and India resorted to this remedy for the first time, and Australia surpassed the United States in the number of new investigations initiated, although the United States still has a much higher number of investigations outstanding.

122. The United States is advocating a Multilateral Steel Agreement in order to deal with the widespread problems of trade distortions such as government subsidies. A previous voluntary restraint arrangement expired as planned in 1992. However, it is not obvious that the U.S. steel industry's problems will be solved by such a trade arrangement: the decline in the market share of integrated producers from 62 to 33 per cent since 1973 is more clearly attributable to competition from mini mills (whose share has risen from 6 to 22 per cent) and "reconstituted mills" (those in Chapter 11 bankruptcy proceedings and those bought out by their management – their share has risen from 20 to 27 per cent) than by imports (whose share rose from 12 to 18 per cent, a level much higher than in the EC or Japan).

123. The ITC turned down a subsequent industry request to vote again on the no-injury findings, but the petitioners still intend to appeal the decisions at the Court of International Trade. In those cases where injury was found, in August 1994 interested parties will have the opportunity to request an administrative review of the order. The administrative review will determine the final amount of the anti-dumping or countervailing duties to be collected and revise the cash deposit rate to represent current levels of selling at less than fair value or subsidies received.

124. This position is supported by the final outcome of the steel cases in which the ITC decisions ran counter to the interests of domestic producers in most cases, despite persistent pressure at the highest level of the domestic industry and Congress. Indeed, in recent decades Congress has removed most Administration discretionary powers in the enforcement of anti-dumping and countervailing duty laws.

125. See Chapter III of the forthcoming OECD Economic Survey of Japan for a detailed look at this question.

126. Indeed, a few years ago fully 40 per cent of all workers receiving the minimum wage were in families with incomes of over $35 000 (in 1987 prices).

References

Adams, James D. (1990), ''Fundamental stocks of knowledge and productivity growth'', *Journal of Political Economy,* 98, 4, August.

Amable, Bruno and Robert Boyer (1992), ''The R&D – Productivity Relationship in the Context of New Growth Theories: Some Recent Applied Research'', xerox, January.

Aschauer, David A. (1989), ''Is Public Expenditure Productive?'', *Journal of Monetary Economics,* 23, March.

Auerbach, Alan, Kevin Hassett and Stephen Oliner (1992), ''Reassessing the social returns to equipment investment'', Working Paper, Federal Reserve Board.

Baily, Martin Neil and Robert J. Gordon (1988), ''The Productivity Slowdown, Measurement Issues, and the Explosion of Computer Power'', *Brookings Papers on Economic Activity,* No. 2.

Baily, Martin Neil, Gary Burtless and Robert E. Litan (1993), *Growth with equity: Economic policymaking for the next century,* Brookings, Washington.

Barro, Robert (1992), ''Human Capital and Economic Growth'', Working Paper, Harvard University, July.

Barro, Robert and Jong-Wha Lee (1993), ''Losers and Winners in Economic Growth'', National Bureau of Economic Research Working Paper No. 4341, April.

Baumol, William J., Sue Anne Batey Blackman and Edward N. Wolff (1989), *Productivity and American Leadership: the Long View,* MIT Press, Cambridge, Massachusetts and London.

Baumol, William J. (1990), ''Entrepreneurship: Productive, Unproductive, and Destructive'', *Journal of Political Economy,* 98, 5, Part 1, October.

Bayoumi, Tamim, Daniel Hewitt and Jerald Schiff (1993), ''Economic Consequences of Lower Military Spending: Some Simulation Results'', IMF Working Paper WP/93/17, March.

Becker, Gary S. and Kevin M. Murphy (1992), ''The Division of Labor, Co-ordination Costs, and Knowledge'', *Quarterly Journal of Economics,* CVII, 4, November.

Bergsten, C. Fred and Marcus Noland (1993), *Reconcilable Differences? U.S.-Japan Economic Conflict,* Institute for International Economics, Washington, June.

Berle, Adolf A. and Gardiner C. Means (1932), *The Modern Corporation and Private Property,* Macmillan, New York.

Berman, Eli, John Bound and Zvi Griliches (1993), ''Changes in the Demand for Skilled Labor within U.S. Manufacturing Industries: Evidence from the Annual Survey of Manufacturing'', National Bureau of Economic Research Working Paper No. 4255, January.

Bernstein, Jeffrey I. and M. Ishaq Nadiri (1991), ''Product Demand, Cost of Production, Spillovers and the Social Rate of Return to R&D'', National Bureau of Economic Research Working Paper No. 3625, February.

Blinder, Alan S. (ed.) (1990), *Paying for Productivity: A Look at the Evidence,* Brookings, Washington.

Clark, Peter and Steve Symansky (1993), ''An analysis of the effects of U.S. fiscal consolidation using MULTIMOD'', IMF working paper prepared for the Project Link meeting in New York, March.

Clinton, William J. and Albert Gore Jr. (1993), ''Technology for America's Economic Growth, A New Direction to Build Economic Strength'', 22 February.

Cohen, Linda R. and Roger G. Noll (1992), ''Research and Development'' in Henry J. Aaron and Charles L. Schultze (eds.), *Setting Domestic Priorities: What Can Government Do?,* Brookings, Washington.

Comment, Robert and G. William Schwert (1993), ''Poison or Placebo? Evidence on the Deterrent and Wealth Effects of Modern Antitakeover Measures'', National Bureau of Economic Research Working Paper No. 4316, April.

Commission of the European Communities (1993), ''Report on United States Trade and Investment Barriers 1993'', Brussels, April.

Committee for Economic Development (1992), *Restoring Prosperity: Budget Choices for Economic Growth,* New York.

Congressional Budget Office (1990), *Using R&D Consortia for Commercial Innovation: Sematech, X-ray Lithography, and High-Resolution Systems,* July.

Congressional Budget Office (1991), *How Federal Spending for Infrastructure and Other Public Investments Affects the Economy,* July.

Congressional Budget Office (1992), *The Economic Effects of Reduced Defense Spending,* February.

Congressional Budget Office (1993*a*), *The Economic and Budget Outlook: Fiscal Years 1994-98,* January.

Congressional Budget Office (1993*b*), *Controlling the Losses of the Pension Benefit Guaranty Corporation,* January.

Congressional Budget Office (1993*c*), ''An Analysis of the President's February Budgetary Proposals'', March.

Congressional Budget Office (1993*d*), *Resolving the Thrift Crisis,* April.

Congressional Budget Office (1993*e*), *Federal Debt and Interest Costs,* May.

Congressional Budget Office (1993*f*), *The Economic and Budget Outlook: An Update,* September.

Currie, Janet and Duncan Thomas (1993), ''Does Head Start Make a Difference?'', National Bureau of Economic Research Working Paper No. 4406, September.

Dean, Edwin (ed.) (1984), *Education and Economic Productivity,* Ballinger, Cambridge, Massachusetts.

Delong, J. Bradford (1988), ''Productivity Growth, Convergence and Welfare: Comment'', *The American Economic Review,* Volume 78, No. 5, December.

DeLong, J. Bradford and Lawrence Summers (1991), ''Equipment Investment and Economic Growth'', *Quarterly Journal of Economics,* CVI, May.

DeLong, J. Bradford and Lawrence Summers (1992), ''Equipment Investment and Economic Growth: How Strong is the Nexus?'', *Brookings Papers on Economic Activity,* No. 2.

Denison, Edward (1985), *Trends in American Economic Growth, 1929-1982,* Brookings, Washington.

Dertouzos, James N., Elaine Holland and Patricia Ebener (1988), *The Legal and Economic Consequences of Wrongful Termination,* Rand Institute for Civil Justice, R-3602-ICJ, Santa Monica, California.

Dertouzos, James N. and Lynn A. Karoly (1992), *Labor-Market Responses to Employer Liability,* Rand Institute for Civil Justice, R-3939-ICJ, Santa Monica, California.

DRI/McGraw-Hill (1993), ''Impacts of Trade Liberalisation under the Uruguay Round'', Study prepared for the Office of the United States Trade Representative, 11 January.

Eberts, Randall W. and Michael S. Fogarty (1987), ''Estimating the Relationship Between Local Public and Private Investment'', Federal Reserve Bank of Cleveland Working Paper No. 8703, May.

Economist (1992), ''America's Parasite Economy'', 10 October.

Eisner, Robert (1993), ''Sense and Nonsense About Budget Deficits'', *Harvard Business Review,* May-June.

Englander, A. Steven and Axel Mittelstadt (1988), ''Total factor productivity: Macroeconomic and structural aspects of the slowdown'', *OECD Economic Studies,* 10, Spring.

Feenstra, Robert C. (1992), ''How Costly is Protectionism?'', *Journal of Economic Perspectives,* 6, 3, Summer.

Fikre, Ted (1991), ''In Brief: Equity Carve-Outs in Tokyo'', *Federal Reserve Bank of New York Quarterly Review,* Winter.

Ford, Robert and Pierre Poret (1991), ''Infrastructure and Private-Sector Productivity'', *OECD Economic Studies,* 17, Autumn.

Fukao, Mitsuhiro (1993), ''International integration of financial markets and the cost of capital'', OECD Economics Department Working Paper No. 128.

Galanter, Marc and Charles R. Epp (1992), ''A beginner's guide to the litigation maze'', *Business Economics,* XXVII, 4, October.

Gibbons, Robert and Kevin J. Murphy (1992), ''Does Executive Compensation Affect Investment?'', National Bureau of Economic Research Working Paper No. 4135, August.

Gordon, Lilli (1993), ''New Deal for Shareholders'', *Wall Street Journal Europe,* 5-6 February.

Goulder, Lawrence and Philippe Thalmann (1990), ''Approaches to Efficient Capital Taxation: Leveling the Playing Field vs. Living by the Golden Rule'', National Bureau of Economic Research Working Paper No. 3559, December.

Gray, Wayne (1987), ''The Cost of Regulation: OSHA, EPA and the Productivity Slowdown'', *American Economic Review,* 77, 5, December.

Gray, Wayne B. and Ronald J. Shadbegian (1993), ''Environmental regulation and manufacturing productivity at the plant level'', National Bureau of Economic Research Working Paper No. 4321, April.

Greenspan, Alan (1993), Speech before the Economics Club of New York, 19 April.

Griliches, Zvi (1990), ''Patent statistics as economic indicators: A survey'', *Journal of Economic Literature,* XXXVIII, 4, December.

Guellec, D. and P. Ralle (1991), ''Endogenous Growth and Product Innovation'', xerox, INSEE/ Commissariat Général au Plan.

Gullickson, William (1992), ''Multifactor Productivity in Manufacturing Industries'', *Monthly Labor Review,* October.

Hahn, Robert W. and John A. Hird (1991), ''The Costs and Benefits of Regulation: Review and Synthesis'', *Yale Journal on Regulation,* 8, 1, Winter.

Hall, Bronwyn H. (1992), ''R&D Tax Policy during the Eighties: Success or Failure?'', National Bureau of Economic Research Working Paper No. 4240, December.

Hall, Bronwyn H. (1993), ''New Evidence on the Impacts of Research and Development'', preliminary draft prepared for the Brookings Panel on Microeconomics, May.

Harris, Ethan, and Charles Steindel (1991), ''The Decline in U.S. Saving and its Implications for Economic Growth'', *Federal Reserve Bank of New York Quarterly Review,* Winter.

Hazilla, Michael and Raymond J. Kopp (1990), ''Social Cost of Environmental Quality Regulations: A General-Equilibrium Analysis'', *Journal of Political Economy,* 98, 4, August.

Helliwell, John *et al.* (1986), ''The supply side in the OECD's Macroeconomic model'', *OECD Economic Studies,* 6, Spring.

Heston, Alan (1993), ''Machinery Investment and Economic Growth'', Working Paper, June.

Hines, James R., Jr. (1991), ''On the sensitivity of R&D to delicate tax changes: The behavior of U.S. multinationals in the 1980s'', National Bureau of Economic Research Working Paper No. 3930, December.

Hood, John (1992), ''Caveat Emptor: The Head Start Scam'', Cato Institute Policy Analysis series no. 187, December.

Hopkins, Thomas D. (1992), ''Costs of Regulation: Filling the Gap'', paper prepared for the Regulatory Information Service Center, Washington, August.

Huber, Peter W. and Robert E. Litan (eds.) (1991), *The Liability Maze: The Impact of Liability Law on Safety and Innovation,* Brookings, Washington.

Hufbauer, Gary Clyde and Jeffrey J. Schott (1993), *NAFTA: An Assessment,* Institute for International Economics, Washington, February.

Ireland, Peter and Christopher Otrok (1992), ''Forecasting the Effects of Reduced Defense Spending'', *Federal Reserve Bank of Richmond Economic Review,* 78, 6, November-December.

Jacobs, Michael T. (1991), *Short-Term America: The Causes and Cures of Our Business Myopia,* Harvard Business School Press, Boston.

Jensen, Michael C. (1991), ''Corporate Control and the Politics of Finance'', *Journal of Applied Corporate Finance,* Vol. 4, No. 2, Summer.

Jones, Charles I. (1992), ''R&D - Based Models of Economic Growth'', xerox, November.

Jorgenson, Dale W. (1991), ''Fragile Statistical Foundations: The Macroeconomics of Public Infrastructure Investment'', paper presented at the American Enterprise Institute Conference on ''Infrastructure Needs and Policy Options for the 1990s'', Washington, 4 February.

Jorgenson, Dale W., F.M. Gollop and Barbara Fraumeni (1987), *Productivity and U.S. Economic Growth,* Harvard University Press, Cambridge, Massachusetts.

Jorgenson, Dale W. and P.J. Wilcoxen (1990), ''Environmental Regulation and U.S. Economic Growth'', *Rand Journal of Economics,* 21, 2, Summer.

Katz, Lawrence F. and Bruce D. Meyer (1990), ''The Impact of Potential Duration of Unemployment Benefits on the Duration of Unemployment'', *Journal of Public Economics,* 41, 1, February.

Kennedy, Paul (1987), *The Rise and Fall of the Great Powers,* Random House, New York.

Kester, W. Carl and Timothy A. Luehrman (1991), ''The price of risk in the United States and Japan'', *Japan and the World Economy,* 3, 3.

Kosters, Marvin (1993), ''The Earned Income Tax Credit and the Working Poor'', *American Enterprise,* 4, 3, May/June.

Kotlikoff, Laurence (1992), *Generational Accounting: Knowing Who Pays, and When, For What We Spend,* Free Press.

Krugman, Paul (1991), ''Myths and Realities of United States Competitiveness'', *Science,* 254, 5033.

Krugman, Paul R. (1992), ''Technology and International Competition: A Historical Perspective'', in Martha Caldwell Harris and Gordon E. Moore (eds.), *Linking Trade and Technology Policies: An International Comparison of the Policies of Industrialized Nations,* National Academy of Engineering, Washington.

Kruse, Douglas L. (1992), ''Profit sharing and productivity: Microeconomic evidence from the United States'', *Economic Journal,* 102, January.

Leamer, Edward E. and Chauncey J. Medberry (1993), ''U.S. Manufacturing and an Emerging Mexico'', National Bureau of Economic Research Working Paper No. 4331, April.

Lebow, David E., John M. Roberts and David J. Stockton (1992), ''Economic Performance Under Price Stability'', Board of Governors of the Federal Reserve System, Division of Research and Statistics, Economic Activity Section Working Paper No. 125, April.

Lee, Thomas H. and Proctor P. Reid (eds.) (1991), *National interests in an age of global technology,* National Academy of Engineering, National Academy Press, Washington.

Levy, Frank and Richard Murnane (1992), ''Education and Training'', in Henry J. Aaron and Charles L. Schultze (eds.), *Setting Domestic Priorities: What Can Government Do?,* Brookings, Washington.

Lichtenberg, Frank and Donald Siegel (1989), ''The Effects of Leveraged Buyouts on Productivity and Related Aspects of Firm Behaviour'', National Bureau of Economic Research Working Paper No. 3022, June.

Lichtenberg, Frank R. (1992), ''R&D Investment and International Productivity Differences'', National Bureau of Economic Research Working Paper No. 4161, September.

Lipsey, Richard and Irving Kravis (1988), ''Is the United States Losing the Economic Race?'', *US Long-Term Economic Outlook,* The Conference Board, New York.

Lundquist, Jerrold T. (1993), ''The Myth of Defense Conversion'', *Wall Street Journal Europe,* 29 March.

MaCurdy, Thomas (1992), ''Work Disincentive Effects of Taxes: A Re-examination of Some Evidence'', *American Economics Association Papers and Proceedings,* 82, 2, May.

Maddison, Angus (1991), ''Standardised estimates of fixed investment and capital stock at constant prices in 6 countries'', working paper, University of Groningen.

Mansfield, Edwin (1986), ''The R&D Tax Credit and Other Technology Policy Issues'', *American Economic Association Papers and Proceedings,* 76, 2, May.

Mansfield, Edwin (1988), ''Industrial R&D in Japan and the United States: A Comparative Study'', *American Economics Association, Papers and Proceedings,* 78, 2, May.

McCauley, Robert N. and Steven A. Zimmer (1992), ''Exchange rates and international differences in the cost of capital'', paper presented to Conference on Exchange Rate Effects on Corporate Financial Performance and Strategies, New York University Stern School of Business, 1 May.

McKibbin, Warwick J. and Philip Bagnoli (1993), ''Fiscal Deficit Reduction: An Evaluation of Alternatives'', Brookings Discussion Papers in International Economics No. 101, July.

McKinsey Global Institute (1992), *Service Sector Productivity,* Washington, October.

Mills, Edwin (1987), ''Has the U.S. Overinvested in Housing?'', *American Real Estate and Urban Economics Association Journal,* 15, 1, Spring.

Morrison, Catherine J. and Ernst R. Berndt (1991), ''Assessing the Productivity of Information Technology Equipment in U.S. Manufacturing Industries'', National Bureau of Economic Research Working Paper No. 3582, January.

Morrison, Steven A. and Clifford Winston (1989), ''Enhancing the Performance of the Deregulated Air Transporation System'', *Brookings Papers on Economic Activity: Microeconomics 1989,* Brookings, Washington.

Munnell, Alicia H. (1993), ''An Assessment of Trends in and Economics Impacts of Infrastructure Investment'' in *Infrastructure Policies for the 1990s,* OECD, Paris.

Nadiri, Ishaq M. and Theofanis P. Mamuneas (1991), ''The Effects of Public Infrastructure and R&D Capital on the Cost Structure and Performance of U.S. Manufacturing Industries'', National Bureau of Economic Research Working Paper No. 3887, October.

National Science Board (1991), *Science and Engineering Indicators – 1991,* Washington.

Nelson, Richard R. and Gavin Wright (1992), ''The Rise and Fall of American Technological Leadership'', *Journal of Economic Literature,* XXX, 4, December.

OECD (1991*a*), *Employment Outlook,* July.

OECD (1991*b*), *Economic Surveys 1990/1991 United States,* November.

OECD (1992*a*), *Education at a Glance,* Centre for Educational Research and Innovation.

OECD (1992*b*), *Economic Surveys 1991/1992 France,* June.

OECD (1993*a*), *Agricultural Policies, Markets and Trade: Monitoring and Outlook 1993,* June.

OECD (1993*b*), ''Investment, Innovation and Competitiveness: Sectoral Performance within the Triad'', Directorate for Science, Technology and Industry, Economic Analysis and Statistics Division, unpublished.

OECD (1993*c*), ''Medium Term Productivity Performance: Trends and Underlying Determinants'', forthcoming.

Office of Management and Budget (1993*a*), *Budget Baselines, Historical Data, and Alternatives for the Future,* January.

Office of Management and Budget (1993*b*), *A Vision of Change for America,* 17 February.

Office of Management and Budget (1993*c*), *Budget of the United States Government, Fiscal Year 1994,* April.

Office of Management and Budget (1993*d*), *Mid-Session Review of the 1994 Budget,* September.

Olson, Mancur (1988), ''The productivity slowdown, the oil shocks, and the real cycle'', *Journal of Economic Perspectives,* 2, 4, Fall.

Osborne, David and Ted Gaebler (1992), *Re-inventing government,* Addison-Wesley, New York.

Papke, Leslie E. (1993), ''What do we know about enterprise zones?'', National Bureau of Economic Research Working Paper No. 4251, January.

Porter, Michael E. (1992), ''Capital Disadvantage: America's Failing Capital Investment System'', *Harvard Business Review,* 70, 5 September-October.

Poterba, James M. (1991), ''Comparing the cost of capital in the United States and Japan: A Survey of methods'', *Federal Reserve Bank of New York Quarterly Review,* 15, Winter.

Reich, Robert B. (1990), ''Who is Us?'', *Harvard Business Review,* 68, 1, January-February.

Report of the Secretary of Transportation to the United States Congress (1993), *The Status of the Nation's Highways, Bridges, and Transit: Conditions and Performance,* January.

Roach, Stephen S. (1988), ''Technology and the Services Sector: America's Hidden Competitive Challenge'' in Bruce R. Guile and James Brian Quinn (eds.), *Technology in Services: Policies for Growth, Trade and Employment,* National Academy of Engineering, Washington.

Roach, Stephen S. (1993*a*), ''Making Technology Work'', Morgan Stanley Special Economic Study, 16 April.

Roach, Stephen (1993*b*), ''Inside the U.S. Economy'', Morgan Stanley U.S. Investment Research, New York, 21 May.

Roe, Mark J. (1991), ''Takeover Politics'', Brookings Discussion Paper in Economics No. 91-4, September.

Romer, Paul M. (1986), ''Increasing returns and long-run growth'', *Journal of Political Economy,* 94, 5, October.

Saunders, Norman C. (1993), ''Employment effects of the rise and fall in defense spending'', *Monthly Labor Review,* 116, 4, April.

Schranz, Mary S. (1993), ''Takeovers Improve Firm Performance: Evidence from the Banking Industry'', *Journal of Political Economy,* 101, 2, April.

Slemrod, Joel (1992), ''Do Taxes Matter? Lessons from the 1980s'', *American Economics Association Papers and Proceedings,* 82, 2, May.

Small, Kenneth A., Clifford Winston and Carol A. Evans (1989), *Road Work: A New Highway Pricing and Investment Policy,* Brookings, Washington.

Solow, Robert M. (1956), ''A contribution to the theory of economic growth'', *Quarterly Journal of Economics,* 70.

Steindel, Charles (1992), ''Manufacturing productivity and high-tech investment'', *Federal Reserve Bank of New York Quarterly Review,* 17, 2, Summer.

Szewczyk, Samuel H. and George T. Tsetsekos (1992), ''State intervention in the market for corporate control: The case of Pennsylvania Senate Bill 1310'', *Journal of Financial Economics,* 31, 1, February.

Tyson, Laura d'Andrea (1992), *Who's Bashing Whom? Trade Conflict in High Technology Industries,* Institute for International Economics, Washington.

Viscusi, W. Kip and Michael J. Moore (1993), ''Product Liability, Research and Development, and Innovation'', *Journal of Political Economy,* 101, 1, February.

U.S. Congress, Joint Committee on Taxation (1992), *Discussion of Revenue Estimation Methodology and Process,* JCS-14-92, 13 August.

U.S. Congress, Office of Technology Assessment (1992*a*), *After the Cold War: Living with Lower Defense Spending,* February.

U.S. Congress, Office of Technology Assessment (1992*b*), *U.S.-Mexico Trade: Pulling Together or Pulling Apart?,* Washington, October.

U.S. Department of Commerce (1993), ''1993 Annual Review of Industrial Policies and the Situation in Industry - United States'', xerox.

U.S. Department of Defense (1992), *Adjusting to the Drawdown,* Report of the Defense Conversion Commission, 31 December.

U.S. Environmental Protection Agency (1990), *Environmental Investments: The Cost of a Clean Environment,* December.

U.S. General Accounting Office (1991), *Canadian Health Insurance,* GAO/HRD-91-90.

U.S. International Trade Commission (1991), ''The Economic Effects of Significant U.S. Import Restraints, Phase III: Services'', Report to the Committee on Finance of the United States Senate, USITC Publication 2422, September.

U.S. International Trade Commission (1992), ''Economy-Wide Modeling of the Economic Implications of a FTA with Mexico and a NAFTA with Canada and Mexico'', USITC Publication 2516, Washington, May.

Zuckman, Jill (1993*a*), ''Clinton School Reform Program Has High Hopes, Low Funds'', *Congressional Quarterly,* 24 April.

Zuckman, Jill (1993*b*), ''Funding Fights to Dominate in Chapter 1 Rewrite'', *Congressional Quarterly,* 8 May.

Annex

Calendar of main economic events

1992

July

The Federal Reserve Board lowers its discount rate from 3½ per cent to 3 per cent, the lowest level for 29 years. In response, major banks reduce their prime lending rate from 6½ per cent to 6 per cent.

Congress passes a bill which extends unemployment benefits after exhaustion of the regular 6 months for a further 20-26 weeks.

Congress adopts, with only minor changes, a resolution calling for tax cuts of $31 billion to stimulate the economy.

August

Subject to ratification by all three legislatures, Trade Ministers sign the North American Free Trade Agreement (NAFTA), effectively incorporating Mexico in the existing free trade pact between the United States and Canada.

Following extensive damage caused by Hurricane Andrew, the President declares Florida and parts of Louisiana a disaster area, thus releasing low-interest loans and federal assistance. Total damage is estimated to exceed $20 billion, of which about $7.3 billion is insured.

September

The Federal Reserve Board adopts new rules which, with effect from 19th December, will allow regulators to close banks if they have less than 2 per cent core capital and fail to strengthen their financial position within 90 days.

The Federal Deposit Insurance Corporation leaves its premium at 0.23 per cent of deposits for the healthiest institutions, but installs, with effect from 1st January 1993, a sliding scale, rising to 0.31 per cent for the weakest banks.

Congress approves a record $11.1 billion relief package to aid victims of the recent hurricanes in Florida and Louisiana (Andrew), Hawaii and Guam (Iniki); $6.3 billion is provided in direct assistance and $4.8 billion in loans.

October

Congress endorses an energy bill aimed at reducing consumption by 6 per cent by 2010 and encouraging a switch to alternative sources. *Inter alia,* the bill requires central and local government and firms with large vehicle fleets to run 3/4 of their fleet on alternative energy by 1999, energy-saving heating and air-conditioning systems to be offered to the public, and tax incentives to encourage energy saving or conversion. In order to finance these reforms, the use of ozone-reducing chemicals will be heavily taxed and tax rates on lottery gains over $5 000 and on dividends will be raised from 20 to 28 and 31 per cent respectively.

November

The United States and the European Community reach agreement whereby the Community is to reduce the volume of subsidised farm exports by 38 per cent reduction from the 1992 level, cut export subsidies by 36 per cent and limit land use for oilseed production.

The United States imposes provisional duties, ranging from 1 to 59 per cent on imports of flat-rolled steel from 12 countries, six of which are EC members.

December

U.S. and EC negotiators sign two documents which embody the political agreement reached on oilseeds and farm trade; subsequently, the United States formally withdraws the additional duties which were to take effect on 5th December.

As a further step towards ratification, the Presidents of the United States and Mexico and the Prime Minister of Canada formally sign the North American Free Trade Agreement.

1993

January

The outgoing Administration presents updated budget forecasts for the next 5 fiscal years (October 1992 to September 1997), projecting deficits of $327, 270, 230, 266 and 305 billion respectively.

The newly elected President notifies Congress that he will not set fixed budget deficit targets, since, under the Gramm-Rudman law, spending cuts of up to $50 billion would otherwise be required in the next 10 months.

In response to complaints from U.S. steelmakers, the Commerce Department imposes provisional duties of up to 109 per cent on steel imports (worth $2 billion) from 19 countries accused of dumping certain steel products on the U.S. market. To become permanent the duties need to be confirmed by the International Trade Commission.

February

President Clinton signs the Family Leave Act, which was twice vetoed in the Bush administration.

The President announces a 25 per cent reduction in the White House staff and a salary cut of 6 to 10 per cent for the remaining 1 044 employees, to take effect by 1st October. The following day he orders federal departments, over the next 4 years, to reduce their staff by 100 000 (from the present 3 million) and cut managerial costs by 3 per cent, saving an estimated $9 billion.

The President presents the proposed federal budget for fiscal 1994 (starting 1st October 1993). For the period 1993-97 the economic plan envisages gross increases in revenue of $246 billion and gross expenditure savings amounting to $247 billion, so that the deficit is projected to decline from $332 billion in fiscal 1993 (5.4 per cent of GDP) to $262 billion the following year and to $206 billion by 1997 (2.7 per cent of GDP).

In his semiannual congressional testimony the Federal Reserve Chairman reports that the Federal Open Market Committee has lowered the preliminary monetary aggregate growth targets for 1993 by ½ percentage point for both M2 and M3 (2 to 6 per cent and ½ to 4½ per cent respectively) but has left the target for domestic non-financial debt (4½ to 8½ per cent) unchanged.

Yen rises to record level against the dollar following comments by the U.S. Treasury Secretary to the effect that a stronger yen/dollar exchange rate would be desirable.

March

The Administration announces a $19.6 billion 4-year programme (including $1.4 billion allocated by Congress last year) to assist workers and communities affected by defence cuts and base closures, offering retraining, investment and development incentives as well as factory conversion.

Following violent tornadoes and heavy blizzards, the State of Florida requests federal disaster assistance and states of emergency are declared in ten other states.

Federal regulators ease lending requirements, effective immediately, for highly rated and adequately capitalised banks and thrifts. About 10 000 institutions are affected and $46 billion in credit is expected to be made available.

The House of Representatives and the Senate pass the $1 500 billion fiscal 1994 budget resolution, which envisages a reduction in the deficit by a total of $496 billion over the next 5 years. The following day the Administration agrees to exempt certain fuels from its planned energy tax.

Partial agreement is reached between the United States and the EC in the trade dispute over public procurement contracts. Agreement is not reached, however, over purchases of telecommunications. On 30th April the United States announces sanctions against Japan and several other countries over similar public procurement contracts for construction and supercomputers; the sanctions are to be imposed within 60 days if the issue remains unresolved.

Following the abandonment of the $16.3 billion stimulus plan, a bill providing $4 billion for extended unemployment benefits is passed and signed into law.

May

To cut debt servicing costs, the Treasury is to reduce the number of 30-year bond offerings by 40 per cent to about $22 billion annually. 7-year bond offerings are also to be abolished, making 10-year government bonds the benchmark funding instrument as in most other major industrialised countries.

Broadly following the House of Representatives' approval in April, the Senate approves $18.3 billion for the Resolution Trust Corporation (RTC) but only $8.5 billion for the Federal Deposit Insurance Corporation to complete the bailout of the thrift industry. In addition, the RTC is to close one year ahead of schedule, on 31st December 1995.

The Administration is asked by the U.S. Supreme Court for its opinion on whether to hear a challenge to California's unitary taxation system. The U.K. Government has threatened retaliatory measures if the long-running dispute is not resolved by the end of the year.

A drastically scaled-down version of the defeated stimulus plan is passed by the House of Representatives, freeing $930 million for, *inter alia,* summer jobs, stipends to poor youths and waste water treatment. The same day the House approves the bill calling for a reduction in the federal budget by $343 billion over the next 5 years, through increased revenue of $275 billion and spending cuts of $68 billion.

June

The Senate passes by 50 to 49 the budget reconciliation bill, preserving the broad outline of the President's deficit-reduction package. However, the Senate version contains more spending cuts than the House version, and a scaled-down gasoline tax, rather than the House version's BTU tax.

July

The United States and Japan reach a trade agreement, establishing a framework for future negotiations, including biannual meetings of the heads of government. Japan promises to achieve, in the "medium-term" (left undefined), a significant increase in imports and decrease of its current-account surplus. The United States promised to reduce the fiscal deficit and promote domestic savings. Consultations will also address foreign direct investment, intellectual property rights, access to technology and long-term buyer-supplier relationships in each country. Non-economic discussions will focus on the environment, technology, human resources development, population growth and AIDS.

Widespread flooding along the Mississippi and Missouri rivers creates damage estimated at about $10 billion. The Administration offers an initial $2.48 billion package of aid to the flooded Midwest.

While downplaying the policy role for the monetary aggregates, the Federal Open Market Committee lowers the 1993 target range for M2 growth by 1 per cent (to 1 to

5 per cent), and lowers the range for M3 by 1/2 per cent (to 0 to 4 per cent). These are also the preliminary targets for 1994. The target range for growth of non-financial debt is lowered by 1/2 per cent, to 4 to 8 per cent.

The International Trade Commission rules that steel imports did not injure U.S. producers in over half of 74 cases, effectively invalidating duties imposed on steel from over 20 nations.

August

The Omnibus Budget Reconciliation Act is passed by Congress and signed by President Clinton, paving the way for some $500 billion in deficit reduction over five years. The final version of the bill called for among other things a rise in the corporate tax rate from 34 to 35 per cent, a personal tax increase for high-income Americans, a 4.3 cent gasoline tax increase, as well as gross cuts in federal spending amounting to more than $300 billion over the next five years.

September

The Administration releases its report on the National Performance Review, with proposals to reduce waste by the executive branch, cut federal costs, trim staff and generally "reinvent government".

President Clinton signs side agreements to the NAFTA, and an appeals court rules that a new environmental impact analysis of NAFTA is not required before Congress votes on the pact.

The outline of the Administration's health care plan is unveiled in a speech by President Clinton to a joint session of Congress. The proposal would extend health care coverage to all Americans, requiring all employers to provide basic health insurance to their employees, and pay 80 per cent of the premium cost. Under the plan, cigarette taxes and reduced inefficiencies would pay the remaining costs, which would result in part from subsidies to small businesses and low-income households.

STATISTICAL ANNEX

Selected background statistics

	Average 1983-92	1983	1984	1985	1986	1987	1988	1989	1990	1991	1992
A. Percentage change from previous year at constant 1987 prices											
Private consumption	2.9	4.6	4.8	4.4	3.6	2.8	3.6	1.9	1.5	–0.4	2.6
Gross fixed capital formation	2.8	6.6	15.9	5.0	0.4	–0.5	4.2	0.1	–1.8	–7.7	6.2
Residential	5.7	40.4	14.4	1.3	12.0	–0.4	–1.1	–3.8	–9.2	–12.8	16.3
Non-residential	2.2	–3.0	16.5	6.4	–4.1	–0.5	6.6	1.7	1.2	–5.9	2.9
GDP	2.9	3.9	6.2	3.2	2.9	3.1	3.9	2.5	1.2	–0.7	2.6
GDP price deflator	3.8	4.1	4.5	3.6	2.7	3.2	3.9	4.5	4.3	3.9	2.9
Industrial production	2.7	3.6	9.4	1.7	0.9	5.0	4.4	1.5	0.0	–1.8	2.4
Employment	1.7	1.3	4.1	2.0	2.3	2.6	2.3	2.0	0.5	–0.9	0.6
Compensation of employees (current prices)	6.5	5.9	9.7	7.0	5.9	6.9	8.3	6.1	6.4	3.2	5.3
Productivity (GDP/employment)[1]	1.1	3.3	1.8	0.5	1.2	0.4	0.8	0.1	–0.1	0.2	3.0
Unit labour costs (compensation/GDP)	3.5	2.0	3.3	3.7	2.9	3.7	4.2	3.5	5.1	3.9	2.6
B. Percentage ratios											
Gross fixed capital formation as per cent of GDP at constant prices	15.7	15.2	16.6	16.9	16.5	15.9	16.0	15.6	15.1	14.1	14.6
Stockbuilding as per cent of GDP at constant prices	0.4	0.1	1.6	0.5	0.2	0.6	0.4	0.6	0.1	–0.2	0.0
Foreign balance as per cent of GDP at constant prices	–2.0	–1.4	–2.9	–3.4	–3.5	–3.1	–2.2	–1.5	–1.1	–0.4	–0.7
Compensation of employees as per cent of GDP at current prices	59.3	59.6	59.0	59.0	59.1	59.4	59.6	59.0	59.5	59.5	59.3
Direct taxes as per cent of household income	12.0	11.9	11.6	12.0	11.8	12.5	11.9	12.5	12.3	11.8	11.6
Household saving as per cent of disposable income	5.5	6.9	8.3	6.6	6.2	4.5	4.5	4.1	4.3	4.9	5.0
Unemployment as per cent of total labour force	6.8	9.6	7.5	7.2	7.0	6.2	5.5	5.3	5.5	6.7	7.4
C. Other indicator											
Current balance (billion dollars)	–97.7	–43.6	–98.8	–121.7	–150.2	–167.3	–127.2	–101.6	–91.9	–8.3	–66.4

1. Ratio of business sector GDP to business sector employment.
Sources: US Department of Commerce, Survey of Current Business and OECD.

Table A. **National product and expenditure**

Seasonally adjusted, percentage changes from previous period, annual rates, 1987 prices

	Average 1982-92	1982	1983	1984	1985	1986	1987	1988	1989	1990	1991	1992
Private consumption	2.8	1.1	4.6	4.8	4.4	3.6	2.8	3.6	1.9	1.5	–0.4	2.6
Public expenditure	2.6	1.5	2.8	3.1	6.1	5.2	3.0	0.6	2.0	3.1	1.5	–0.1
Gross fixed investment	1.9	–8.0	6.6	15.9	5.0	0.4	–0.5	4.2	0.1	–1.8	–7.7	6.2
Residential	3.5	–18.1	40.4	14.4	1.3	12.0	–0.4	–1.1	–3.8	–9.2	–12.8	16.3
Non-residential	1.6	–4.6	–3.0	16.5	6.4	–4.1	–0.5	6.6	1.7	1.2	–5.9	2.9
Final domestic demand	2.6	–0.3	4.6	6.2	4.8	3.4	2.3	3.1	1.7	1.3	–1.2	2.5
Stockbuilding[1]	–0.0	–1.1	0.6	1.6	–1.1	–0.3	0.4	–0.1	0.2	–0.5	–0.3	0.3
Total domestic demand	2.5	–1.4	5.2	7.8	3.6	3.0	2.7	3.0	1.8	0.8	–1.4	2.9
Exports of goods and services	5.6	–9.0	–3.6	6.9	1.2	6.6	10.5	15.8	11.9	8.2	6.4	6.4
Imports of goods and services	6.8	0.0	12.5	25.0	6.3	6.6	4.6	3.7	3.8	3.6	–0.5	8.7
Foreign balance[1]	–0.2	–0.8	–1.3	–1.7	–0.6	–0.2	0.3	0.9	0.6	0.4	0.7	–0.3
GDP	2.4	–2.2	3.9	6.2	3.2	2.9	3.1	3.9	2.5	1.2	–0.7	2.6

	1992 levels (1987 $ billions)	1990	1991				1992				1993	
		Q4	Q1	Q2	Q3	Q4	Q1	Q2	Q3	Q4	Q1	Q2
Private consumption	3 341.8	–2.7	–2.8	1.8	1.3	0.0	4.3	1.8	4.2	5.6	0.8	3.2
Public expenditure	945.2	5.8	2.8	1.4	–2.0	–4.7	3.0	–1.0	4.1	–1.4	–6.4	4.3
Gross fixed investment	726.4	–12.2	–16.4	–1.8	1.0	0.8	6.9	16.9	3.1	14.0	10.7	7.8
Residential	197.2	–24.3	–25.5	1.2	17.3	20.3	16.8	21.8	1.2	32.8	1.5	–8.4
Non-residential	529.2	–7.7	–13.2	–2.7	–3.8	–5.1	3.5	15.1	3.8	7.6	14.4	14.4
Final domestic demand	5 013.4	–2.6	–3.8	1.2	0.6	–0.8	4.4	3.3	4.0	5.5	0.8	4.1
Stockbuilding[1]	6.5	–0.6	0.1	–0.1	0.4	0.2	–0.2	0.4	–0.1	0.0	0.4	–0.3
Total domestic demand	5 019.9	–5.1	–3.6	0.8	2.4	–0.1	3.4	4.7	3.8	5.4	2.5	2.8
Exports of goods and services	578.0	9.6	–0.8	19.4	3.0	13.3	4.9	–0.6	6.5	8.8	–2.4	4.8
Imports of goods and services	611.6	–9.1	–11.1	11.7	11.8	6.3	3.8	15.9	9.2	5.6	11.6	13.1
Foreign balance[1]	–33.6	0.5	0.3	0.2	–0.2	0.2	0.0	–0.5	–0.1	0.1	–0.4	–0.3
GDP	4 986.3	–3.2	–2.4	1.5	1.4	0.6	3.5	2.8	3.4	5.7	0.8	1.8

1. Changes as a percentage of previous period GDP.
Source: US Department of Commerce, Survey of Current Business.

Table B. **Labour Market (s.a.)**

	1984	1985	1986	1987	1988	1989	1990	1991	1992	1992 Q2	1992 Q3	1992 Q4	1993 Q1	1993 Q2
1. Number of persons, millions														
Population of working age[1,2]	176.4	178.2	180.6	182.8	184.6	186.4	188.0	189.8	191.6	191.3	191.8	192.3	192.8	193.3
Civilian labour force[1]	113.5	115.5	117.8	119.9	121.7	123.9	124.8	125.3	127.0	127.0	127.3	127.3	127.3	127.9
Unemployment[1]	8.5	8.3	8.2	7.4	6.7	6.5	6.9	8.4	9.4	9.5	9.6	9.3	8.9	8.9
Employment[1]	105.0	107.2	109.6	112.4	115.0	117.3	117.9	116.9	117.6	117.5	117.7	118.0	118.4	119.0
Employment[3]	94.5	97.5	99.5	102.2	105.5	108.3	109.4	108.3	108.5	108.4	108.6	108.9	109.4	110.0
Federal government	2.8	2.9	2.9	2.9	3.0	3.0	3.1	3.0	3.0	3.0	3.0	3.0	2.9	2.9
State and local	13.2	13.5	13.8	14.1	14.4	14.8	15.2	15.4	15.7	15.6	15.7	15.8	15.8	15.9
Manufacturing	19.4	19.3	19.0	19.0	19.3	19.4	19.1	18.5	18.0	18.1	18.0	17.9	17.9	17.8
Construction	4.4	4.7	4.8	5.0	5.1	5.2	5.1	4.7	4.5	4.5	4.5	4.5	4.5	4.6
Other	54.7	57.2	59.0	61.2	63.7	65.9	66.9	66.7	67.4	67.2	67.5	67.8	68.2	68.8
2. Percentage change from previous period (s.a.a.r.)														
Population of working age[1,2]	1.2	1.0	1.3	1.2	1.0	1.0	0.9	0.9	1.0	0.9	1.0	1.1	1.0	1.0
Civilian labour force	1.8	1.7	2.1	1.7	1.5	1.8	0.8	0.4	1.3	2.5	1.0	–0.0	–0.2	1.9
Employment[1]	4.1	2.0	2.3	2.6	2.3	2.0	0.5	–0.9	0.6	1.5	0.7	1.0	1.2	2.1
Employment[3]	4.8	3.2	2.1	2.7	3.3	2.6	1.0	–1.1	0.2	1.3	0.8	1.1	1.9	2.0
Federal government	1.2	2.4	0.8	1.5	0.9	0.6	3.3	–3.9	0.1	–0.7	–2.0	–1.5	–1.3	–4.1
State and local government	0.9	2.3	2.0	2.0	2.5	2.6	2.9	1.4	1.6	1.9	2.7	1.4	0.9	1.8
Manufacturing	5.1	–0.6	–1.5	0.3	1.7	0.5	–1.7	–3.5	–2.2	–1.0	–2.1	–2.0	0.6	–2.7
Construction	11.1	6.7	3.1	3.1	2.9	1.5	–1.2	–9.2	–3.9	–0.4	–2.4	0.7	1.9	6.5
Other	5.3	4.5	3.3	3.6	4.1	3.5	1.4	–0.2	0.9	1.9	1.5	2.0	2.6	3.3
3. Unemployment rates														
Total	7.5	7.2	7.0	6.2	5.5	5.3	5.5	6.7	7.4	7.5	7.5	7.3	7.0	7.0
Married men	4.6	4.3	4.4	3.9	3.2	3.1	3.4	4.4	5.0	5.0	5.2	4.9	4.6	4.5
Females	7.6	7.4	7.1	6.2	5.6	5.4	5.5	6.3	6.9	7.0	7.1	6.9	6.7	6.6
Youths	18.9	18.6	18.4	16.9	15.3	15.0	15.5	18.7	20.0	20.7	20.3	19.4	19.6	20.1
4. Activity rate[4]	59.5	60.1	60.7	61.5	62.3	62.9	62.7	61.6	61.4	61.4	61.4	61.4	61.4	61.6

1. Household survey.
2. Non-institutional population aged 16 and over.
3. Non-agricultural payroll.
4. Employment as percentage of population aged from 16 to 64.

Source: Department of Labor, Monthly Labor Review.

Table C. **Costs and prices**

Percentage changes from previous period, s.a.a.r.

	1984	1985	1986	1987	1988	1989	1990	1991	1992	1992			1993	
										Q2	Q3	Q4	Q1	Q2
Rates of pay														
Major wage settlements [1]	3.7	3.2	2.3	3.1	2.6	3.2	3.5	3.5	3.0	4.0	4.0	1.6	2.0	3.6
Hourly earnings index [2]	3.7	3.0	2.3	2.5	3.3	4.0	3.7	3.1	2.5	1.9	2.7	2.5	2.9	1.7
Wages and salaries per person	5.3	4.6	4.1	4.6	4.8	3.4	4.7	3.4	5.7	4.2	4.4	16.8	–15.8	12.8
Compensation per person	5.4	4.9	3.6	4.2	5.9	4.0	5.8	4.1	4.6	4.3	4.5	5.2	4.0	2.6
Productivity, non-farm business														
Hourly	2.1	0.9	2.0	0.8	0.9	–0.9	0.5	1.1	3.2	2.9	3.6	4.3	–1.7	–1.4
Per employee	3.3	0.1	0.8	1.4	1.2	–1.0	–0.4	–0.2	2.5	2.1	3.4	4.9	–1.0	0.9
Unit labour cost, non-farm business	1.9	3.3	3.0	2.5	3.3	4.3	5.0	3.9	2.0	1.8	2.4	0.6	4.5	2.9
Prices														
GDP deflator	4.5	3.6	2.7	3.2	3.9	4.5	4.3	3.9	2.9	2.8	1.2	3.3	3.6	2.3
Private consumption deflator	4.0	3.9	3.1	4.2	4.2	4.9	5.1	4.3	3.3	3.6	1.5	4.0	3.0	2.5
Consumer price index	4.3	3.5	1.9	3.7	4.1	4.8	5.4	4.2	3.0	3.3	3.2	2.9	3.4	3.1
Food	3.9	2.3	3.2	4.2	4.1	5.8	5.8	2.9	1.2	0.6	1.3	2.1	2.9	2.6
Wholesale prices	2.4	–0.5	–2.9	2.6	4.0	5.0	3.6	0.2	0.6	4.4	2.4	–0.1	1.8	3.9
Crude products	2.2	–7.5	–8.4	6.7	2.5	7.4	5.7	–7.0	–0.8	12.4	3.5	–0.1	1.1	12.3
Intermediate products	2.5	–0.4	–3.5	2.4	5.5	4.6	2.2	–0.0	0.2	4.1	3.7	–1.8	1.9	2.7
Finished products	2.1	0.9	–1.4	2.1	2.5	5.1	4.9	2.1	1.2	3.8	1.2	1.6	1.4	3.7

1. Total effective wage adjustment in all industries under collective agreements in non-farm industry covering at least 1 000 workers, not seasonally adjusted.
2. Production or non-supervisory workers on private non-agricultural payrolls.

Sources: Department of Labor, Bureau of Labor Statistics, Monthly Labor Review; US Department of Commerce, Survey of Current Business.

Table D. **Monetary Indicators**

	1984	1985	1986	1987	1988	1989	1990	1991	1992	1992			1993	
										Q2	Q3	Q4	Q1	Q2
Monetary aggregates (percentage changes from previous period s.a.a.r)														
M1	7.1	9.0	13.5	11.6	4.3	1.0	3.7	6.0	12.4	11.0	12.2	17.8	6.7	10.9
M2	8.2	8.9	8.2	6.6	5.2	3.9	5.3	3.1	2.0	0.3	0.9	2.8	–1.8	2.2
M3	10.3	8.9	8.2	6.9	6.4	4.5	2.6	1.6	0.5	–0.6	0.1	–0.1	–3.6	2.6
Velocity of circulation														
GDP/M1	7.0	6.9	6.4	6.1	6.3	6.7	6.8	6.7	6.3	6.3	6.2	6.1	6.1	6.0
GDP/M2	1.7	1.6	1.6	1.6	1.6	1.7	1.7	1.7	1.7	1.7	1.7	1.8	1.8	1.8
GDP/M3	1.3	1.3	1.3	1.3	1.3	1.3	1.4	1.4	1.4	1.4	1.5	1.5	1.5	1.5
Federal Reserve Bank reserves ($ billion)														
Non-borrowed	22.3	27.8	33.6	38.6	37.8	38.7	39.9	42.7	50.0	49.1	50.1	53.5	54.8	56.3
Borrowed	3.7	1.3	0.8	0.8	2.4	1.1	0.9	0.4	0.2	0.2	0.3	0.1	0.1	0.1
Total	26.1	29.1	34.5	39.4	40.1	39.8	40.9	43.1	50.2	49.3	50.4	53.7	54.9	56.4
Required	25.4	28.3	33.5	38.4	39.1	38.9	39.9	41.9	49.2	48.3	49.5	52.6	53.7	55.4
Excess	0.7	0.8	0.9	1.0	1.0	1.0	1.0	1.2	1.0	1.0	1.0	1.1	1.2	1.0
Free (excess – borrowed)	–3.1	–0.5	0.1	0.3	–1.3	–0.2	0.0	0.8	0.9	0.9	0.7	1.0	1.1	0.9
Interest rates (%)														
Federal funds rate	10.2	8.1	6.8	6.7	7.6	9.2	8.1	5.7	3.5	3.8	3.3	3.0	3.0	3.0
Discount rates[1]	8.8	7.7	6.3	5.7	6.2	7.0	7.0	5.4	3.3	3.5	3.0	3.0	3.0	3.0
Prime rate[2]	12.0	9.9	8.3	8.2	9.3	10.9	10.0	8.5	6.3	6.5	6.0	6.0	6.0	6.0
3-month Treasury Bills	9.5	7.5	6.0	5.8	6.7	8.1	7.5	5.4	3.4	3.7	3.1	3.1	3.0	3.0
AAA rate[3]	12.7	11.4	9.0	9.4	9.7	9.3	9.3	8.8	8.1	8.3	8.0	8.0	7.7	7.4
10-year Treasury Bonds	12.4	10.6	7.7	8.4	8.8	8.5	8.6	7.9	7.0	7.4	6.6	6.7	6.3	6.0

1. Rate for Federal Reserve Bank of New York.
2. Prime rate on short-term business loans.
3. Corporate Bonds, AAA rating group, quoted by Moody's Investors Services.

Source: Board of the Governors of the Federal Reserve System, Federal Reserve Bulletin.

Table E. **Balance of payments,**

Millions

	1979	1980	1981	1982	1983
Exports, fob[1]	184 439	224 250	237 044	211 157	201 799
Imports, fob[1]	212 007	249 750	265 067	247 642	268 901
Trade balance	–27 568	–25 500	–28 023	–36 485	–67 102
Services, net[2]	33 877	36 165	44 755	42 118	41 220
Balance on goods and services	6 308	10 667	16 732	5 632	–25 882
Private transfers, net	–921	–1 044	–4 517	–8 738	–9 067
Official transfers, net	–5 674	–7 305	–7 187	–8 337	–8 676
Current balance	–285	2 318	5 030	–11 442	–43 623
US assets abroad other than official reserves	–64 922	–78 813	–108 972	–117 370	–57 660
US private assets, net[3]	–61 176	–73 651	–103 875	–111 239	–52 654
Reported by U.S. banks	–26 213	–46 838	–84 175	–111 070	–29 928
US government assets[4]	–3 746	–5 162	–5 097	–6 131	–5 006
Foreign assets in the United States					
Liabilities to foreign official monetary agencies[5]	–13 624	14 882	5 298	2 988	5 243
Other liabilities to foreign monetary agencies[6]	52 416	42 615	78 072	88 826	77 534
Reported by U.S. banks	32 607	10 743	42 128	65 633	50 342
Allocation of SDR's	1 140	1 150	1 090	–	–
Errors and omissions	26 449	25 387	24 992	41 360	19 099
Change in reserves (+ = increase)	1 133	8 154	5 176	4 965	1 195
a) Gold	–	–	–	–	–
b) Currency assets	–257	6 471	861	1 040	–3 305
c) Reserve position in IMF	189	1 667	2 492	2 552	4 435
d) Special drawing rights	1 136	16	1 823	1 372	65

1. Excluding military goods.
2. Services include reinvested earnings of incorporated affiliates.
3. Including: Direct investment financed by reinvested earnings of incorporated affiliates; foreign securities; U.S. claims on unaffiliated foreigners reported by U.S. nonbanking concerns; and U.S. claims reported by U.S. banks, not included elsewhere.
4. Including: U.S. credits and other long-term assets; repayments on U.S. credits and other long-term assets, U.S. foreign currency holdings and U.S. short-term assets, net.

Source : U.S. Department of Commerce, Survey of Current Business.

OECD basis

of dollars

1984	1985	1986	1987	1988	1989	1990	1991	1992
219 926	215 915	223 344	250 208	320 230	361 697	388 705	415 962	439 272
332 418	338 088	368 425	409 765	447 189	477 365	497 558	489 398	535 547
–112 492	–122 173	–145 081	–159 557	–126 959	–115 668	–108 853	–73 436	–96 275
34 279	23 403	21 726	19 135	25 175	40 133	51 342	61 725	65 188
–78 212	–98 770	–123 355	–140 421	–101 788	–75 537	–57 511	–11 710	–31 088
–9 758	–9 544	–10 112	–10 543	–11 862	–12 316	–12 373	–12 996	–13 792
–10 856	–13 406	–14 063	–12 507	–13 006	–13 291	–20 542	21 024	–17 567
–98 825	–121 720	–147 531	–163 473	–126 657	–101 142	–90 427	–3 682	–62 447
–26 094	–30 212	–91 382	–71 550	–88 795	–89 651	–54 163	–67 982	–48 802
–20 605	–27 391	–89 360	–72 556	–91 762	–90 922	–56 467	–71 379	–47 843
–11 127	–1 323	–59 975	–42 119	–56 322	–51 255	7 469	–4 753	32 372
–5 489	–2 821	–2 022	1 006	2 967	1 271	2 304	3 397	–959
2 401	–1 963	33 453	47 714	40 225	8 343	32 042	16 807	37 838
98 870	132 084	187 543	184 585	179 731	205 204	65 471	48 573	80 093
33 849	41 045	79 783	89 026	70 235	63 382	16 370	–13 678	14 667
–	–	–	–	–	–	–	–	–
26 038	24 826	15 408	–4 097	–126	19 646	47 369	–1 078	–13 051
3 132	3 858	–313	–9 148	3 913	25 293	2 158	–5 763	–3 901
–	–	–	–	–	–	–	–	–
1 156	3 869	942	–7 589	5 065	25 229	2 697	–6 307	–4 276
995	–909	–1 501	–2 070	–1 024	–471	–731	366	2 691
979	897	246	510	–127	535	193	176	–2 316

5. Including: U.S. Government securities and other U.S. Government liabilities, U.S. liabilities reported by U.S. banks not included elsewhere and other foreign official assets.
6. Including direct investment; U.S. Treasury securities; other U.S. securities; U.S. liabilities to unaffiliated foreigners reported by U.S. non-banking concerns; U.S. liabilities reported by U.S. banks not included elsewhere.

Table F. **Public sector**

	1960	1970	1980	1989	1990	1991	1992
A. Budget indicators:							
General government accounts (% GDP)							
Current receipts	27.0	29.7	30.5	30.9	30.9	30.8	30.7
Non-interest expenditures	25.0	29.6	30.6	30.4	31.2	31.9	33.2
Primary budget balance	2.0	0.1	–0.1	0.5	–0.4	–1.1	–2.5
Net interest	–1.3	–1.2	–1.2	–2.0	–2.1	–2.3	–2.2
General government budget balance	0.7	–1.1	–1.3	–1.5	–2.5	–3.4	–4.7
of which:							
Central government	0.7	–1.3	–2.2	–2.3	–3.0	–3.7	–5.0
Excluding Social security[1]	–	–	–2.2	–3.6	–4.1	–4.4	
B. The structure of expenditure and taxation (% GDP)							
Government expenditure							
Transfers	5.7	8.3	11.7	11.7	12.3	12.7	14.4
Subsidies	–0.1	0.3	0.2	0.1	0.1	0.0	0.0
General expenditures							
Education	3.5	5.3	5.2	5.1	5.3	5.4	
Transportation	2.0	2.0	1.7	1.5	1.5	1.5	
Health	0.8	2.2	3.1	3.9	4.2	4.7	

	United States			OECD average		
	1989	1990	1991	1989	1990	1991
Tax receipts						
Income tax	10.6	10.6	10.4	11.4	11.6	11.6
Social security tax	8.7	8.7	8.9	9.1	9.2	9.5
Consumption tax	4.2	4.2	4.4	11.1	11.0	11.2

	Prior to Tax Reduction	Under the Tax Reduction
C. Tax rates (%)		
Average rate of income tax[2]	13.0	11.9
Top rate	50.0	28.0
Lower rate	11.0	15.0
Average marginal rate[2]	20.2	18.6
Income tax elasticity[2]	1.55	1.56
Social security tax rate	7.15	7.15
VAT rate	–	–
Corporation tax rate	51.0	45.0
Effective tax rate on corporate investment	33.3	36.5
Equipment	10.0	39.6
Non-residential housing	34.4	43.1
Owner-occupied housing	22.5	23.7

	1960	1970	1980	1989	1990	1991	1992
Income tax as % of total tax	32.7	35.2	36.9	34.8	35.7	35.8	34.8
D. Government debt (% GDP)							
General government gross debt	60.3	45.4	37.8	54.0	56.2	59.8	63.2
Net debt	46.6	28.5	18.8	30.4	32.9	34.3	38.0

1. OECD estimates derived from fiscal year off-budget items (primarily retirement pension balance), converted to a calendar year basis.
2. Federal government.

Sources: Economic Report of the President, February 1990; Department of Treasury, Office of Tax Analysis; Revenue Statistics of OECD Member Countries, 1965-1992, OECD 1993, and OECD calculations.

Table G. **Financial markets**

	1970	1975	1980	1988	1989	1990	1991	1992
A. Financial and corporate flows								
Share of private financial institutions' financial assets in national net assets (%)[1]	43.0	40.0	37.5	59.7	62.3	64.2	71.3	72.4
Market value of equities including corporate farm equities (billions of dollars)[1]	0.648	0.684	1.293	2.577	3.211	3.005	3.901	4.252
Debt-to-equities ratio in non-financial corporate business excluding farms (%)[1]	56.8	82.3	67.6	78.2	68.3	75.6	58.3	54.8
Ratio of market value to net worth[1]	80.6	41.9	41.8	63.0	75.9	71.5	99.5	111.9
B. Foreign sector (billions of dollars)								
Net foreign assets outstanding[1,3]	68.7	81.4	260.6	–280.8	–385.7	–407.3	–446.9	–617.7
Changes in net foreign investment[2]	3.0	24.0	25.7	–126.8	–98.7	–43.1	–4.8	–68.9
of which net financial investment of:								
Private sectors	14.3	92.3	96.7	89.3	190.5	195.1	277.0	312.9
Public sectors	–22.3	–80.1	–63.7	–195.5	–220.9	–224.9	–300.1	–404.7
Foreign purchases of U.S. corporate equities[2]	0.7	3.1	4.2	–0.5	7.0	–14.5	9.2	–5.7
U.S. purchases of foreign equities[2]	1.1	–0.9	2.4	0.9	17.2	7.4	30.2	31.5
C. Net worth (billions of dollars)[1]								
Total, all sectors	3.056	5.536	10.631	17.108	18.236	18.228	18.363	18.327
Private, consolidated	3.462	6.172	11.664	19.210	20.537	20.748	21.276	21.526
Household	3.367	5.157	9.644	17.199	18.917	18.839	20.629	21.414
Total owner-occupied real estate	0.872	1.580	3.306	5.643	6.082	6.005	6.468	6.698
Home mortgages as a per cent of owner-occupied real estate	31.3	27.7	27.7	37.3	38.8	43.2	42.0	43.4
D. Debt to net worth ratios, Private sector (%)[4]								
Household	14.1	14.0	14.6	18.5	18.5	20.1	19.0	19.3
Non-farm non-corporate business	32.6	43.6	43.2	66.8	64.9	69.5	71.3	73.7
Farm business	19.2	17.5	18.2	18.8	18.3	18.3	18.3	18.5
Non-financial corporate business excluding farms	45.8	34.5	28.2	49.3	51.9	54.1	58.1	61.3
Private financial institutions	77.0	92.4	87.5	119.8	120.0	118.3	106.5	108.5

1. Data are year-end outstandings.
2. Data are annual flows.
3. Net foreign assets exclude U.S. holdings of foreign equities and foreign holdings of U.S. equities.
4. Debt is credit market debt.

Source: Balance Sheets for the U.S. Economy, 1945-92.

Table H. **Labour market indicators**

	Peak	Trough	1988	1989	1990	1991	1992
A. Evolution							
Standardised unemployment rate	1982: 9.6	1969: 3.4	5.4	5.2	5.4	6.7	7.3
Unemployment rate							
Total	1982: 9.5	1969: 3.4	5.4	5.2	5.4	6.6	7.3
Male	1983: 9.7	1969: 2.7	5.3	5.1	5.5	6.9	7.6
Female	1982: 9.4	1969: 4.7	5.6	5.3	5.4	6.3	6.9
Youth[1]	1982: 17.0	1969: 7.4	10.6	10.5	10.7	12.9	13.7
Share of long-term unemployment[2]	1983: 13.4	1969: 1.9	7.4	5.8	5.6	6.3	11.2
Productivity index, 1987 = 100[3]			101.6	102.1	102.6	102.8	103.7

	1970	1980	1988	1989	1990	1991	1992
B. Structural or institutional characteristics							
Participation rate[4]							
Global	60.4	63.8	65.9	66.5	66.4	66.0	66.3
Male	79.7	77.4	76.2	76.4	76.1	75.5	
Female	43.3	51.5	56.6	57.4	57.5	57.3	
Employment/population between 16 and 64 years	57.4	59.2	62.3	63.0	62.7	61.6	61.4
Employment by sector							
Agriculture – per cent of total	4.5	3.6	2.9	2.9	2.8	2.9	2.9
per cent change	–3.6	0.6	–2.1	1.4	–0.6	1.0	–0.3
Industry – per cent of total	34.3	30.5	26.9	26.7	26.2	25.3	24.6
per cent change	–1.8	–1.9	1.6	1.1	–1.2	–4.4	–2.0
Services – per cent of total	61.1	65.9	70.2	70.5	71.0	71.8	72.5
per cent change	3.0	1.7	2.7	2.4	1.2	0.3	1.6
of which:							
Government – per cent of total	0.2	0.2	0.2	0.2	0.2	0.2	0.2
per cent change	3.0	1.8	2.2	2.3	3.0	0.5	1.4
Voluntary part-time work[5]	13.9	14.2	14.0	14.1	13.7	13.7	13.4
Social insurance as a percent of compensation	10.8	16.3	16.4	16.6	16.7	17.1	17.2
Government unemployment insurance benefits[6]	12.3	12.6	7.9	8.3	9.4	11.2	14.3
Minimum wage:							
as a percentage of average wage[7]	49.6	46.6	36.1	34.7	36.8	40.1	40.2

1. People between 16 and 24 years as a percentage of the labour force of the same age group.
2. People looking for a job since one year or more as a percentage of total unemployment.
3. Production as a percentage of employment.
4. Labour force as a percentage of the corresponding population aged between 16 and 64 years.
5. As a percentage of salaried workers.
6. Value of the unemployment benefits per unemployed divided by the compensation per employee.
7. Private non-agricultural sector.

Sources: Department of Labor, Bureau of Labor Statistics, Data Resources Incorporated, and OECD.

BASIC STATISTICS

BASIC STATISTICS:
INTERNATIONAL COMPARISONS

	Units	Reference period[1]	Australia	Austria	Belgium	Canada
Population						
Total	Thousands	1990	17 085	7 718	9 967	26 620
Inhabitants per sq. km	Number	1990	2	92	327	3
Net average annual increase over previous 10 years	%	1990	1.5	0.2	0.1	1
Employment						
Total civilian employment (TCE)[2]	Thousands	1990	7 850	3 412	3 726	12 572
Of which : Agriculture	% of TCE		5.6	7.9	2.7	4.2
Industry	% of TCE		25.4	36.8	28.3	24.6
Services	% of TCE		69	55.3	69	71.2
Gross domestic product (GDP)						
At current prices and current exchange rates	Bill US $	1990	294.1	157.4	192.4	570.1
Per capita	US $		17 215	20 391	19 303	21 418
At current prices using current PPP's[3]	Bill US $	1990	271.7	127.4	163	510.5
Per capita	US $		15 900	16 513	16 351	19 179
Average annual volume growth over previous 5 years	%	1990	3.1	3.1	3.2	3
Gross fixed capital formation (GFCF)	% of GDP	1990	22.9	24.3	20.3	21.4
Of which: Machinery and equipment	% of GDP		9.7	10.1	10.4	7.2
Residential construction	% of GDP	1990	4.8	4.6	4.3	6.8
Average annual volume growth over previous 5 years	%	1990	2.4	4.6	9.5	5.8
Gross saving ratio[4]	% of GDP	1990	19.7	26	21.8	17.4
General government						
Current expenditure on goods and services	% of GDP	1990	17.3	18	14.3	19.8
Current disbursements[5]	% of GDP	1990	34.9	44.9	53.1	44
Current receipts	% of GDP	1990	35.1	46.7	49.5	41.6
Net official development assistance	Mill US $	1990	0.34	0.25	0.45	0.44
Indicators of living standards						
Private consumption per capita using current PPP's[3]	US $	1990	9 441	9 154	10 119	11 323
Passenger cars per 1 000 inhabitants	Number	1989	570	416	416	613
Telephones per 1 000 inhabitants	Number	1989	550 (85)	540	500 (88)	780 (88)
Television sets per 1 000 inhabitants	Number	1988	217	484 (89)	255	586
Doctors per 1 000 inhabitants	Number	1990	2.3	2.1	3.4	2.2
Infant mortality per 1 000 live births	Number	1990	8.2	7.8	7.9	7.2 (89)
Wages and prices (average annual increase over previous 5 years)						
Wages (earnings or rates according to availability)	%	1990	5.6	5	3	4.3
Consumer prices	%	1990	7.9	2.2	2.1	4.5
Foreign trade						
Exports of goods, fob*	Mill US $	1990	39 813	40 985	118 291[7]	127 334
As % of GDP	%		13.5	26	61.5	22.3
Average annual increase over previous 5 years	%		11.9	19.1	17.1	7.8
Imports of goods, cif*	Mill US $	1990	38 907	48 914	120 330[7]	116 561
As % of GDP	%		13.2	31.1	62.5	20.4
Average annual increase over previous 5 years	%		11	18.6	16.5	8.8
Total official reserves[6]	Mill SDR's	1990	11 432	6 591	8 541[7]	12 544
As ratio of average monthly imports of goods	ratio		3.5	1.6	0.9	1.3

* At current prices and exchange rates.
1. Unless otherwise stated.
2. According to the definitions used in OECD Labour Force Statistics.
3. PPP's = Purchasing Power Parities.
4. Gross saving = Gross national disposable income minus Private and Government consumption.
5. Current disbursements = Current expenditure on goods and services plus current transfers and payments of property income.
6. Gold included in reserves is valued at 35 SDR's per ounce. End of year.
7. Including Luxembourg.
8. Included in Belgium.

Denmark	Finland	France	Sweden	Switzerland	Turkey	United Kingdom	United States
5 141	4 986	56 420	8 559	6 796	56 473	57 411	251 523
119	15	103	19	165	72	235	27
0	0.4	0.5	0.3	0.6	2.4	0.2	1
2 638	2 457	21 732	4 508	3 563	19 209	26 577	117 914
5.6	8.4	6.1	3.3	5.6	47.8	2.1	2.8
27.5	31	29.9	29.1	35	19.9	29	26.2
66.9	60.6	64	67.5	59.5	32.3	68.9	70.9
129.3	137.3	1 190.8	228.1	224.8	108.4	975.1	5 392.2
25 150	27 527	21 105	26 652	33 085	1 896	16 985	21 449
85.2	82.2	980.4	144.6	142.1	189.7	911.8	5 392.2
16 570	16 487	17 376	16 896	20 911	3 318	15 882	21 449
1.5	3.4	2.9	2.1	2.8	5.9	3.2	3
17.7	26.3	21.2	20.7	27.1	22.7	19.2	16.1
8.1	10	9.7	8.9	9.1	11.7 (87)	8.5	7.8 (89)
3.7	7.1	5.2	5.5	17.9[9]	5.8 (87)	3.4	4.4 (89)
0.8	4.8	5.8	4.9	6	4.7	5.8	2.7
18	23.1	21	17.3	33	22.2	15.6	14.4
25.2	21.1	18	27.1	13.3	19.4	19.9	18.1
56.5	37.5	46.2 88)	59.1	30.7	..	38.1	34.6 (89)
56.1	41.2	46.5 88)	63.9	34.2	..	40	31.8 (89)
0.93	0.64	0.79	0.9	0.31	..	0.27	0.21
8 639	8 602	10 482	8 748	11 933	1992	10 051	14 465
370	439	494	462	479	37	449	748
880 (88)	620 (85)	610 (87)	889 (83)	880 (88)	120 (88)	524 (84)	650 (84)
526	486	399	395	408	172	435	812
2.7 (87)	1.9	2.6 (89)	3.1 (89)	2.9 (89)	0.9	1.4 (89)	2.3
7.5 (89)	6.1 (89)	7.2 89)	5.9	7.3	6.5 (89)	7.9	9.2
6	8.2	3.7	8.2	..	..	8.5	2.6
3.9	5	3.1	6.2	2.5	53.7	5.9	4
34 988	26 583	216 157	57 422	63 847	12 836	185 710	393 812
27.1	19.4	18.2	25.2	28.4	11.8	19	7.3
15.6	14.3	16.5	13.7	18.4	9.9	12.9	13.1
31 647	26 950	225 260	54 659	69 811	22 224	225 327	494 842
24.5	19.6	18.9	24	31	20.5	23.1	9.2
11.8	15.3	16.8	14	17.8	14.2	15.5	7.4
7 445	6 779	25 851	12 644	20 541	4 252	25 201	50 791
2.8	3	1.4	2.8	3.5	2.3	1.3	1.2

Including non-residential construction.

0. Federal Government Statistics.

ources: Population and Employment: OECD La

GDP, GFCF, and General Government:

Indicators of living standards: Miscellar

Wages and Prices: OECD Main Econor

Foreign trade: OECD Monthly Foreign

Total official reserves: IMF Internationa

August, 1992

EMPLOYMENT OPPORTUNITIES

Economics Department, OECD

The Economics Department of the OECD offers challenging and rewarding opportunities to economists interested in applied policy analysis in an international environment. The Department's concerns extend across the entire field of economic policy analysis, both macro-economic and micro-economic. Its main task is to provide, for discussion by committees of senior officials from Member countries, documents and papers dealing with current policy concerns. Within this programme of work, three major responsibilities are:

– to prepare regular surveys of the economies of individual Member countries;
– to issue full twice-yearly reviews of the economic situation and prospects of the OECD countries in the context of world economic trends;
– to analyse specific policy issues in a medium-term context for theOECD as a whole, and to a lesser extent for the non-OECD countries.

The documents prepared for these purposes, together with much of the Department's other economic work, appear in published form in the *OECD Economic Outlook, OECD Economic Surveys, OECD Economic Studies* and the Department's *Working Papers* series.

The Department maintains a world econometric model, INTERLINK, which plays an important role in the preparation of the policy analyses and twice-yearly projections. The availability of extensive cross-country data bases and good computer resources facilitates comparative empirical analysis, much of which is incorporated into the model.

The Department is made up of about 75 professional economists from a variety of backgrounds and Member countries. Most projects are carried out by small teams and last from four to eighteen months. Within the Department, ideas and points of view are widely discussed; there is a lively professional interchange, and all professional staff have the opportunity to contribute actively to the programme of work.

Skills the Economics Department is looking for:

a) Solid competence in using the tools of both micro-economic and macro-economic theory to answer policy questions. Experience indicates that this normally requires the equivalent of a PH.D. in economics or substantial relevant professional experience to compensate for a lower degree.

b) Solid knowledge of economic statistics and quantitative methods; this includes how to identify data, estimate structural relationships, apply basic techniques of time series analysis, and test hypotheses. It is essential to be able to interpret results sensibly in an economic policy context.

c) A keen interest in and knowledge of policy issues, economic developments and their political/social contexts.

d) Interest and experience in analysing questions posed by policy-makers and presenting the results to them effectively and judiciously. Thus, work experience in government agencies or policy research institutions is an advantage.

e) The ability to write clearly, effectively, and to the point. The OECD is a bilingual organisation with French and English as the official languages. Candidates must have excellent knowledge of one of these languages, and some knowledge of the other. Knowledge of other languages might also be an advantage for certain posts.

f) For some posts, expertise in a particular area may be important, but a successful candidate is expected to be able to work on a broader range of topics relevant to the work of the Department. Thus, except in rare cases, the Department does not recruit narrow specialists.

g) The Department works on a tight time schedule and strict deadlines. Moreover, much of the work in the Department is carried out in small groups of economists. Thus, the ability to work with other economists from a variety of cultural and professional backgrounds, to supervise junior staff, and to produce work on time is important.

General Information

The salary for recruits depends on educational and professional background. Positions carry a basic salary from FF 262 512 or FF 323 916 for Administrators (economists) and from FF 375 708 for Principal Administrators (senior economists). This may be supplemented by expatriation and/or family allowances, depending on nationality, residence and family situation. Initial appointments are for a fixed term of two to three years.

Vacancies are open to candidates from OECD Member countries. The Organisation seeks to maintain an appropriate balance between female and male staff and among nationals from Member countries.

For further information on employment opportunities in the Economics Department, contact:

Administrative Unit
Economics Department
OECD
2, rue André-Pascal
75775 PARIS CEDEX 16
FRANCE

Applications citing "ECSUR", together with a detailed *curriculum vitae* in English or French, should be sent to the Head of Personnel at the above address.

MAIN SALES OUTLETS OF OECD PUBLICATIONS
PRINCIPAUX POINTS DE VENTE DES PUBLICATIONS DE L'OCDE

ARGENTINA – ARGENTINE
Carlos Hirsch S.R.L.
Galería Güemes, Florida 165, 4° Piso
1333 Buenos Aires Tel. (1) 331.1787 y 331.2391
Telefax: (1) 331.1787

AUSTRALIA – AUSTRALIE
D.A. Information Services
648 Whitehorse Road, P.O.B 163
Mitcham, Victoria 3132 Tel. (03) 873.4411
Telefax: (03) 873.5679

AUSTRIA – AUTRICHE
Gerold & Co.
Graben 31
Wien I Tel. (0222) 533.50.14

BELGIUM – BELGIQUE
Jean De Lannoy
Avenue du Roi 202
B-1060 Bruxelles Tel. (02) 538.51.69/538.08.41
Telefax: (02) 538.08.41

CANADA
Renouf Publishing Company Ltd.
1294 Algoma Road
Ottawa, ON K1B 3W8 Tel. (613) 741.4333
Telefax: (613) 741.5439
Stores:
61 Sparks Street
Ottawa, ON K1P 5R1 Tel. (613) 238.8985
211 Yonge Street
Toronto, ON M5B 1M4 Tel. (416) 363.3171
Telefax: (416)363.59.63

Les Éditions La Liberté Inc.
3020 Chemin Sainte-Foy
Sainte-Foy, PQ G1X 3V6 Tel. (418) 658.3763
Telefax: (418) 658.3763

Federal Publications Inc.
Suite 103, 388 King Street W
Toronto, ON M5V 1K2 Tel. (416) 581.1552
Telefax: (416) 581.1743

Les Publications Fédérales
1185 Université
Montréal, QC H3B 3A7 Tel. (514) 954.1633
Telefax : (514) 954.1635

CHINA – CHINE
China National Publications Import
Export Corporation (CNPIEC)
16 Gongti E. Road, Chaoyang District
P.O. Box 88 or 50
Beijing 100704 PR Tel. (01) 506.6688
Telefax: (01) 506.3101

DENMARK – DANEMARK
Munksgaard Book and Subscription Service
35, Nørre Søgade, P.O. Box 2148
DK-1016 København K Tel. (33) 12.85.70
Telefax: (33) 12.93.87

FINLAND – FINLANDE
Akateeminen Kirjakauppa
Keskuskatu 1, P.O. Box 128
00100 Helsinki
Subscription Services/Agence d'abonnements :
P.O. Box 23
00371 Helsinki Tel. (358 0) 12141
Telefax: (358 0) 121.4450

FRANCE
OECD/OCDE
Mail Orders/Commandes par correspondance:
2, rue André-Pascal
75775 Paris Cedex 16 Tel. (33-1) 45.24.82.00
Telefax: (33-1) 45.24.81.76 or (33-1) 45.24.85.00
Telex: 640048 OCDE

OECD Bookshop/Librairie de l'OCDE :
33, rue Octave-Feuillet
75016 Paris Tel. (33-1) 45.24.81.67
(33-1) 45.24.81.81

Documentation Française
29, quai Voltaire
75007 Paris Tel. 40.15.70.00

Gibert Jeune (Droit-Économie)
6, place Saint-Michel
75006 Paris Tel. 43.25.91.19

Librairie du Commerce International
10, avenue d'Iéna
75016 Paris Tel. 40.73.34.60

Librairie Dunod
Université Paris-Dauphine
Place du Maréchal de Lattre de Tassigny
75016 Paris Tel. (1) 44.05.40.13

Librairie Lavoisier
11, rue Lavoisier
75008 Paris Tel. 42.65.39.95

Librairie L.G.D.J. - Montchrestien
20, rue Soufflot
75005 Paris Tel. 46.33.89.85

Librairie des Sciences Politiques
30, rue Saint-Guillaume
75007 Paris Tel. 45.48.36.02

P.U.F.
49, boulevard Saint-Michel
75005 Paris Tel. 43.25.83.40

Librairie de l'Université
12a, rue Nazareth
13100 Aix-en-Provence Tel. (16) 42.26.18.08

Documentation Française
165, rue Garibaldi
69003 Lyon Tel. (16) 78.63.32.23

Librairie Decitre
29, place Bellecour
69002 Lyon Tel. (16) 72.40.54.54

GERMANY – ALLEMAGNE
OECD Publications and Information Centre
August-Bebel-Allee 6
D-53175 Bonn 2 Tel. (0228) 959.120
Telefax: (0228) 959.12.17

GREECE – GRÈCE
Librairie Kauffmann
Mavrokordatou 9
106 78 Athens Tel. (01) 32.55.321
Telefax: (01) 36.33.967

HONG-KONG
Swindon Book Co. Ltd.
13–15 Lock Road
Kowloon, Hong Kong Tel. 366.80.31
Telefax: 739.49.75

HUNGARY – HONGRIE
Euro Info Service
POB 1271
1464 Budapest Tel. (1) 111.62.16
Telefax : (1) 111.60.61

ICELAND – ISLANDE
Mál Mog Menning
Laugavegi 18, Pósthólf 392
121 Reykjavik Tel. 162.35.23

INDIA – INDE
Oxford Book and Stationery Co.
Scindia House
New Delhi 110001 Tel.(11) 331.5896/5308
Telefax: (11) 332.5993

17 Park Street
Calcutta 700016 Tel. 240832

INDONESIA – INDONÉSIE
Pdii-Lipi
P.O. Box 269/JKSMG/88
Jakarta 12790 Tel. 583467
Telex: 62 875

IRELAND – IRLANDE
TDC Publishers – Library Suppliers
12 North Frederick Street
Dublin 1 Tel. (01) 874.48.35
Telefax: (01) 874.84.16

ISRAEL
Electronic Publications only
Publications électroniques seulement
Sophist Systems Ltd.
71 Allenby Street
Tel-Aviv 65134 Tel. 3-29.00.21
Telefax: 3-29.92.39

ITALY – ITALIE
Libreria Commissionaria Sansoni
Via Duca di Calabria 1/1
50125 Firenze Tel. (055) 64.54.15
Telefax: (055) 64.12.57
Via Bartolini 29
20155 Milano Tel. (02) 36.50.83

Editrice e Libreria Herder
Piazza Montecitorio 120
00186 Roma Tel. 679.46.28
Telefax: 678.47.51

Libreria Hoepli
Via Hoepli 5
20121 Milano Tel. (02) 86.54.46
Telefax: (02) 805.28.86

Libreria Scientifica
Dott. Lucio de Biasio 'Aeiou'
Via Coronelli, 6
20146 Milano Tel. (02) 48.95.45.52
Telefax: (02) 48.95.45.48

JAPAN – JAPON
OECD Publications and Information Centre
Landic Akasaka Building
2-3-4 Akasaka, Minato-ku
Tokyo 107 Tel. (81.3) 3586.2016
Telefax: (81.3) 3584.7929

KOREA – CORÉE
Kyobo Book Centre Co. Ltd.
P.O. Box 1658, Kwang Hwa Moon
Seoul Tel. 730.78.91
Telefax: 735.00.30

MALAYSIA – MALAISIE
Co-operative Bookshop Ltd.
University of Malaya
P.O. Box 1127, Jalan Pantai Baru
59700 Kuala Lumpur
Malaysia Tel. 756.5000/756.5425
Telefax: 757.3661

MEXICO – MEXIQUE
Revistas y Periodicos Internacionales S.A. de C.V.
Florencia 57 - 1004
Mexico, D.F. 06600 Tel. 207.81.00
Telefax : 208.39.79

NETHERLANDS – PAYS-BAS
SDU Uitgeverij
Christoffel Plantijnstraat 2
Postbus 20014
2500 EA's-Gravenhage Tel. (070 3) 78.99.11
Voor bestellingen: Tel. (070 3) 78.98.80
Telefax: (070 3) 47.63.51

**NEW ZEALAND
NOUVELLE-ZÉLANDE**
Legislation Services
P.O. Box 12418
Thorndon, Wellington Tel. (04) 496.5652
Telefax: (04) 496.5698

NORWAY – NORVÈGE
Narvesen Info Center – NIC
Bertrand Narvesens vei 2
P.O. Box 6125 Etterstad
0602 Oslo 6 Tel. (022) 57.33.00
Telefax: (022) 68.19.01

PAKISTAN
Mirza Book Agency
65 Shahrah Quaid-E-Azam
Lahore 54000 Tel. (42) 353.601
Telefax: (42) 231.730

PHILIPPINE – PHILIPPINES
International Book Center
5th Floor, Filipinas Life Bldg.
Ayala Avenue
Metro Manila Tel. 81.96.76
Telex 23312 RHP PH

PORTUGAL
Livraria Portugal
Rua do Carmo 70-74
Apart. 2681
1200 Lisboa Tel.: (01) 347.49.82/5
Telefax: (01) 347.02.64

SINGAPORE – SINGAPOUR
Information Publications Pte. Ltd.
41, Kallang Pudding, No. 04-03
Singapore 1334 Tel. 741.5166
Telefax: 742.9356

SPAIN – ESPAGNE
Mundi-Prensa Libros S.A.
Castelló 37, Apartado 1223
Madrid 28001 Tel. (91) 431.33.99
Telefax: (91) 575.39.98

Libreria Internacional AEDOS
Consejo de Ciento 391
08009 – Barcelona Tel. (93) 488.30.09
Telefax: (93) 487.76.59

Llibreria de la Generalitat
Palau Moja
Rambla dels Estudis, 118
08002 – Barcelona
(Subscripcions) Tel. (93) 318.80.12
(Publicacions) Tel. (93) 302.67.23
Telefax: (93) 412.18.54

SRI LANKA
Centre for Policy Research
c/o Colombo Agencies Ltd.
No. 300-304, Galle Road
Colombo 3 Tel. (1) 574240, 573551-2
Telefax: (1) 575394, 510711

SWEDEN – SUÈDE
Fritzes Information Center
Box 16356
Regeringsgatan 12
106 47 Stockholm Tel. (08) 690.90.90
Telefax: (08) 20.50.21

Subscription Agency/Agence d'abonnements :
Wennergren-Williams Info AB
P.O. Box 1305
171 25 Solna Tel. (08) 705.97.50
Téléfax : (08) 27.00.71

SWITZERLAND – SUISSE
Maditec S.A. (Books and Periodicals - Livres
et périodiques)
Chemin des Palettes 4
Case postale 266
1020 Renens Tel. (021) 635.08.65
Telefax: (021) 635.07.80

Librairie Payot S.A.
4, place Pépinet
CP 3212
1002 Lausanne Tel. (021) 341.33.48
Telefax: (021) 341.33.45

Librairie Unilivres
6, rue de Candolle
1205 Genève Tel. (022) 320.26.23
Telefax: (022) 329.73.18

Subscription Agency/Agence d'abonnements :
Dynapresse Marketing S.A.
38 avenue Vibert
1227 Carouge Tel.: (022) 308.07.89
Telefax : (022) 308.07.99

See also – Voir aussi :
OECD Publications and Information Centre
August-Bebel-Allee 6
D-53175 Bonn 2 (Germany) Tel. (0228) 959.120
Telefax: (0228) 959.12.17

TAIWAN – FORMOSE
Good Faith Worldwide Int'l. Co. Ltd.
9th Floor, No. 118, Sec. 2
Chung Hsiao E. Road
Taipei Tel. (02) 391.7396/391.7397
Telefax: (02) 394.9176

THAILAND – THAÏLANDE
Suksit Siam Co. Ltd.
113, 115 Fuang Nakhon Rd.
Opp. Wat Rajbopith
Bangkok 10200 Tel. (662) 225.9531/2
Telefax: (662) 222.5188

TURKEY – TURQUIE
Kültür Yayinlari Is-Türk Ltd. Sti.
Atatürk Bulvari No. 191/Kat 13
Kavaklidere/Ankara Tel. 428.11.40 Ext. 2458
Dolmabahce Cad. No. 29
Besiktas/Istanbul Tel. 260.71.88
Telex: 43482B

UNITED KINGDOM – ROYAUME-UNI
HMSO
Gen. enquiries Tel. (071) 873 0011
Postal orders only:
P.O. Box 276, London SW8 5DT
Personal Callers HMSO Bookshop
49 High Holborn, London WC1V 6HB
Telefax: (071) 873 8200
Branches at: Belfast, Birmingham, Bristol, Edinburgh, Manchester

UNITED STATES – ÉTATS-UNIS
OECD Publications and Information Centre
2001 L Street N.W., Suite 700
Washington, D.C. 20036-4910 Tel. (202) 785.6323
Telefax: (202) 785.0350

VENEZUELA
Libreria del Este
Avda F. Miranda 52, Aptdo. 60337
Edificio Galipán
Caracas 106 Tel. 951.1705/951.2307/951.1297
Telegram: Libreste Caracas

Subscription to OECD periodicals may also be placed through main subscription agencies.

Les abonnements aux publications périodiques de l'OCDE peuvent être souscrits auprès des principales agences d'abonnement.

Orders and inquiries from countries where Distributors have not yet been appointed should be sent to: OECD Publications Service, 2 rue André-Pascal, 75775 Paris Cedex 16, France.

Les commandes provenant de pays où l'OCDE n'a pas encore désigné de distributeur devraient être adressées à : OCDE, Service des Publications, 2, rue André-Pascal, 75775 Paris Cedex 16, France.

09-1993

PRINTED IN FRANCE

•

OECD PUBLICATIONS
2 rue André-Pascal
75775 PARIS CEDEX 16
No. 46897
(10 93 02 1) ISBN 92-64-14005-0
ISSN 0376-6438

•